D0217085

"Faggioli offers a highly sophisticated analysis of the new ecclesial movements while telling the story of the Catholic Church over the past one and a half centuries. His international perspective informs his use of methods that are historical, sociological, and theological. This book stands in a category of its own among works on this subject."

— Dennis M. Doyle
Professor of Religious Studies
University of Dayton

"Massimo Faggioli has become one of the most respected theological interpreters of Vatican II and the battle over its meaning. This new book explores a wider set of issues with a related agenda. How are we to assess the variety of new Catholic movements and their relationship to the legacy of Vatican II? His analysis and findings will undoubtedly shape the future debate."

— Bradford Hinze
Fordham University

"Massimo Faggioli brings his fresh, creative voice to the much neglected subject of 'new ecclesial movements.' 'Sorting out' movements 'intimately intertwined' with 'the modern papacy and the contemporary church' requires skills as a theologian and historian, which Faggioli has in abundance. Movements have already transformed Catholicism in Europe and Latin America, and in the future they will either complement or substitute traditional parishes, support or undermine Catholic institutions. Those who wish to understand and share responsibility for the future of Catholicism, in the United States and elsewhere, would do well to consider Faggioli's nuanced assessment of these mostly Euro-centered movements."

— David J. O'Brien
College of the Holy Cross (Emeritus)

Sorting Out Catholicism
A Brief History of the New Ecclesial Movements

Massimo Faggioli

Translated by
Demetrio S. Yocum

A Michael Glazier Book

LITURGICAL PRESS
Collegeville, Minnesota

www.litpress.org

A Michael Glazier Book published by Liturgical Press

Cover design by Stefan Killen Design. Cover photos: (top) © Getty and (bottom) © Thinkstock.

This work was originally published in Italian as *Breve storia dei movimenti cattolici* by Massimo Faggioli. Copyright (c) 2008 by Carocci editore S.p.A., Roma.

Excerpts from documents of the Second Vatican Council are from *Vatican Council II: Constitutions, Decrees, Declarations; The Basic Sixteen Documents*, edited by Austin Flannery, OP, © 1996. Used with permission of Liturgical Press, Collegeville, Minnesota.

Unless otherwise noted, quotations from papal documents have been translated by Demetrio S. Yocum.

© 2014 by Order of Saint Benedict, Collegeville, Minnesota. All rights reserved. No part of this book may be reproduced in any form, by print, microfilm, microfiche, mechanical recording, photocopying, translation, or by any other means, known or yet unknown, for any purpose except brief quotations in reviews, without the previous written permission of Liturgical Press, Saint John's Abbey, PO Box 7500, Collegeville, Minnesota 56321-7500. Printed in the United States of America.

1   2   3   4   5   6   7   8   9

Library of Congress Cataloging-in-Publication Data

Faggioli, Massimo.
   [Breve storia dei movimenti cattolici. English]
   Sorting out Catholicism : a brief history of the new ecclesial
movements / Massimo Faggioli ; translated by Demetrio S. Yocum.
     pages   cm
   Includes bibliographical references and index.
   ISBN 978-0-8146-8305-7 — ISBN 978-0-8146-8330-9 (ebook)
    1. Catholic Church—Societies, etc.—History—19th century.   2. Catholic Church—Societies, etc.—History—20th century.   3. Catholic Action—Europe.   I. Title.

BX808.F33513   2014
282.09'04—dc23   2014020481

Contents

Prologue
to the New English Edition

Sorting Out Catholicism: A Brief History of the New Ecclesial Movements is not merely the English translation of the book published in Italy in the spring of 2008 under the title of *Breve storia dei movimenti cattolici* (and translated into Spanish in 2011). Not only because the second part of this book is essentially new and the result of later reflections following 2008, but also because this book, which Hans Christoffersen, academic publisher of Liturgical Press, has graciously accepted for publication, is the attempt to "translate" for an English-speaking public the research that I began in an Italian and European context.

Moreover, this book is not intended as a comprehensive history of all the Catholic movements that emerged and developed in the twentieth century. In fact, only a few references are made to crucial phenomena in American Catholicism, such as Dorothy Day's Catholic Worker; to more recent evangelical Catholic movements; and, in general, to the more ecumenical and interdenominational character of some of the new Catholic movements and intentional communities outside Europe and in the United States specifically. The main topic of this book deals with the new Catholic movements that originated in Europe in the period between the 1930s and 1970s, which had a relatively direct relationship with the theological and ecclesiological roots of Catholic Action as a form of lay apostolate guided by the Church hierarchy (bishops and popes), and that have since become international Catholic movements, in the sense that they have spread from Europe to the rest of the world. In other words, my research focuses on the transition from a hierarchically led lay apostolate called Catholic Action to new forms of lay apostolate (such as the Focolare movement and the Community of Sant'Egidio) or mixed lay-clerical institutions and congregations (such as Opus Dei and the Legionaries of Christ), without exploring further the kind of evangelical movements that are taking shape today in the Catholic Church, especially outside of Europe.

Further, this book is perhaps more important today than at the time of its first publication in Italy in 2008. Today, world Catholicism is experiencing a particular historical moment in which the influence of Catholic movements is particularly strong, thanks to the New Evangelization launched by Saint John Paul II, resumed by Pope Benedict XVI, and reinvigorated by Pope Francis. American Catholicism is taking an unprecedented leading role for the Church worldwide. Hence, the publication of this book in North America is part of my attempt to act as liaison, or as mediator, of theological ideas and different religious experiences between two continents, Europe and North America, much more distant than what we normally think, even inside the same Catholic world.

What has not changed, however, is the central thesis of the book, namely, that the new ecclesial movements are one of the key experiences for understanding the complexity of the relationship between Catholicism and the modern world in the twentieth century and the relationship between the Second Vatican Council and the experience of the preconciliar and postconciliar Catholic Church and what this experience says about the hermeneutics of Vatican II. The perspective of the research has expanded, as did the intent to understand this particular issue within a scope that is not only European. It is up to the Anglophone reader to judge whether this book is able to account for the argument, intended for a segment of the world, specifically the English-speaking North American one, ever more important for the future of world Catholicism.

For Catholic and non-Catholic readers in the English-speaking world, where Catholic movements of the evangelical type are increasingly flourishing, the usefulness of this book is essentially twofold. First, it allows us, *from a historical point of view*, to draw a comparison between three different moments of the organization of the laity in the Catholic Church: the era of Catholic Action (from the 1920s to the Second Vatican Council); the era of the international new Catholic movements (emerging between World War II and the 1970s); and the current era, characterized by new Catholic movements that have permanently lost their ties with the first period. The second reason is to offer—*from a theological perspective* and to theologians and those who observe the Catholic Church phenomenon with an eye on the history of the Church—an insight into the ecclesiological effects of the first wave of the new Catholic movements on the balance, typical of Catholicism, between institution and charism. This rationale can be useful for the purpose of forming an opinion on Catholic evangelical movements, even though this book does not directly address that topic, mainly because it takes its start from the perspective of the movements of European origin that eventually spread worldwide.

But this book also tries to address the issue of the role of Catholics (organized in different ways: movements, associations, theological traditions) at the intersection between Church, society, and the power of the State and government. The history of the ecclesial movements is relevant to the issue of the possibility for Catholics to influence "the world" without being completely absorbed by politics but also without being constrained by the institutional mechanisms of the Church.[1] In other words, the phenomenon of the ecclesial movements is a key aspect of a larger issue at the core of the debate about the nature of Catholicism in a secular age. There is no doubt that one of the typical features of our time is a political disillusionment that sometimes becomes an antipolitical sentiment—the ultimate secularism. Catholicism is part of this phenomenon, and in some cases the new ecclesial movements fit the current trend of a Catholicism that undermines political commitment in favor of a revaluation of Christian charity in a world made of small, almost utopian, communities. Engagement with the world or withdrawal from politics, inclusiveness and radical evangelism, social gospel and political homelessness—these are issues that are, in different measures, part of the spiritual and intellectual experience of the ecclesial movements between the end of the nineteenth century and today. This book is just a brief history of different answers to those questions.

---

[1] I refer here to the debate with William Cavanaugh and Michael Baxter: see Massimo Faggioli, "A View from Abroad," in *America* (February 24, 2014): 20–23; Michael Baxter and William T. Cavanaugh, "Reply to 'A View from Abroad' by Massimo Faggioli," in *America* (April 21, 2014): 8; Katie Grimes, in *America* (April 28–May 5, 2014): 6.

I would like to express my gratitude to Enrico Galavotti, Alberto Melloni, Joseph Ruggieri, and Silvia Scatena for the many conversations, friendships, and personal experiences at the John XXIII Foundation for Religious Studies in Bologna between 1996 and 2008.

The English translation of a book that has found many interested readers in Europe and the Spanish-speaking world is the result of Phyllis Zagano's initial interest and curiosity. The department of theology at the University of St. Thomas (St. Paul, Minnesota) has always shown interest in, and patience with, my research agenda. And without my colleagues' support, little of this work would have ever been accomplished. The Vatican II Studies group and the Ecclesiological Investigations group at the American Academy of Religion have become a precious point of reference for my journey.

Special thanks go to Amy Uelmen for all her comments and advice in favor of the "inculturation" of this book in the English-speaking world. My heartfelt thanks go also to Ladislas Orsy, SJ, who gave me the opportunity to present my research on the new Catholic movements at a meeting of the Peter and Paul Seminar at Georgetown University many years ago, in April 2004. Friendships that have developed and accompanied me during the writing of this book include the ones with Kevin Ahern, Thomas Bremer, Kathleen Cummings, Dennis Doyle, Brian Flanagan, Bradford Hinze, Cathleen Kaveny, Gerard Mannion, Mark Massa, SJ, John O'Malley, SJ, James McCartin, Katarina Schuth, Maureen Sullivan, and Terrence Tilley. Their warmth and support have made my transition to America an experience intellectually and humanly irreplaceable and indispensable for the scholar that I strive to be every day.

Particular and sincere thanks to my editor, Lauren L. Murphy, and my translator, Demetrio S. Yocum: their dedication is what the author of a book to be translated in another language always hopes to find.

This book is dedicated to my wife Sarah and our daughter Laura. They always know how to support and share with me their wisdom and grace.

Minneapolis
April 27, 2014
Canonization of St. John XXIII and St. John Paul II

ॐ

Some of the following chapters have appeared elsewhere. They have been revised and updated for the present book: chapter 2, "Movimenti religiosi," in *Dizionario del sapere storico-religioso del Novecento*, edited by Alberto Melloni (Bologna: Il Mulino, 2010), 1145–53; chapter 9, "Die neuen geistlichen Bewegungen in der katholischen. Kirche und die Priesterausbildung in den Seminaren," *Una Sancta. Zeitschrift für ökumenische Begegnung* 66, no. 2 (2011): 155–63; chapter 10, "Il movimentismo cattolico e l'"apologetica dell'inimicizia' nella chiesa post-conciliare," in *Tutto è grazia. In omaggio a Giuseppe Ruggieri*, edited by Alberto Melloni (Milan: Jaca Book, 2010), 441–56; chapter 11, "Inclusion and Exclusion in the Ecclesiology of the New Catholic Movements," in *Ecclesiology and Exclusion*, edited by Dennis Doyle, Pascal D. Bazzell, and Timothy J. Furry (Maryknoll, NY: Orbis, 2012), 199–213. I wish to thank the publishers and editors of these volumes for granting their permission to republish my articles here in their expanded and updated version.

PART 1

The History of the Movements

CHAPTER 1

Reasons for a Historical Survey
of the Movements

Undoubtedly, it is not an easy task to categorize the new Catholic movements. Neither their self-definition nor the way they are defined in the Code of Canon Law are of much help. The lowest common denominator can be summarized as a group of faithful Catholics who share the following characteristics: "A charismatic founder, a particular charism, some form of ecclesial reality or expression, a predominantly lay membership, a radical commitment to the Gospel, a form of teaching or training closely linked to its charism, a specific focus and a commitment to bringing its own emphasis or understanding into the life of the Church."[1]

As a result, the new Catholic movements that are the subject of this book are movements such as Communion and Liberation, Opus Dei, the Community of Sant'Egidio, the Focolare Movement, the Neocatechumenal Way, the Cursillos de Cristianidad, the Regnum Christi Movement, the Legionaries of Christ, and others originating and emerging within the Catholic Church between the 1920s and 1970s still active and present beyond their country of origin. In Europe, these movements are often presented as the pope's new "elite troops," the

---

[1] Charles Whitehead, "The Role of Ecclesial Movements and New Communities in the Life of the Church," in *New Religious Movements in the Catholic Church*, ed. Michael A. Hayes (London and New York: Burns & Oates, 2005), 18. See also Brendan Leahy, *Ecclesial Movements and Communities: Origins, Significance, and Issues* (Hyde Park, NY: New City Press, 2011), 14–22.

new vanguard, or the newly created "battalions of the Church"—but also as "divisions within the Church."

But what are these new "divisions"? A similar question at the beginning of the twenty-first century is no longer posed by dictators concerned about the political-diplomatic structure of the twentieth-century Church: there is no longer someone like Joseph Stalin who sardonically seeks information on the *force* capability of Catholicism. The way to measure or "weigh up" the Church has changed. Even before the absence of dictators interested in a clash with the Church of Rome, there is no longer the old Catholic Church, nor its diplomacy, always active on the international political Cold War chessboard. And gone is the Church's patient dialogue and silent martyrdom that clashed with a programmatically hostile political system and that symbolically confirmed the end of "Christianity" as a European political and religious power.

The question on the divisions of the Church instead arises in the context of the political and cultural debate on the *militant* fiber of the Church—and more generally on the role of the Churches and Catholicism in the Western world—in the age of globalization and the meeting between civilizations and religions, in the political, cultural, and symbolic arena at the dawn of the third millennium. But the divisions of the Church are also clearly visible by taking into account the polarizing effect of the movements, the recurring tensions among them—and with the bishops.[2] In theological debates in the Church, as in the public sphere, the "movement" element (here intended as "group of Christians that presupposes a firm commitment and a rule of life that may be habitual or in written form") is increasingly taking the characteristics of a cumbersome novelty, to which, along with the acknowledged signs of dynamism, the most various labels, hardly ever sympathetic or benevolent, are also attached: radicalism, fundamentalism, papalism and ultramontanism, intellectual narrow-mindedness, sectarianism, ecclesiastical careerism, thirst for power, or worse still.[3]

---

[2] As we have recently seen, for example, between 2010 and 2011 with the very acute tension between the bishops of Japan and the Neocatechumenal movement.

[3] For an example of this "conspiracy mythology," see Gordon Urquhart, *The Pope's Armada: Unlocking the Secrets of Mysterious and Powerful New Sects in the Church* (New York: Prometheus Press, 1999).

Some consider the ecclesial movements at large as negative, while others simply weigh the risks of one or the other group. Extremely rare are those who intend to offer an assessment without being moved by disparaging or apologetic intents. This reason only provides ample ground for a better understanding of the historical dimension of the phenomenon.

Similarly, in the contemporary Catholic Church the phenomenon of ecclesial movements proves to be central to the understanding of some fundamental dynamics. Not only the large growth of these realities but also the rise of their influence, beyond the numbers they express, represent a phenomenon that reveals a shift of the center of gravity: in the relationship of the Catholic Church with the secular or post-denominational society; in the balance between local dimensions (parish, diocese) and the personal (or virtual) reality of being Church; in the relationship between theology, liturgy, and devotional styles in the contemporary Catholic Church; in the connection between the European "roots" of the Catholic movements and their "branches" in North America, Latin America, Asia, and Africa.

The transitions represented by Pope John Paul II's death and the beginning of Benedict XVI's pontificate in April 2005 and by the resignation of Benedict XVI in February 2013 followed by the election of Pope Francis on March 13, 2013, require that the question about the historical range of the post–Vatican II pontificates be also directed to investigating one of the most important and tangible aspects of the Catholic Church at the end of the twentieth century. It is necessary to ask whether the visibility of the new ecclesial groups also translates into a real impact and concrete significance of the phenomenon of the movements within the Church. Conversely, we cannot fail to investigate the movements as a relevant phenomenon given that they have often been idealized, demonized, and at times trivialized, not only in consideration of their numerical size and social rootedness, but also in evaluating their forward thrust over the long-term period of the post–Vatican II Catholic Church and the future of the Church in the twenty-first century.[4]

---

[4] See John L. Allen Jr., *The Future Church: How Ten Trends Are Revolutionizing the Catholic Church* (New York: Doubleday, 2009), 425.

To answer these questions, it is essential to:

- research the historical roots of the phenomenon both in the distant past and in the present more close at hand
- deconstruct both the foundational myths as well as the anti-movement propaganda
- identify the common/different socio-political coordinates between the various movements
- put forward the current trends and possible objectives but also the tensions between the ecclesiological model "papacy–bishops–ordained ministry" and the more "fluid" one embodied by the movements

The reality of the movements visible on the scene of international Catholicism goes deeper and far beyond most of the well-known names always in the public eye, at the funerals of popes, or at Catholic rallies in the streets of Rome and elsewhere. Christianity in the twentieth century, better still in the second half of the twentieth century, has taken on the traits of a reality "on the move," that is, dynamic and driven—whether one accepts or not the pro-movement line of the Church—by progressive forces as well as conservative ones: relatively visible and solid, variously structured, with or without labels, yet in a way all characterized by a "dialectical" or antagonistic relationship (either deliberate or spontaneous, depending on the history of each of these movements) with the local and episcopal structure of the Catholic Church.

The historiographical and mass media *vulgata* (official version)—both the apologetically slanted and the more critical one—claims that John Paul II's long pontificate gave a decisive boost to the development of these particular associations within the Catholic Church. Equally accepted is the view of the pontificate of his successor, Benedict XVI, who would have harvested the fruits, sharing the same strategic vision that animated the Polish pope in his relationship with the movements,[5] albeit

---

[5] Substantially different opinions on John Paul II's pontificate can be found in Alberto Melloni, *Chiesa madre, chiesa matrigna. Un discorso storico sul cristianesimo che cambia* (Turin: Einaudi, 2005); Daniele Menozzi, *Giovanni Paolo II. Una transizione incompiuta?* (Brescia: Morcelliana, 2006); Giovanni Miccoli, *In difesa della*

without the charismatic leadership style of his predecessor.[6] It is a way of interpreting the relations between the two pontiffs, which, however, does not necessarily correspond to the recent history of the movements within the Roman Catholic Church. Rather, it shows how the "movement" element has become a kind of litmus test that does not reveal the index of bitterness of the object observed but that of the observer.

In any case, the movements today seem to have become the index to evaluate the health of the Church and its ability to draw the faithful at moments and in associations different from the local units of parishes and dioceses created in ancient times on the model of the Roman Empire, strengthened in the Middle Ages during the clash with princes and emperors, and perfected on the model of Church that came out from the Council of Trent. Through the movements, observers can analyze one of the most evident, but at the same time "unreadable," Church phenomena characterized by a light but not random structure and essentially difficult to exploit by the media beyond the sporadic events of mixed political-religious street gatherings.

The topic has its own present-day relevance, which not only derives from the superficial and partial view of the popular press on the numerical strength or the political orientation of each ecclesial movement. Rather, it stems from passing the mark of the end of a century, the twentieth century, which has seen dramatic changes in the "identity" of the Catholic Church as well as the Christian Churches.[7] It is therefore useful to offer an overview of the journey of the movement phenomenon within the Church, bearing in mind that the movement element, intended as dialectical or transversal to the institutional and historical Churches, cuts across contemporary Christianity as a whole, through languages and continents. It certainly affects Catholicism in a particular way, given the particular historical and institutional model on which it exerts its influence.

---

fede. La chiesa di Giovanni Paolo II e di Benedetto XVI (Milan: Rizzoli, 2007); Andrea Riccardi, *Giovanni Paolo II. La biografia* (Cinisello B.: San Paolo, 2011).

[6] See Joseph Ratzinger, "I movimenti ecclesiali e la loro collocazione teologica," in *I movimenti nella chiesa*. Atti del convegno mondiale dei movimenti ecclesiali (Rome, May 27–29, 1998), Pontificio Consiglio per i Laici (Vatican City, 1999), 23–51 (English translation: "The Ecclesial Movements: A Theological Reflection on Their Place in the Church," *Communio* 25 [Fall 1998]: 480–504).

[7] See *Le chiese del Novecento*, ed. Giuseppe Ruggieri (Bologna: EDB, 2003).

Hence, it is worth asking, at the onset of this study, some questions that are at the heart of the matter and that should guide the path of inquiry on ecclesial movements.

1. Christianity's Return to Being a "Movement"

During the course of the twentieth century we have started to understand the importance of the "movement" phenomenon as a co-essential element of Christianity, together with the *societas perfecta iuridice* ("juridically perfect institution") of the Counter-Reformation shaped by the Council of Trent (1545–63).[8] The Church of the Counter-Reformation, which in many ways remained unchanged from the end of the Ancien Régime until the Second Vatican Council (1959–65),[9] saw itself as a legal institution that already consisted of its own institutional, political, and sociological legitimacy and therefore, from the outset, excluded the possibility of an extraordinary element, or one that was not yet legally regulated with regard to the canonical norm of the institutional church. This new awareness of the movement element was the result of the crisis of this Tridentine and post-Tridentine ecclesiology, which between the nineteenth century and the beginning of the twentieth century had begun to show its significant delays regarding the cultural, social, moral, and epistemological evolution of the Western world. On the one hand, these delays stemmed from the Church's institutional self-referentiality; on the other, from its loyalty to the political and social system of the Ancien Régime.

A few decades later, in the 1970s, the post–Vatican II era, and with the advent of sociological, ethnographical, and anthropological disciplines devoted to the study of Christian origins,[10] the studies of

---

[8] See Giuseppe Alberigo, Massimo Marcocchi, Claudio Scarpati, *Il concilio di Trento. Istanze di riforma e aspetti dottrinali* (Milan: Vita e pensiero, 1997); John W. O'Malley, *Trent: What Happened at the Council* (Cambridge, MA: Belknap Press of Harvard University Press, 2013).

[9] See *Storia del concilio Vaticano II*, 5 vols., ed. Giuseppe Alberigo (Leuven-Bologna: Peeters-Il Mulino, 1995–2001); English version: *History of Vatican II*, 5 vols., ed. Giuseppe Alberigo, English ed. Joseph A. Komonchak (Maryknoll, NY: Orbis, 1995–2006); John W. O'Malley, *What Happened at Vatican II* (Cambridge, MA: Belknap Press of Harvard University Press, 2008).

[10] See Claudio Gianotto, "Il movimento di Gesù," *Concilium: "Movimenti" in the Church*, ed. Alberto Melloni (2003/3): 36–51; Massimo Faggioli, "Studi sui movimenti

early Christianity as a movement, the so-called Jesus movement, offered a "radical" reading (focused on the true roots of Christianity) of a phenomenon, that of the "new movements," that in those years was beginning to take a more visible and concrete shape. It also captured the desire for reform in the postconciliar Church.

To what extent have the contemporary ecclesial movements revived the Jesus movement or the apostolic and post-apostolic moment? In speaking of language, symbolism, ecclesiology, liturgy, to what extent do contemporary ecclesial movements draw on a religious movement born before the fateful union of Christianity with the Roman Empire and, ultimately, with political power? To what extent are the current ecclesial movements the offspring of the golden age of the Catholic Action tradition during the central decades of the twentieth century? Are they to be considered as a continuation of this tradition or a replacement of the basic theological, social, and institutional aspects of the typical form of lay association within the Catholic Church?

In other words, is the Catholic movement culture a conscious (or unconscious) development of the "end of the Constantinian era" (dating back to the covenant between the Church and the Western powers, initiated by Emperor Constantine), as suggested by the Dominican theologian Marie-Dominique Chenu?[11] Or is the movement culture in the Church instead to be interpreted as the rejection of the idea of leaving behind the Constantinian era and the attempt to recover on the social and communal level what had been lost on the political level?

What are the effects of the impact of the movements on the Church as a whole? Are they "stirring" the Catholic Church and bringing innovations that go beyond the traditional Catholic socio-communal model? Or are the movements contributing to slowing down a Catholic Church that seems to have forgotten and shelved that period of opportunities and dialogue represented by the 1960s and 1970s?

---

religiosi," in *Dizionario delle scienze storico-religiose nel Novecento*, ed. Alberto Melloni (Bologna: Il Mulino, 2010), 1145–53.

[11] See Marie-Dominique Chenu, "La fine dell'era costantiniana," in *Un concilio per il nostro tempo* (Brescia: Querininana, 1962), 46–68 (original French edition: "La fin de l'ère constantinienne," in Jean-Pierre Dubois-Dumée et al., *Un concile pour notre temps* [Paris: Cerf, 1961], 59–87). See also Gianmaria Zamagni, *Fine dell'era costantiniana. Retrospettiva genealogica di un concetto critico* (Bologna: Il Mulino, 2011).

2. Framing the Movement

It has become more difficult to try to assess and describe ecclesial movements. Apart from this reason, in the limited space of this book the reader will surely not find a new categorization of the movements, according to the different types of membership and leadership, theological-spiritual guidance, political orientations, and areas of expansion. There are already many definitions for "Catholic movements" based on sound analytical and theological foundations, among which are the following:

- reform, social, and Church movements[12]
- movements of pilgrims and converts[13]
- lay, spiritual, and ecclesial movements[14]
- movements of institutional, spiritual-emotional, and ascetic-sectarian mobilization[15]
- movements of spiritual and apostolic commitment, of Christian animation of temporal realities, of Christian inspiration that operates in temporal realities[16]
- movements of spiritual and apostolic intra-ecclesial commitment, and movements of Christian animation of temporal realities[17]

A brief overview of the typologies makes it clear that within ecclesial movements there are today many different and contradictory

---

[12] See Alberto Melloni, "Movimenti. De significatione verborum," *Concilium: "Movimenti" in the Church*, ed. Alberto Melloni (2003/3): 13–34.

[13] See Danièle Hervieu-Léger, *Le pèlerin et le converti. La religion en mouvement* (Paris: Flammarion, 1999).

[14] See Jean B. Beyer, "De motu ecclesiali quaesita et dubia," *Periodica* 78 (1989): 437–52.

[15] See Gianni Ambrosio, "Cammino ecclesiale e percorsi aggregativi," in *La Scuola Cattolica* 116 (1988): 441–60.

[16] See Agostino Favale, *Movimenti ecclesiali contemporanei. Dimensioni storiche, teologico-spirituali ed apostoliche*, 2nd ed. (Rome: LAS, 1982; 4th ed., 1991); Agostino Favale, *Segni di vitalità nella Chiesa. Movimenti e muove comunità* (Rome: LAS, 2009).

[17] See Piersandro Vanzan, "Elementi comuni e identificativi dell'attuale fenomeno movimentista intraecclesiale con cenni a rischi e speranze," in *Fedeli Associazioni Movimenti* (Milan: Glossa, 2002), 187–206.

elements among them: traditionalist nostalgias and liturgical aestheticisms (not only of the supporters of the preconciliar Mass in Latin, such as the New Liturgical Movement); anxieties of Church reform in an ecumenical sense; revivals of clericalism; contractors of pastoral and social services at the expense of the government and the state; strong personalities' protagonisms and antagonisms; political and ecclesiastical powers—and abuse of powers. At the heart of a movement there is often the simple need to live the Gospel outside the imposed or socially inherited conventions, in communities that go beyond "associative" boundaries and symbolic dictates of a specific creed.

For this reason, one of the central questions for understanding the various orientations, worldviews, and visions of the Church of these movements remains the articulation of the relationship between the Catholic movement of the early twentieth century and the contemporary movements in terms of referential political ideologies, ecclesiology, types of membership, ecclesial praxis and ecclesiastical politics, explicit goals, and latent functions.

One of the most successful interpretive keys is still that of a transition from a Catholic movement of *lay mobilization* (with all the hierarchical dependencies on the ecclesiastical authority) between the late nineteenth and early twentieth centuries to the *theological movements* for biblical, ecumenical, liturgical, patristic *ressourcement* of the early twentieth century and the *postconciliar movements* that have excluded from their horizon the urgency of a "reform" (in the institutional sense) of the Catholic Church to engage primarily instead in self-reform efforts guided by the charismatic and spiritual renewal, the service to others, ascetic practices, and the "return to the sources."

Nevertheless, it is evident that, in order to frame the contemporary ecclesial movements and their distinctive features, the crucial aspect to consider is the legacy and reception (whether conscious or not) of the theology of Vatican II or, conversely, the revival of the intransigent culture typical of the late nineteenth century.

3. Chronology and Historical Framing of the Phenomenon

To identify the "genome" of the ecclesial movements today, we need to take a step forward with regard to the state of the studies currently available: from a sociological categorization it is necessary to switch to a historical approach that seeks to identify not just the "schools" or the movements' ideological leanings but also the various stages of the formation of this type of magma difficult to classify.

The centrality of the question of the movements in the post-conciliar Church and at the turn of the twenty-first century is clear to all. In a climate such as the present one, where sociology and ethnography have largely replaced history for the understanding of religious phenomena, the risk is to stop at the snapshot taken in different places and at particular times of the religious-political media-friendly presentations of Western Catholicism. The fact is that even the new ecclesial groups, simply labeled as "movements," have a history that may reveal much about their genesis, their development, their role, and their current configuration.

To begin to understand the phenomenon in its entirety, we need not only a chronology of events, individuals, and their connections but also a historical view able to recognize defining moments as well as disruptions. The enticement to match the history of the movements in the Church with the history of individual pontificates suffers from two pathologies of classic "ecclesiastical historiography": the sluggishness of the historian, who squeezes every event and phenomenon within the reassuring frame of contemporary pontifical annals, and the myopia typical of those who consider phenomena internal to the Catholic Church as always original, fundamental, and therefore independent from the broader political and cultural phenomena and the "spirit of the age" (from which even the Church can hardly escape). There is a clear need for a historical framing that reestablishes a specific historical development of the ecclesial movements, though without denying the contribution of the popes, thus incorporating them in the larger course of contemporary history.

4. A History beyond the Foundational Myths

A historical view is all the more necessary, considering the subject at hand. Such an approach is essential in order to do away with an exclusively sociological analysis and to leave behind the obstructive mythology represented by both the insiders' apologetic historiography and the hagiography of the founders—products that currently make up the vast majority of the bibliography on ecclesial movements.

Each movement tends to represent itself on the basis of *ad hoc* historical/biographical reconstructions, in most cases the result of celebratory and laudatory approaches. Only a few isolated analyses, fruit of a theological vision faithful to the ecclesiology of Vatican II, diverge from this "internal" or "official" approach. These studies underline the "subversive" potential of the movements within the Catholic Church, almost fearing the re-proposal of the *duo genera christianorum*, that is, the "two kinds of Christians" (clergy on one side and laity on the other side, clearly separated). In this perspective, the programmatic division between clergy and laity has been replaced in our contemporary age by the separation between "ordinary Christians," namely, the "the loose" laity (unorganized, unaffiliated), and the elite troops formed by the members of ecclesial movements.

Beyond the self-representations or hostile attitudes, which are the effect of conspiracy theories, if it is true that there is a division between the diocesan/parish realities and that of the movements, the map of the positions within the Church is more complex, variable, and reluctant to embrace dogmatic or ideological classifications as well as the contraposition between ecclesial movements and the "Church of Vatican II."

5. Movements beyond Lobbies

The movement-structure does not fit well into rigid classifications, nor is there a correspondence between movement-structure and its position in the "political spectrum" of the contemporary Church. One of the fascinating aspects of the study of the movements lies largely in the discovery of the variety, flexibility, and adaptability of the movement-structure in relation to the typology of its members (clergy and laity together), its agenda (spiritual, ecclesiastical, political, humanitarian), its position inside or outside the administrative system of the Catholic Church or the local churches and their institutional bodies, and its referential theological and political cultures.

A historical look free from the need to retrace the exploits of a single association or founder allows us to look at the movements as divisions of the Church or vanguards of mobilization but also as a source of *division* (possible or real) within the Church. Hence, "division" is intended both as specific fields of the apostolate and also as the divisive effect caused by the movements, seen as compact entities and therefore potentially divided or "total institutions" of a contemporary Church still struggling to find moments and places of synthesis, sharing, and communion. From this point of view, it is increasingly important to keep in mind that the different initial conditions of Catholicism more locally defined (by the cultural environment, the religious landscape of a given area, the legal status of the relations between Church and state, etc.) play a major role on the effects that a Catholic movement has on any given local church. In this sense, the differences between the practical ecclesiology of European Catholicism and that of the non-European Churches are still little explored.

6. The "Spring of the Movements" and the Second Vatican Council

One of the key issues is the link between the event of the Second Vatican Council, on the one hand, and the first new associative experiences in the 1920s and the 1930s together with the blossoming of movements starting from the end of the 1960s, on the other. Enthusiasts claim that the movements are the true "fruit of Vatican II," in that they are *the* practical implementation of the new ecclesiology of the people of God, of the new theology of the laity, and of a Church open to the world and to young people. Critics draw attention instead to the unrelated nature of certain typical aspects of the ecclesial movement culture with respect to Vatican II: the central role of the charismatic leader, disregard for the authority of the diocesan bishops, and leader-centered and antimodern political culture (which is often accompanied by a totally depoliticized and alienating *Weltanschauung*). Beyond any simplification, the Second Vatican Council plays a central role in the identification and self-identification—explicit or implicit—of the movements.

Even if we take into account the potential added value given by the movements to the reception-rejection of the Second Vatican Council, however, it is important to give to the interpretation of the phenomenon of the movements its own autonomy with regard to the controversy surrounding the council, especially in relation to the protagonists of this controversy. To apply to the movements the "logic of alliances," pitting "pre–Vatican II nostalgics" against "Vatican II loyalists," means to hide the incongruities between the official proclamations of loyalty to the conciliar principles and the unconscious yet deep and creative reception (or rejection in some cases) of Vatican II in most of the contemporary ecclesial movements.

7. Ecclesial Movements within the Twentieth-Century Movement Culture

The deep roots of the Catholic movement culture date back to the intransigent culture of the late nineteenth and early twentieth centuries, the beginning of the crisis of the episcopal authority in the government of the Church marked by the First Vatican Council (1869–70), and the recognition of the anti-institutional nature of the Jesus of Nazareth movement as its original feature. But the contributions to the organizational and political culture of the movements in the Church do not come only from the theological and ecclesial world but tap into the political and social culture of Europe and the contemporary Western world as well.[18]

The issue touches on the relationship between the origin of the culture of "mass mobilization" in the language and political practice of the first half of the century and the characteristics of the movements in the Church: the leader's role and group ideology, the relationship between the vanguard and the ecclesial community, and the "representations" of the idea of Church.

For the period between World War II and Vatican II, there is also the question of the existence and nature of the transition from a "movement culture of the elites"—the liturgical, ecumenical, biblical, patristic movements, all originating in Europe and North America, as the vanguard of the openings of the council[19]—to a "base movement culture" born in Mediterranean countries (such as Italy and Spain) less marked by the coexistence with other Churches and Christian denominations and geographically and culturally closer to the Roman See. For the subsequent period, we must also ask whether ecclesial movements have anything in common with the outburst of the "revenge of God" that Gilles Kepel located at the beginning of the 1970s in Judaism, Christianity, and Islam.[20] The decline of the ecumenical dream on the

---

[18] See Peter L. Berger, *The Homeless Mind: Modernization and Consciousness* (New York: Random House, 1973).

[19] See Étienne Fouilloux, "Mouvements théologico-spirituels et concile (1959–1962)," in *À la veille du Concile Vatican II. Vota et réactions en Europe et dans le catholicisme oriental*, ed. Mathijs Lamberigts and Claude Soetens (Leuven: Peeters, 1992), 185–99.

[20] See Gilles Kepel, *La revanche de Dieu: Chrétiens, juifs et musulmans à la reconqête du monde* (Paris: Editions du Seuil, 1991). English translation: *The Revenge of*

one hand and the globalization of the religious language on the other encourages people to question the trans-denominational and multi-religious scope of the movement element in the twentieth-century religious world, which has borne some fruits within the Catholic Church. But losing sight of what happened in the global religious landscape of the past few decades would make it impossible to grasp certain parallel and crucial elements.

8. Retreat? Or New Birth?

Both the apologetic and the demonizing views of the movements tend to emphasize the power of these organizations, associating them with a facet of the new strength of the contemporary Church: new spiritual forces, agencies of organized activism, political lobbying, and forms of rejection or non-reception of Vatican II—or all of these elements combined. It is undeniable, beyond the more or less reliable figures that are periodically made public regarding the nature of these groups, that the international expansion of the movements and their development are difficult to trace without referring to the most publicized names and "labels" spread by the media.

Worth asking is whether this phenomenon is after all indicative of a change of Catholicity and of some of its specific "vanguards" or "rearguards." It is an effort that must be made, in a society more refractory to the language of faith, whereby to "believe" and to "belong" are no longer coextensive but two different entities, where to belong not always presupposes a belief and to believe does not always mean belonging.[21]

Nevertheless, they are two entities that meet at an intersection: less cumbersome than the self-representations of the Catholic kind but broader and more diverse than the theories of both the secularization and part of the de-privatization of religion.[22]

God: The Resurgence of Islam, Christianity, and Judaism in the Modern World; trans. Alan Braley (University Park: Pennsylvania State University Press, 1994).

[21] See Grace Davie, *Religion in Britain since 1945: Believing without Belonging* (Oxford: Blackwell, 1994).

[22] See José Casanova, *Public Religions in the Modern World* (Chicago: University of Chicago Press, 1994).

CHAPTER 2

ॐ

Religious Movements and Catholic Movements in the History of Scholarly Literature

1. "Religious Cults," "New Religious Movements," and "Ecclesial Movements"

According to Dominican theologian Yves Congar, Catholic theological reflection on the laity and the Church as "people of God" originated first thanks to biblical research, followed by historical studies, and finally by pastoral experience. The phenomenon of religious movements is far older than its current thriving in contemporary Christianity, or in the postconciliar period when it comes to the Catholic Church. In a broader sense, the development of studies on "religious movements" in the course of the twentieth century shows, if compared to Congar's reading (entirely in line with the history of Catholic ecclesiology), a more tortuous course amid sociological, historical, and theological approaches, albeit with a clear predominance of the sociological.

The trajectory of the studies on religious movements in the twentieth century developed along three main lines, each of which has coincided with a season of religious-historical studies: a *first phase* corresponding to the first half of the century and characterized by socio-economic studies of the Churches as "religious cults" and, simultaneously, by the beginning of the reflection on the Catholic laity as a movement within the Roman Catholic Church; a *second phase*, from the Second World War to the 1980s, of studies on new religious movements as entities external to the Churches and the historical Christian confessions/denominations; and a *third phase*, starting from the beginning of the 1980s, of attempts to map the new ecclesial movements either inside the historical Christian Churches (and especially Western Catholic Christianity) or tangential to the Churches (such as the Pentecostal and charismatic undercurrents).

With an ever-increasing intensity, the studies of Church history, Christianity, and history of religions written in the course of the twentieth century dealt with the phenomenon of "religious movements." In these studies, they were intended as dialectical or transversal forces with respect to an ecclesial "institution," or a "universal" religious affiliation with its own rules and hierarchies, doctrinal traditions, and liturgies. The focus of the analysis was never the question of the definition of "movement" but rather tended to define a behavior, an *ethos*, and a *Weltanschauung* against a specific Church or religious background.

Throughout the century, these studies have maintained a large part of a genetic heritage that dates back to the early studies of social sciences at the beginning of the twentieth century. One of the features of the twentieth century (the advent of the masses in the public arena and, in terms of political struggle, the creation of mass political parties, which marked a "revolution" in the phenomenology of social life in the Western world) seems to have infiltrated somehow not only the reality of Churches and religions but also the studies dealing with the contemporary religious landscape. The result seems to have been the application of analyses and models typical of political mass movements to religious or ecclesial movements that hardly ever are—from both a statistical point of view and internal dynamics—mass phenomena. Recent studies rarely point this out, despite the fact that the "movements" tend to define themselves as mass movements for reasons related to the need for visibility, which is directly proportional to the recognition that the public and the Church is willing to offer them.

The development of the studies dealing with "Christian religious movements" and "ecclesial movements" has followed a course that can be divided into several periods, with each one marked by a particular historical-political climate, specific ecclesiological notions, and different disciplinary approaches.

2. Juridical Ecclesiology and Movements as "Sects"

In the first period, which goes from the beginning of the twentieth century until the outbreak of the Second World War, the studies of the phenomena of religious movements arose from a sociological approach of a particular European and German school, one that marked the study of religious movements throughout the century, even if later it incorporated the contribution of the social sciences (in particular of anthropology and psychology of religion) of the Anglo-Saxon and North American school.

It was an approach that originated—in terms of language, method, sources, and goals—outside the theological sciences of the denominational Churches. At the beginning of the twentieth century, the dominant juridical ecclesiology in the Catholic Church tended to emphasize the unity of the ecclesiastical institution as *societas iuridice perfecta* (a "perfect community/institution") thus institutionally ignoring the existence of phenomena such as groups, associations, and organizations that somehow escaped the ordering principle of the law enacted by the ecclesiastical authority while reviving the prophetic and charismatic dimension of the religious experience lived in a community of life. This was a community that corresponded neither to the ecclesiastical districts nor to the dimensions of ecclesial life in the society of European and Western *christianitas*—a Christianity that had become "Christendom." The growth of lay activism in the Church in these early decades of the century was framed within Catholic Action as a "militant mass organization." The modernist crisis and the Roman reaction against biblical studies and the history of early Christianity—both condemned as "modernist" in 1907 by Pope Pius X—prevented the rise of ideas capable of recovering the movement-oriented dimension of the communities of that which would later be identified as "Judeo-Christianity."

On the Protestant side, Rudolf Sohm's axiom of an irreducible contradiction between the legal dimension of the Church and the essence of the Church ("ecclesiastical law stands in contradiction to the nature of *Ecclesia*"[1]) brought the perception that the tension between the believer's belonging to the institution and new associative forms among the believers in the Church was overcome. In the conclusion of his work on the social doctrines of the Churches and Christian groups, in 1912 Ernst Troeltsch created a tripartite division—"Church, sect, mysticism"—for the three main types of autonomous social conformation

---

[1] See Rudolf Sohm, *Kirchenrecht* (Leipzig: Duncher & Humblot, 1892).

of the Christian idea.[2] Troeltsch's opinion—"while Catholicism always knows how to reduce sects and mysticism to powerlessness, both become increasingly stronger in Protestantism"—seems, after a century, certainly outdated in light of the twentieth-century development of the "sectarian" type of movements within the Catholic Church, which, thanks to a transformation achieved after the Second Vatican Council, grew closer to a certain part of the neo-evangelical Protestant world. During the first decades of the twentieth century, ecclesiological studies characterized by a "hierarchological" approach and the ineptness of the social sciences with respect to the tools of the Catholic intellectual marked the continuation of a "sectarian" criterion (not too different from the "heresiological" approach typical of ecclesiastical historiography focusing on minorities defined and condemned as heretical) regarding the issue of religious movements.

All of this happened at a time when the phenomenon of the "movements of renewal" made their appearance, albeit in the form of an underground force restricted to a few activists of Francophone and German circles. As such, they lacked a legal structure as well as an active organizational dimension of mobilization but would later develop into the movements for biblical, patristic, liturgical, ecumenical reform, and more generally of *ressourcement* of Catholic theology in the twentieth century.[3]

Throughout the century, the fruit of these reform movements will help to give new life to the vision of Max Weber, who in the 1920s had seen within each religious "community" three different forces at work: prophecy, lay traditionalism, and lay intellectualism;[4] a reading of his that seems to be validated by more recent ones regarding the phenom-

---

[2] See Ernst Troeltsch, *Die Soziallehren der christlichen Kirchen und Gruppen* (Tübingen: Mohr, 1912); English translation: *The Social Teaching of the Christian Churches*, trans. Olive Wyon, with an introductory note by Charles Gore (New York: The Macmillan Company, 1931).

[3] See Étienne Fouilloux, "I movimenti di riforma nel pensiero cattolico del XIX e XX secolo," in *I movimenti nella storia del cristianesimo. Caratteristiche—variazioni—continuità*, ed. Giuseppe Alberigo and Massimo Faggioli, *Cristianesimo nella Storia* 24, no. 3 (2003): 659–76; Gabriel Flynn and Paul D. Murray, eds., *Ressourcement: A Movement for Renewal in Twentieth-Century Catholic Theology* (Oxford: Oxford University Press, 2012).

[4] See Max Weber, *Wirtschaft und Gesellschaft* (Tübingen: Mohr, 1922); English translation: *Economy and Society: An Outline of Interpretive Sociology*, ed. Guenther

enon of "religious movements" at the end of the twentieth century. The main differences between the Weberian model and Troeltsch's analysis did not eliminate the evidence of the essential function, for an analysis of religious movements in the twentieth century, of the *Church-sect theory* that has in Weber's and Troeltsch's findings its starting point.

3. "Theology of the Laity" and Social Origins of Religious Groups

Between the 1930s, the Second World War, and the 1960s, the relevant ideas regarding religious movements, on the Catholic front, were to be found in what has been defined by the French-speaking world as "theology of the laity." From a theological point of view, a first breach of the conception of the "hierarchological" Church came with the notion of the "apostolate of the laity," which envisioned a new leading role for the "learning" Church, *ecclesia discens* (as opposed to the "teaching" Church, *ecclesia docens*), but always under the guidance of the ecclesiastical authority, the bishops, and especially the Roman papacy,[5] aiming to establish a new "kingdom" in society inspired by the teachings of the magisterium.[6] The development of the concept of "universal priesthood of the faithful" rarely considered the existence of a mission of the laity independent from Catholic Action.[7] The experience of World War II contributed to the development, especially in France, of the idea of a new role for the organized Catholic laity within the ecclesial structure. New insights came from Yves Congar, who distanced himself from the previous series of works on the mission of the laity, thus opening a new space for reflection on the theology of the laity right at the time of the first major crisis of both the Italian Catholic Action (1952–54) and the *Association Catholique de la Jeunesse Française* (1956).[8]

Roth and Claus Wittich, trans. Ephraim Fischoff et al. (Berkeley: University of California Press, 1978).

[5] See Paul Dabin, *L'Action Catholique* (Paris, 1929); Paul Dabin, *L'apostolat laïque* (Paris, 1931).

[6] See Émile Guerry, *L'Action Catholique* (Paris: Desclée De Brouwer, 1948).

[7] See Michel Ernest, *Von der kirchlichen Sendung* (Berlin: Schneider, 1934).

[8] See Yves Congar, *Jalons pour une théologie du laïcat* (Paris: Cerf, 1953); *Lay People in the Church: A Study for a Theology of the Laity*, trans. Donald Attwater (Westminster, MD: Newman Press, 1957).

On the sociological side, and in the footsteps of Weber and Troeltsch, research in North America began to identify, with Helmut Richard Niebuhr, a connection between social background and denominational paths within the same confessional family. At the beginning of his book, Niebuhr wrote: "Denominationalism in the Christian Church is such an unacknowledged hypocrisy. . . . It represents the accommodation of Christianity to the caste-system of human society."[9] The analysis of the social and economic roots of denominational affiliations was one of the elements—typical of a culture of the human sciences that had not yet removed historical materialism—that was no longer to be found in studies on religious movements after the 1980s, both in Europe and in America. In his analysis, Niebuhr transposed the dialectic between "movement" and "institution" to that between "denomination/sect" and "Church," identifying in the first term the dynamic element that could call Christians back to their mission and in the second one the burden of the institutional tradition engaged in self-preservation. By defining denominations, Churches, and sects as "sociological groups whose principle of differentiation is to be sought in their conformity to the order of social classes and castes," Niebuhr concluded: "Denominationalism thus represents the moral failure of Christianity."[10] Unlike the later stage of the critical studies on the dynamics within the Christian Churches, the players here identified as "cult-like groups" were labeled not (as happened soon after Vatican II) as retrograde forces with respect to the new centrality of the Bible, alien to the spirit of liturgical reform, and indifferent to the ecclesiology of the "Church as the people of God" but rather as the dynamic element capable of recovering the evangelical character of being Christians.

4. The Turning Point of the 1960s and 1970s

During the sixties and seventies, along with the decolonization of Christianity in Africa and the "liberationism" of Latin American theology, we witness an "awakening" of the North American religious world as well as the fragmentation within the Western historical

---

[9] See Helmut Richard Niebuhr, *The Social Sources of Denominationalism* (New York: Meridian Books, 1957), 6. The first edition was published by H. Holt and Company in New York, 1929.

[10] See ibid., 25.

Churches. During this time, North American sociologists began to bring their attention to the phenomenon of new religious movements external to the historical Churches, confessions, and denominations.[11] Going beyond the phase of studies on religious movements as phenomena of social deviance (but retaining the methodological approach used for the analysis of small groups), groundbreaking studies in the United States on the new religious movements were conducted by Peter Berger. On the basis of a theory of secularization as the product of Weber's "rationalization" of society and starting from the assumption of the conservative and inhibitory potential inherent in every religion, Berger located the causes of the proliferation of religious movements in the religious "privatization" and "pluralism" that considers religious affiliation a choice.[12] Starting in the 1970s, the question of religions (in the plural) was placed in a pluralistic context in which the plurality of religions and religious movements fulfilled the idea of a post-traditional religious world, according to an "evolutionary" perspective disconnected from any ecclesiological notion.[13]

On both sides of the Atlantic, research on the movement-oriented character of religion in the 1970s tended to see in the fragmentation of the religious landscape the signs of a cultural and institutional crisis, the dynamics of which were not religious in nature but the result of social conflicts. The explosion of these contradictions, which in the religious groups and movements stemmed from a religious approach toward socialization, helped to radically undermine traditional forms of social legitimacy of the religious and/or institutional authority.[14]

As regards the movements within the Christian Churches and denominations, an important contribution came, albeit indirectly, from

[11] See Lorne L. Dawson, *Comprehending Cults: The Sociology of New Religious Movements* (Toronto: Oxford University Press, 1998), 37.

[12] See Peter L. Berger, *The Sacred Canopy: Elements of a Sociological Theory of Religion* (Garden City, NY: Doubleday, 1967); Peter L. Berger, Brigitte Berger, Hansfried Kellner, *The Homeless Mind: Modernization and Consciousness* (New York: Random House, 1973).

[13] See Robert N. Bellah, *Beyond Belief: Essays on Religion in a Post-Traditional World* (Berkeley: University of California Press, 1970).

[14] See Gian Enrico Rusconi and Chiara Saraceno, *Ideologia religiosa e conflitto sociale* (Bari: De Donato, 1970); Franco Garelli, "Gruppi giovanili ecclesiali: tra personale e politico tra funzione educativa e azione sociale," *Quaderni di sociologia* 3–4 (1977): 275–95.

the sociological studies of early Christianity as a "movement," a study that originated with the contributions of the second half of the 1970s, and the transition from the *new quest* for the historical Jesus to the *third quest*. This approach to Christianity intended as a movement, starting from its origins in the Syrian-Palestinian region, has led to a series of studies on the various epochs of the history of the Church and Churches focused on the support of groups, fraternities, and lay congregations.

We can make only a brief reference here to the wealth of studies on the mendicant orders in the high Middle Ages—orders with which the leaders and apologists of Catholic ecclesial movements of the post-conciliar period have been increasingly eager to be identified in their official reconstructions and foundational myths. During the 1980s and 1990s, the rhetoric of the new Catholic movements as "heirs" of the medieval mendicant orders, the religious orders of the early modern age, and Tridentine Catholicism (especially of the Jesuits in the case of Opus Dei, which tried to reclaim for twentieth-century Catholicism the same role played by the Society of Jesus in the post-Trent period) became part of the apologetics of the postconciliar Catholic movements. This rhetoric allowed the movements to avoid, once again, coming to terms with the ecclesiological turning point represented by the Second Vatican Council.

5. Religious Movements, Fundamentalism, and *Revanche de Dieu*

The 1980s and 1990s saw an ebbing away of the movement-oriented approach for studies of religious movements: a wealth of studies, of which it is impossible to give an exhaustive picture here, abandoned the unruly and revolutionary viewpoint to embrace a type of analysis aimed at framing the phenomenon in the context of "postmodernity." The international research on new religious movements, which somehow incorporates also the new Catholic movements, moved primarily in two directions.

On the one hand, facing the offensive brought against the "new cults" based on considerations of public order and safety (after the mass suicide in Guyana that took place in 1978), a response was prepared to deal with the "cult controversy" of the new religious movements in North America and Europe.[15] The phenomenon of new religious movements was based on the idea of the transformation of the sacred, in

---

[15] See James A. Beckford, *Cult Controversies: The Societal Response to New Religious Movements* (London: Tavistock Publications, 1985).

particular due to the de-modernizing thrust generated by modernity itself. The new forms of religion can be interpreted as "religions of the crisis," emblematic of a period of disorientation characterized by the gnostic-type tension of "waiting for the end." In Italy, the Group for Research and Study of Sects (GRIS), recognized by the Italian Episcopal Conference (CEI), and the Center for the Studies of New Religions (CESNUR), led by Massimo Introvigne, have provided a significant contribution to this "prefectorial" approach to the phenomenon of new religions, an approach that has many links with North American scholars of new religious movements.[16]

On the other hand, the subject of study became the link between secularization and membership/religious faith in the West and the thriving of the movements in the English-speaking world, albeit with a less radical perspective than the one that characterized the 1970s. From a sociological perspective, a foundation was proposed that distinguished between faith and religious affiliation and saw the proliferation of movements as a result of the American counterculture of the 1960s, as a challenge to the secularization of society, and as a response to the secularization of the Churches. In this view, the image of postmodern Christianity is precisely that of a "religion of emotional communities," a religion wary of any doctrinal formalization, and therefore flexible, fluid, nomadic, and precarious.[17] The religious movements (in this case, those *inside* the Churches) are seen as the response to the end of inherited religious identities; thus individualization and subjectification are part of the contemporary religious landscape, in which the movement element uncovers the crisis of the "institution" and the deterioration of secularism. Since 1993, the Centre d'Etudes Interdisciplinaires des Faits Religieux at the École des hautes études en sciences sociales in Paris, coordinated by Danièle Hervieu-Léger, has been investigating the evolution of movements within the Catholic Church as it morphs into a "mosaic Church," an assemblage of many different ecclesial groups and communities.

---

[16] See Massimo Introvigne, *Le nuove religioni* (Milan: SugarCo, 1989); Massimo Introvigne, Jean-François Mayer, and Ernesto Zucchini, *I nuovi movimenti religiosi. Sètte cristiane e nuovi culti* (Leumann: Elledici, 1990).

[17] See Grace Davie, *Religion in Britain* (Oxford: Blackwell, 1994); Danièle Hervieu-Léger, *Vers un nouveau christianisme? Introduction à la sociologie du christianisme occidental* (Paris: Cerf, 1986); Danièle Hervieu-Léger, *Le pèlerin et le converti. La religion en mouvement* (Paris: Cerf, 1999).

The reflection on the relationship between movement-oriented phenomenology and *revanche de Dieu* ("revenge/comeback of God") has been analyzed in relation to the galaxy of the monotheistic religions, which in the 1970s identified the starting point for a new type of relationship between politics and religion and hence a new space for the politicized vanguards within Judaism, Christianity, and Islam.[18] The connections here are clearly with the studies of Protestant and evangelical fundamentalism in the United States, with which, however, the studies of the new Catholic movements have always had very little contact, if any at all.[19]

6. Movements in the Catholic Church

Starting from the early 1970s and during the 1980s, with the pontificate of Paul VI and especially with that of John Paul II, the Catholic Church has seen a flourishing of groups, movements, and associations that have become the strategic vanguard for the New Evangelization. One of the most recent hypotheses about the movements argues that the Catholicism of post–Vatican II, strongly rejuvenated by these movements, has led to an "evangelical" shift within the Catholic Church, especially in North America. In reality, a combination of demands for conciliar renewal of the Catholic Church, social action in solidarity with the poor, and new forms of ecclesial associations inspired by a charismatic spirituality had already emerged since the late 1970s in Latin America and beyond.[20]

Studies of ecclesial movements have been slow to follow this post-conciliar development, and not without a series of major cultural, ideological, and methodological obstacles to moving forward. One of the most accredited hypotheses on the movements' genesis within the Catholic Church is that of the "diaspora" originating from the Catholic

---

[18] See Gilles Kepel, *La Revanche de Dieu: Chrétiens, juifs et musulmans à la reconquête du monde* (Paris: Le Seuil, 1991); English edition: *The Revenge of God: The Resurgence of Islam, Christianity, and Judaism in the Modern World*, trans. Alan Braley (University Park: Pennsylvania State University Press, 1994).

[19] See George M. Marsden, *Understanding Fundamentalism and Evangelicalism* (Grand Rapids, MI: W. B. Eerdmans, 1991); *The Fundamentalism Project*, 5 vols., ed. Martin Marty and R. Scott Appleby (Chicago: University of Chicago Press, 1991–95).

[20] See Leo-Jozef Suenens and Helder Camara, *Charismatic Renewal and Social Action: A Dialogue* (Ann Arbor, MI: Servant Publications, 1979).

movement (in the singular) of the early twentieth century and Catholic Action, which gave rise, at the end of the century, to a wide galaxy of groups, associations, movements, and names. On the one hand, in post-conciliar Catholicism the historiography of Catholic Action focused on the statutory aspects of the history of the organized Catholic laity as a "modern mass organization," first "external" and then clericalized by the Church hierarchy in the first half of the twentieth century. On the other, it celebrated an "inside look" approach to the history of the movement.[21] These two approaches—the "predetermined clericalization of the movement" and the apologetic "inside look"—are reflected also in the scientific research on other subjects related to Catholic movements that only rarely attempts sociological and psychological investigations of the phenomenon or tries to create subdivisions of new religious and ecclesial movements using legal, socio-psychological, and political typologies.

In the mapping of the associative phenomena organized within the Roman Catholic Church, the prevalent view, at least from a quantitative position, is definitely the one based on "official" reconstructions "approved" by the movements under investigation. Appreciative assessments of the movements and the political attitude of John Paul II's pontificate toward the movements have appeared since 1982. These reconstructions tend to align with theological and pastoral positions common to the movements that identify their mission with the recent ecclesiastical magisterium. As such, studies shaped by a juridical approach can only partially understand and analyze, with varying degrees of completeness and multidisciplinary approach, a phenomenon, such as that of the Catholic movements, characterized by great diversity and heterogeneity in terms of national and linguistic origins, theological cultures, political leanings, exclusively lay or mixed membership, canonical regulation, and associative or, rather, "leader-centered" type of institutional structure.[22]

---

[21] See Liliana Ferrari, *L'Azione Cattolica in Italia* (Queriniana: Brescia, 1982); Liliana Ferrari, *Una storia dell'Azione cattolica. Gli ordinamenti statutari da Pio XI a Pio XII* (Genova: Marietti, 1989); Mario Casella, *L'Azione Cattolica nell'Italia contemporanea* (Rome: AVE, 1992); Ernesto Preziosi, *Obbedienti in piedi. La vicenda dell'Azione cattolica in Italia* (Turin: SEI, 1996); Mario Casella, *L'Azione Cattolica del Novecento, 1919–1969* (Rome: AVE, 2003).

[22] See *I movimenti della Chiesa negli anni Ottanta* (Milan: Jaca Book, 1982); Agostino Favale, *Movimenti ecclesiali contemporanei. Dimensioni storiche, teologico-spirituali ed apostoliche*, 2nd ed. (Rome: LAS, 1982; 4th ed., 1991).

Further, the individual movements have enjoyed *ad hoc* historical-biographical reconstructions, in most cases the result of apologetic approaches, and have usually carefully avoided investigation from an anthropological-ethnographic perspective. As regards the phenomenon of Communion and Liberation, the critical trend started by Salvatore Abbruzzese's reflections in 1989 was to some extent brought to an end by Massimo Camisasca's three commemorative volumes in the form of an official historical reconstruction, published between the end of John Paul II's pontificate and the beginning of Benedict XVI's.[23] Other examples provide confirmation of the theory of an existing trend in the studies that promise an "inside look" analysis characterized by an apologetic and defensive attitude not only in the face of "secularist" criticism but also of the one originating from within the Catholic Church.[24] Without even considering the wealth of studies on Opus Dei, if we look at the Focolare movement, Christoph Hegge's study together with Enzo Fondi and Michele Zanzucchi's official history represent a "handbook" to the Opera di Maria (the official name of the Focolare movement), welcoming the definition of "ecclesial movement" and "characterized by an 'open-minded' vision of the church, that of Vatican II."[25] Recently, the valuable study by Thomas Masters and Amy Uelmen has provided a viable model for a local "inside look" at the Focolare movement with an interesting approach to "inculturation" of the movement in the United States.[26] One of the very few studies devoted to the history of an ecclesial movement, written

[23] See Salvatore Abbruzzese, *Comunione e Liberazione. Identité catholique et disqualification du monde* (Paris: Cerf, 1989); Massimo Camisasca, *Comunione e Liberazione. Le origini (1954–1968)* (Cinisello B.: San Paolo, 2001); *Comunione e Liberazione: La ripresa (1969–1976)* (Cinisello B.: San Paolo, 2003); *Comunione e Liberazione: Il riconoscimento (1976–1984)* (Cinisello B: San Paolo, 2006).

[24] See *New Religious Movements in the Catholic Church*, ed. Michael A. Hayes (London and New York: Continuum, 2005).

[25] See Enzo Fondi and Michele Zanzucchi, *Un popolo nato dal Vangelo* (Cinisello B.: San Paolo, 2003), 542; Christoph Hegge, *Rezeption und Charisma: Der theologische und rechtliche Beitrag Kirchlicher Bewegungen zur Rezeption des Zweiten Vatikanischen Konzils* (Würzburg: Echter, 1999).

[26] See Thomas Masters and Amy Uelmen, *Focolare: Living a Spirituality of Unity in the United States* (Hyde Park, NY: New City Press, 2011). See also, for a "new movement" in United States, Kristy Nabhan-Warren, *The Cursillo Movement in America: Catholics, Protestants, and Fourth-Day Spirituality* (Chapel Hill: University of North Carolina Press, 2013).

with a scientific approach, comprehensive sources, and the necessary detachment, is that by Bern Svend Anuth on the Neocatechumenal Way.[27] Distinct from the "inside look" or "official" approach are some isolated studies, which are the result of a theological vision faithful to the episcopal ecclesiology of Vatican II, underlining the "subversive" potential of the movements within the Catholic Church, as if fearing a reinstatement of the *duo genera christianorum*. Typical of this approach is the "Geistliche Gemeinschaften und Bewegungen" (Spiritual Communities and Movements) of the *Lexicon für Theologie und Kirche*, as well as the geography traced in the early 1990s by Antonio Giolo and Brunetto Salvarani and, more recently, by Brendan Leahy.[28] But they represent voices and perspectives that, during the 1990s until now, have remained isolated and silenced by the noise coming from both an apologetic and denigrating-demonizing type of literature.

---

[27] See Bernd Sven Anuth, *Der Neokatechumenale Weg: Geschichte, Erscheinungsbild, Rechtscharakter* (Würzburg: Echter, 2006).

[28] See Antonio Giolo and Brunetto Salvarani, *I cattolici sono tutti uguali? Una mappa dei movimenti della Chiesa* (Genova: Marietti, 1992); Brendan Leahy, *Ecclesial Movements and Communities: Origins, Significance, and Issues* (Hyde Park, NY: New City Press, 2011).

CHAPTER 3

ॐ

"Catholic Movement," "Catholic Action," and the Reform Movements of the Late Nineteenth and Early Twentieth Centuries

1. Emergence of Catholic Movements

Those interested in understanding the relationship between the development of religious movements and the political, social, and cultural history of the contemporary age well know that an exclusively twentieth-century framing of the phenomenon of ecclesial movements turns out to be of little help. Viewing contemporary ecclesial movements as an exclusively twentieth-century phenomenon presupposes a character of absolute novelty while painting a picture of Catholicism as unquestionably "open to society" and supporting the view of a direct affiliation with the "progressive" theology of the laity of Franco-Belgian origin.

It is true that in the twentieth century the phenomenon takes on new forms, dimensions, and vitality in the "hierarchological ecclesiology" (in Yves Congar's words) of the long nineteenth century that emerged in the aftermath of the shock caused by the French Revolution. But it is equally true that the size of the movement is related to the historicity of Christianity and its long-term duration, where "tradition" is not at all the same—except for the reactionaries and traditionalist Catholics—as immutability and preservation. To quote one of the greatest scholars of European Catholicism in the twentieth century, Émile Poulat, "There has always been *some* movement in the

Church, as there has always been change. There have always been *some* movements in the Church, and always *some* changes."[1]

For a history of religious phenomena and in particular of religious and ecclesial movements, a general division into historical periods, albeit in the form of hypothesis, must be willing to remain open with regard to the end of the twentieth century and try to catch the signals of continuity and change between the nineteenth century, characterized by the clashes between liberal states and the Catholic Church in Europe, and the twentieth century, which in turn witnessed the complex relationship between churches, totalitarian regimes, and worldwide ideological conflict.[2] Undoubtedly, there are elements of continuity between the two souls of the Catholic movement of the late nineteenth century and the movements of the late twentieth century.

The modernization theories, typical of the 1960s, of the "eclipse of the sacred"[3] in contemporary society have already been thoroughly refuted and have been replaced by analyses—more attentive to religion as a global phenomenon—of the de-privatization of religion.[4] What still remains inadequate, however, are the purely sociological interpretations that freeze in a snapshot a phenomenon that by definition is dynamic and frame the experience of the movements in a post–Second World War or only post–Vatican II period. This view is understandably accepted and accredited by single movements for autobiographical and "institutional" reasons, but it cannot be justified in the context of the tumultuous history of Catholicism and its conflict with modern society in the nineteenth and twentieth centuries.

For this reason, the roots for the understanding of the phenomenon of the Catholic movements, which spanned the entire twentieth century, at the very least are to be found in the previous century and

---

[1] Émile Poulat, "La grande avventura del movimento cattolico in Francia (XIX e XX secolo)," *Concilium: "Movimenti" in the Church*, ed. Alberto Melloni (2003/3): 75–86, here at 75.

[2] See Giovanni Miccoli, *Fra mito della cristianità e secolarizzazione: studi sul rapporto chiesa-società nell'età contemporanea* (Casale Monferrato: Marietti, 1985); and *In difesa della fede. La chiesa di Giovanni Paolo II e Benedetto XVI* (Milan: Rizzoli, 2007).

[3] See Sabino Acquaviva, *L'eclissi del sacro nella civiltà industriale* (Milan: Edizioni di Comunità, 1961); translated into other languages and reprinted several times: Milan 1966, 1971, 1976, 1981, 1992.

[4] See the now classic work by Josè Casanova, *Public Religions in the Modern World* (Chicago: University of Chicago Press, 1994).

in the reaction of European Catholicism to the epochal trauma of the French Revolution and of the political revolutions in Europe in the first half of the nineteenth century.

One of the arguments most commonly accepted, and not without foundation, on the genesis of the movements in the Church is the one that sees a shift from the broad current of the late nineteenth- and early twentieth-centuries "Catholic movement" (in the singular) to the many branches of the second half of the twentieth-century "Catholic movements" (in the plural).[5] It is a model that reconciles the elements of continuity and discontinuity between the two moments, albeit without dwelling on the enormous changes pertaining to the social context and the political-cultural climate of the Catholic Church in the late nineteenth and early twentieth centuries. Further, it does not take into consideration the relationship between the two different souls of the movement of the late nineteenth century and the wide galaxy of contemporary ecclesial groups.

The issue of continuity also arises in relation to the various stages of that first blossoming of the laity in the shadow of the initiatives of the papacy and of Catholic bishops in Europe. It is, however, clear that one of the first issues that needs to be addressed to understand the phenomenon of the movements in the Church of the twentieth century is that of the continuity between the history of the "Catholic movement" emerging in the late nineteenth and early twentieth centuries on one side and, on the other, the associations that were found in the second half of the twentieth century after the war and Vatican II—associations that now, at the beginning of the twenty-first century, are the face of the "Catholicism of the movements."

2. The "Catholic Movement" of Leo XIII and Pius X

The term "movement"—in the singular—originated in France around the time of the political crisis of 1830 to distinguish the "Party of the Movement" from the "Party of the Resistance" and, still in France, was later adopted by Auguste Comte for his studies of social phenom-

---

[5] See Antonio Giolo and Brunetto Salvarani, *I cattolici sono tutti uguali? Una mappa dei movimenti della Chiesa* (Genova: Marietti, 1992).

ena.[6] The use of the term "movements" (in the plural) will become widespread only in the late twentieth century to identify new communities, realities of association, advocacy agencies, and theological-spiritual leanings within the Catholic Church.

In reality, in the Church of Rome the organized laity began to "find its voice" only in the mid-twentieth century—but in a very different sense from that *pris de la parole* ("speaking up") that was one of the hallmarks of the early 1960s (and even of the Catholic 1960s).[7] In the conflict between the Catholic Church and the liberal states, and starting with Leo XIII, the papacy and the bishops had no scruples in mobilizing the laity to defend the prerogatives of the Church and use the same laity as an antiliberal and anti-Marxist vehicle for its antiliberal and anti-Marxist social teaching.[8]

The recruitment initiatives of Leo XIII (1878–1903) and the consolidating efforts of Pius X (1903–14) met with significant differences and discontinuities but according to a political-ecclesiological model fundamentally homogeneous and consistent. An ecclesiology marked by a prevailing juridical approach led to accentuating the unity of the ecclesiastical institution as *societas iuridice perfecta* ("a juridically perfect society/community"), thus aiming to institutionally incorporate the existence of phenomena such as groups, associations, and organizations that—in that model of Church—did not escape from the ordering principle of the vertical-hierarchical ecclesial authority.[9] In the Church shaped by the First Vatican Council (1869–70) no legal legitimacy, ecclesiastical praxis, or theological justification was given to support the experiences of Catholics released from the local

---

[6] See Alberto Melloni, *Chiesa madre, chiesa matrigna. Un discorso storico sul cristianesimo che cambia* (Turin: Einaudi, 2005), 86.

[7] Michel de Certeau (1925–86) stated that "in May 1968, the floor was taken exactly as the Bastille was taken in 1789"; see Michel de Certeau, *La Prise de parole, pour une nouvelle culture* (Paris: Desclée De Brouwer, 1968).

[8] See *Le pontificat de Léon XIII: renaissances du Saint-Siège?*, ed. Philippe Levillain and Jean-Marc Ticchi (Rome: École Française de Rome, 2006).

[9] See Severino Dianich, "L'ecclesiologia in Italia dal Vaticano I al Vaticano II," in *Dizionario storico del movimento cattolico in Italia, 1860–1980*, ed. Francesco Traniello and Giorgio Campanini, vol. 1/1 (Genova: Marietti, 1981), 162–80; Giuseppe Alberigo, "Le concezioni della Chiesa e i mutamenti istituzionali," in *Chiesa e papato nel mondo contemporaneo*, ed. Giuseppe Alberigo and Andrea Riccardi (Roma-Bari: Laterza, 1990), 65–121.

dimension of obedience to the diocesan bishops and parish priests, the more so if these experiences were designed to recover the prophetic and charismatic dimension of the religious experience lived in a community of life organically and hierarchically not related to the Church as a legal institution. The reaction against the French Revolution and the liberal revolutions, and the ensuing definitions of Vatican I on the primacy and infallibility of the pope, imprinted on the conscience of the Catholic Church an "intransigent" label from within, no less than from outside.

During the nineteenth and early twentieth centuries, the Catholic Church was unable to conceive of the conditions of existence of a "community" of faithful (either lay or clerical) that did not coincide with either the ecclesiastical districts and religious orders subject to a bishop or well-identified hierarchical superior or with the context of ecclesial life in the society of European and Western *christianitas*, soon to become the myth of Christendom. The development of lay activism in the Church during the late nineteenth century and the first two decades of the twentieth century was framed within a "Catholic action" that increasingly took on the characteristics of a militant mass organization.

The birth of a movement culture as a defense weapon of Catholicism in a secularized and de-confessionalized[10] Europe represented a dimension of the encounter between Catholicism and mass society in the Western world, especially in Europe.[11] The struggle not only took place at the political level, with the denial of legitimacy of the new nation-states and, first, of Italy, but also within the ranks of the Church against those members who were more willing to come to terms with the new situation as well as with the new discoveries of science and modern culture.

The papacy's harsh repression against the ferment of the theology of "modernism" in Europe[12] meant also an embargo against biblical

---

[10] "Confessionalization" in the sense of *Konfessionalisierung*, which was introduced in historiography in the eighties by Wolfgang Reinhard and Heinz Schilling; see *Die katholische Konfessionalisierung*, ed. Wolfgang Reinhard and Heinz Schilling (Münster: Aschendorff, 1995).

[11] See Elias Canetti, *Masse und Macht* (Hamburg: Claassen, 1960); English edition: *Crowds and Power*, trans. Carol Stewart (New York: Continuum, 1973).

[12] Pius X's encyclical condemning the "modernist" doctrines, *Pascendi Dominici Gregis*, was issued on September 8, 1907.

studies and the history of early Christianity, a restriction that helped to prevent, first, the emergence of a theological reflection and, then, a juridical-canonical one capable of recovering the "movement" dimension of the Christian communities.[13] In the Catholic Church between Vatican I and Vatican II the vertical dimension always had the better of any horizontality of the relationship of faith between and within local communities (either parish/diocesan or religious).

Thus, the emergence of the Catholic movement between the late nineteenth and early twentieth centuries was neither characterized by a leading role of the laity nor witnessed the emergence of new theological, cultural, and spiritual sensibilities in the Catholic Church; these remained confined within specific, limited, and permanent circles and environments, which gave life—after surviving the repression from Rome and in the following decades—to the Church of the Second Vatican Council and to some of its "reform movements" but never gained that public visibility and power that characterize the mass movements of contemporary Catholicism.

The origins of the Catholic movement represented an attempt on the part of the Catholic Church to respond on the "social" level (and therefore not directly "political," given that the Church hierarchy recognized neither its "constitutional" nor theological legitimacy) to the political and cultural offensive of liberalism and socialism in Europe, which were compared to the challenge against the Church led first by Luther and then by the French Revolution: "The Catholic movement is, in a certain sense, the lay Catholic response to the liberal secularization of state and society."[14]

3. From Pius IX to Pius X: The Catholic Movement from the Counter-Revolution to the "Social Question"

The fifty years from the decade of the unification of Italy and Vatican I to the First World War represent the cradle of the Catholic movement in Europe. Not surprisingly, its gestation coincided with

---

[13] See *Pio X e il suo tempo*, ed. Gianni La Bella (Bologna: Il Mulino, 2003); Maurilio Guasco, *Modernismo: i fatti, le idee, i personaggi* (Cinisello B.: San Paolo, 1995); Claus Arnold, *Kleine Geschichte des Modernismus* (Freiburg: Herder, 2007).

[14] See Francesco Traniello and Giorgio Campanini's introduction to *Dizionario storico del movimento cattolico in Italia*, ix.

the age of nationalisms and with the reaction of the Catholic Church against them. The typical line of action of the Catholic movement was modeled, and not only in Italy, by the papacy's direct policy in opposition to the "liberal states" governed by constitutions and elective parliaments.

In the mid-nineteenth century, the papacy's reaction to the French Revolution and the age of constitutions and declarations of rights marked a Catholic culture proclaiming itself to be unavailable to compromise with modern freedoms. Toward the end of the century, the tactic employed in relation to the "social question" had brought into play a new participant, the Catholic movement that, without rejecting its intransigent origins, developed new forms of association and mobilization, all under the strict control of the ecclesiastical hierarchy, the pope, and the bishops. Its direct dependence on the papacy and bishops was clear in terms of the purposes of mobilization and the choice of the organizational structure as well as for the selection of the leadership of the movement.

The movement culture of the late nineteenth and early twentieth centuries never questioned its place in the organized hierarchical pyramid erected by the Catholic ecclesiology, because the movement itself emerged in a political and cultural—and therefore also theological—climate that repudiated the "modern freedoms" that materialized in contraposition to the political and social model of European *christianitas*.

The emergence of the Catholic movement was sought by the Church hierarchy and came into view as an "extension" of the pope's arm, created to deal with socio-political issues as the Catholic socio-economic movement and divorced from any kind of ecclesial, spiritual, theological, or liturgical reflection. It was a socio-economic movement that left to the Church hierarchy the decision to establish possible relationships with political-parliamentary groups, relationships that the papacy took upon itself, without delegating this task to the Catholic laity.

It is important to remember that the Catholic movement in the late nineteenth century and Pius XI's pontificate existed in a context shaped by the Roman policy *non expedit* ("it is not expedient" for Catholics to participate, as elector or elected, in politics, including voting). The ban on the participation of Catholics in Italian national elections, a ban that was particularly effective between 1874 and 1905, reverberated on the "social" choice of Catholics, a choice that no longer had a "political" component to it and that would find legitimacy in the Catholic Church only after many decades. This division of political and social lines of action between the Catholic hierarchy and the laity not only was fraught with consequences for the political life of European nations but also imprinted specific traits on the "genome" of the Catholic movement. First and foremost, it marked the instability of the Catholic movement in the first half of the twentieth century—especially when engaged in the political sphere.

The importance of managing political issues directly between the papacy and the states, without political or partisan interventions of any kind, was contrasted on the one hand by the weakness of a *political movement* created by the Church hierarchy, restricted to implement the directives of the hierarchy, and at the mercy of the hierarchy to the extreme point of self-sacrifice. On the other hand, there was an *economic movement* that at that time was able to consolidate, in a fierce political climate, the base of its economic and financial "hard power." What happened at the beginning of the twentieth century at the Opera dei Congressi (Work of the Congresses) in Italy, with the dissolution of its absolute power on the altar of the papacy's liberty to deal with political powers, would happen again, in Italy, to the Associazione Scout Cattolici Italiani (Association of Italian Catholic Boy Scouts) as well as to Luigi Sturzo's Partito Popolare during the Fascist regime and the clash of dictatorships between the two world wars.

The relationship between Catholic movements and the ecclesiastical hierarchy, which became less severe starting with the Second Vatican Council, was one of functional dependency. This relationship of dependency and obedience to the ecclesiastical hierarchy would eventually take on, with John Paul II's pontificate, more diverse and nuanced traits, but it was still marked by a new and tacit pact of coexistence between the Holy See and the new ecclesial movements.

4. Origins of the Organized Catholic Laity

This response of the Catholic Church to the liberal secularization of state and society had a more direct impact on the Italian social scenario but spread throughout Western Europe as well. The wave of nationalisms forced the Roman Catholic Church to redefine its strategies of political and territorial presence through the creation of the episcopal conferences conceived as Rome's *longa manus* ("long arm") in opposition to the national states, "agents" of the Catholic cause among the liberal elites (and not as advocates of the local churches against the universalism of Rome as in the late twentieth century).[15]

Similarly, the establishment of an organized Catholic laity was part of the papal strategy to fight back against the subversive maneuvers of modernity and its opposition to the Catholic Church and the tradition it embodied. In France, the tones of an "intransigent" Catholicism, originating from the refusal to participate in the civic life of the new state, took on a different color with Leo XIII's pontificate as the result of the confluence of different currents inspired by Rome, especially the *ralliement* ("rallying") of French Catholics to the unconditional acceptance of the French Republic and "social Catholicism." But the direction and the relationship that saw the activism of the Catholic laity closely linked to the Holy See was undivided in France, as in a Germany that had just gone through the *Kulturkampf,* the "culture war" against Catholicism enacted in the 1870s by the prime minister of Prussia, Otto von Bismarck.[16]

In Italy, the history of the relationship between the Church of Rome and the role of the Catholic laity was peculiar, considering the special relationship between the Rome of the popes and the newborn Italian state. More than elsewhere, the new "lay" organizations on the Italian peninsula were directly dependent on the pope and the Roman headquarters of the Church. The Catholic Youth Organization (Società della Gioventù Cattolica [SGCI]), which came to light in 1868 and was approved by Pius IX in May of the same year, organized the first congress of Italian Catholics in 1874 in Venice, from which the Opera dei Congressi (Work of the Congresses) later emerged. According to the SGCI statutes, a central governing role was given to a "high council,"

---

[15] See Giorgio Feliciani, *Le conferenze episcopali* (Bologna: Il Mulino, 1974).

[16] See Yvon Tranvouez, *Catholiques d'abord: approches du mouvement catholique en France (XIXe–XXe siècle)* (Paris: Editions Ouvrières, 1988); Gérard Cholvy, *Histoire des organisations et mouvements chrétiens de jeunesse en France (XIXe–XXe siècle)* (Paris: Cerf, 1999), esp. 111–47; Angelika Steinmaus-Pollak, *Das als katholische Aktion organisierte Laienapostolat: Geschichte seiner Theorie und seiner kirchenrechtlichen Praxis in Deutschland* (Würzburg: Echter, 1988); Andreas Wollasch, *Der Katholische Fürsorgeverein für Mädchen, Frauen und Kinder (1899–1945)* (Freiburg i.B.: Lambertus, 1991).

recognized by the ecclesiastical authority, which attached to it a priest known as the ecclesiastical assistant. Still in 1868, an internal regulation was approved, and later renewed in 1872, in which the autonomy of the laity regarding the internal management of the organization was accompanied by a clear dependence of the same laity on the Church hierarchy in matters pertaining to the "educational contents."[17] Dedicated to the education of young people and the public profession of faith, and by following the teachings of Vatican I, SGCI was the expression of a Catholic culture that relied more on its devotion to the pope and the Holy See than on the diocesan bishops. As such, it was an aspect of the Catholic "modernization without modernity," an offspring of Vatican I, which will reemerge in many ecclesial movements of the late twentieth century as well as in the Judaic, Christian, and Islamic fundamentalist movements within the context of the *revanche de Dieu* ("revenge/comeback of God") of the late twentieth century.

The difficulty of placing the nascent Catholic movement of the late nineteenth century within the frame of modernity or anti-modernity becomes apparent even with regard to other elements: its *lay origin*, which, however, represented a change from the past, and its organizational dimension at the *national level*, which signaled (as the creation of national episcopal conferences around the same time) the inevitability of coming to terms with the emergence of nation-states, even if they were still identified with the "conspiracy" forces at work against the Catholic Church.

The encyclical *Rerum Novarum* by Leo XIII (1891), which celebrated this new activism outlining at the same time the programmatic guidelines of Catholic social action, defined the signs of the times. The Catholic movement was a network of associations that was *not* committed to redefining the ways of belonging to the Church of Rome or its forms of devotions, theologies, or relations with other Christian denominations. It was instead a network of Catholic entities that represented the "public" face and the hub of a Catholic Church made of associations, cooperatives, groups, alliances, clubs, and unions. As the official lay organization obedient to the pope and, at the same time, a religious, social, political association, the Opera dei Congressi

---

[17] See Ernesto Preziosi, *Obbedienti in piedi. La vicenda dell'Azione Cattolica in Italia* (Turin: SEI, 1996).

was the organized expression of the intransigent Catholic social culture—at a time when "social Catholicism" had not yet acquired its
connotation of "left-wing Catholicism," which it will take in the political language of the second half of the twentieth century. At the end
of the nineteenth century, the loyalty to the Church in the person of
the pope was combined with an "intransigent" opposition to liberal
governments, its ideology, its laws, and in service to the dioceses and
bishops. In effect, in the Church of Vatican I, it was inconceivable to
contrast the sense of belonging to the local diocesan church with the
loyalty to the pope, which had become the distinctive trait of Catholic
"confessionalization."

Organized in a hierarchical and centralized structure, with headquarters in Venice and a peripheral configuration divided into local,
regional, diocesan, and parish committees, the Opera dei Congressi
periodically held national congresses. After 1880, it developed rapidly
and established itself particularly in the regions of Lombardy and
Veneto, while promoting a broad economic and social policy with the
establishment of rural banks, mutual aid societies, and cooperatives.[18]
Hence, "intransigent" culture and new pastoral sensitivity toward "social" issues, which were the basic components of the Catholic movement of the late nineteenth century, were two sides of the same coin.

The ambiguous ecclesial-political position of the Catholic movement of the late nineteenth century encountered a first test in 1896,
when Romolo Murri founded the Italian Catholic Federation of University Students (FUCI).[19] At that time, the emergence within the
Catholic movement of the Christian-democratic leanings that were
headed by Romolo Murri and Filippo Meda—inclined toward a more
social and political openness—created, after 1896, a conflict situation
with the Opera dei Congressi, triggering a crisis within the movement.

The loyalty to the pope and the attention to the social question
constituted the evidence of the dangerousness of the Catholic movement as a subversive and "anti-system" force. After the shock caused

[18] For the role of this network of social Catholicism in the life of Angelo Giuseppe
Roncalli (later John XXIII), see Massimo Faggioli, *John XXIII: The Medicine of Mercy*
(Collegeville, MN: Liturgical Press, 2014), 29–32.

[19] Long before he was suspended *a divinis* in 1907, and excommunicated in 1909,
following his election as Member of Parliament; see Daniela Saresella, *Romolo Murri
e il movimento socialista, 1891–1907* (Urbino: Quattro venti, 1994).

by the deaths in the street clashes of 1898 in Italy, the participation of "social" Catholics in the strikes between 1901 and 1902 constituted cause for concern for the Vatican hierarchy (even though some bishops gave support to the protesters). It was only the beginning of a new trajectory. In 1901, Leo XIII's encyclical *Graves de Communi Re* reaffirmed the hierarchical relationship of interdependence between the papacy, bishops, and Catholic movement:

> And this action of Catholics certainly will exert a wider influence if all societies, while preserving its autonomy, will move under the impulse of one direction. And in Italy we want this direction to be led by the Opera dei Congressi and the Catholic Committees, that time and again earned Our praise, to which Our Predecessor and We ourselves entrusted the task of directing the Catholic movement always under the auspices and guidance of the Bishops.[20]

In 1902, with Leo XIII's *Instructions* to the Catholic movement, the pope took "the first step toward the establishment of a new relationship between the institutional Church and the Catholic movement."[21]

After the election of Pius X (August 4, 1903), the direction impressed by the papacy with regard to the Catholic movement was intended to restrict the freedom of "experimentation" of the Catholic laity and especially to reiterate its subordination to the directives of the Church hierarchy, particularly of the pope. In terms of "active militancy," whether in the religious or political and social spheres, the laity was given a subordinate role.[22] In July 1904, the dissolution of the Opera dei Congressi by the Vatican Secretariat of State, attributable to the pontificate's refusal to accept both the changes in the relationship between clergy and laity and the levels of autonomy of the laity in its approach to Italian politics, marked a rupture in the development of the lay Catholic movement and of the "Catholic action" (lowercase).

In the reorganization of the Catholic movement, Pius X's 1905 *Norms* to the laity, constituted a Magna Carta for organized Catholic movements, giving rise to a model (which remained in force for a long time) of association-movements recognized by the ecclesiastical

---

[20] Leo XIII, encyclical *Graves de Communi Re*, January 18, 1901, no. 23.

[21] Liliana Ferrari, *Una storia dell'Azione cattolica. Gli ordinamenti statutari da Pio XI a Pio XII* (Genova: Marietti, 1989), 18.

[22] See Pius X's encyclical letter *Il fermo proposito*, June 11, 1905.

hierarchy: the bishops took the direction of Catholic action, and the priests were present at different levels of the associations as ecclesiastical assistants and representatives of the ecclesiastical authority, which appointed them with the right of veto.

Pius X's contribution was central to continuing and strengthening the line of a Catholic movement subject to the Vatican policy directed toward the social question. At that time, one of the most significant experiences of social Catholicism, the Social Weeks, came to light: in France in 1904, in Spain in 1906, in Italy in 1907, in Belgium in 1908, and in Mexico and Uruguay in 1908.

But Pius X was also decisive in intervening directly with the Catholic movement to deal with outbreaks of rebellion and leaders accused of doctrinal deviations, which fell back into the antimodernist campaign launched by the encyclical *Pascendi* of 1907. The condemnation of social, theological, and cultural modernism meant also the inclusion of representatives of the Catholic movement more attuned to the new demands of social and political engagement.

From an institutional point of view, the restructuring of Catholics' lay action saw the creation of three new unions: the Italian Catholic Popular Union, the Italian Catholic Union of Electoral Associations, and the Italian Catholic Union of the Social and Economic Institutions (or Catholic and Economic Social Union). These three unions had specific tasks, namely, of organization and coordination in the electoral process and in the social sphere. In addition to these three unions, there was the Catholic Youth Organization, which during Pius X's pontificate took on the traits of a mass organization and was at the origin of the future "Italian Catholic Action."

5. Origin and Crisis of the "Reform Movements"

The picture of the emergence of ecclesial movements would be incomplete if we failed to mention the defeated, so to speak, minority of the history of Catholic movements. At the heart of the contemporary Catholic movements there is no doubt the activist, "Romanocentric" and "Romanized," current of the Catholic movement. But the other element that helped to shape contemporary Catholicism was the intellectual-spiritual current, which found itself on the margins of mainstream Catholicism and forced to longer or shorter periods of clandestineness. This second current of thought of the modern Catholic movements originated at the same time as the first one but went in the opposite direction when it came to the relationship with the "modern times."

Alongside the socio-economic, Ultramontanist, and papalist arm, and the solidaristic activism loyal to the papacy's political course of action and vetoes, there emerged a series of reflections and contributions undoubtedly movement oriented in character with regard to new methods and initiatives, courage, and ability to envision the situation besetting the Church between the late nineteenth and early twentieth centuries.

During this time, the reform movements came alive and, in the course of the twentieth century, eventually brought to Roman Catholicism the boldest content for the liturgical reform (starting from the use of national languages for liturgical celebrations), the return of Catholics to the reading of the Scriptures, the desire for an ecumenical thrust able to re-create the visible unity among Christians. Not coincidentally, these movements originated outside of Italy (especially in France, Belgium, and Germany), animated by single theologians and monks or small groups, active in centers and journals (such as the *École Biblique de Jérusalem*, founded in 1890, and the *Revue biblique*, founded in 1892) and monasteries (as Solesmes in France; Beuron in southern Germany; Louvain in Belgium; and a few years later, in 1926, Saint John's Abbey in Collegeville, Minnesota, the cradle of the liturgical movement in North America).

We can situate at the end of the nineteenth century the first stage of the formation of these semi-clandestine groups that placed themselves on a different but parallel side to the Catholic movement demanded by Pope Leo XIII and structured by Pius X along the lines of a pronounced devotion to the pope and a "Romanization" of Catholicism as a whole.[23] The 1890s and Pius X's pontificate saw the birth of the early advocates of ecumenism (such as the French Dominican Yves Congar) and the initiatives of the founders of the Catholic biblical movement (among whom was another French Dominican, Marie-Joseph Lagrange) and of the liturgical movement (the Benedictines Dom Prosper Guéranger and Dom Lambert Beauduin).[24]

---

[23] See Étienne Fouilloux, "I movimenti di riforma nel pensiero cattolico del XIX e XX secolo," in *I movimenti nella storia del cristianesimo. Caratteristiche—variazioni—continuità*, ed. Giuseppe Alberigo and Massimo Faggioli, *Cristianesimo nella Storia* 24, no. 3 (2003): 659–76.

[24] See André Haquin, *Dom Lambert Beauduin et le renouveau liturgique* (Gembloux: Duculot, 1970); Maria Paiano, *Liturgia e società nel Novecento: percorsi del movimento*

If the Catholic Church of the Catholic social movement was anti-modern, anti-Protestant, antiliberal, and not without anti-Semitic and anti-Jewish impulses, the reform movements were intended to renew and rejuvenate the face of Catholicism: recovering the true, ecumenical Tradition of the undivided Church and abandoning other traditions, the real *parvenues* of modern Catholicism, and returning to the biblical sources (*ressourcement*), the writing of the fathers of the Church in the patristic period, to break away with the official neo-Thomistic theology.[25] The reform movements were not opposed to opening up to the ideas of the time, in order to "break down the ramparts" (in the words of Hans Urs von Balthasar) of the fortress of a Catholicism perched in a fierce defense of its Roman and papalist identity.

The paths of these two different types of movements—the intransigent "Catholic" one, and the reformist-intellectual one—for a long time remained parallel. Only in the mid-twentieth century, during the Second Vatican Council and the postconciliar period, did these two currents experience a phase of approach and confluence, which, unfortunately, did not last long, giving way instead to a new generation of movements—heirs of the intransigent Catholic social supply chain rather than the theological-intellectual one.[26]

---

liturgico di fronte ai processi di secolarizzazione (Rome: Edizioni di Storia e Letteratura, 2000); Bernard Montagnes, *Marie-Joseph Lagrange. Une biographie critique* (Paris: Cerf, 2005).

[25] See Giovanni Miccoli, "Santa Sede, questione ebraica e antisemitismo fra Otto e Novecento," in *Gli ebrei in Italia*, ed. Claudio Vivanti, vol. 2 *Dall'emancipazione ad oggi*, Storia d'Italia, Annali 11/2 (Turin: Einaudi, 1997); Renato Moro, *La Chiesa e lo sterminio degli ebrei* (Bologna: Il Mulino, 2002), 48–58.

[26] See *La theologie catholique entre intransigeance et renouveau. La reception des mouvements preconciliaires a Vatican II*, ed. Gilles Routhier, Philippe Roy, Karim Schelken (Leuven: Louvain-la-Neuve, 2011).

ᘒ

Catholic Movement and Political
Ideologies of the Twentieth Century

One of the key elements for understanding Catholic movements is
the role played by modern political ideologies and the reaction of
the Roman papacy to them in the late nineteenth and early twentieth
centuries. The result of this dialectic has given shape to much of the
history of Catholic movements, starting from the crisis that the movements for liturgical, ecumenical, and biblical, patristic *ressourcement*
reform experienced between the pontificate of Pius X and that of
Pius XII.

Already severely subdued, albeit in an indirect way, by Pius X's condemnation of modernism starting from 1907, these movements represented the response of an elite to the epochal crisis of the relationship
between the Church and the modern world. Formed by groups of
intellectuals and theologians, and perceived by Rome as foreign to
the design of the *reconquista* of modern society, these groups had a
complicated life in the institutional Church, as they were strangers to
both the rejection of the principles of modernity and the adoption of
modern tools of mass organization and consensus building in a society characterized by political mobilization. The proposals and the
reform experiments of the Catholic Church, and its theology, liturgy,
and relations with non-Catholic Christians, were rejected because they
conveyed to Rome a weakening of the ecclesial body. Between the two
world wars, the Catholic magisterium's reading of the contemporary
world was marked by certain apocalyptic tendencies, as evidenced in
the tone used by the bishops in their pastoral letters. As a result, the
"besieged citadel" of Catholicism chose the language and the strategy
of mobilization instead of reconciliation with the "modern world."

The master plan for the action of the Church in the European nations caught between nationalist ideologies and the Bolshevik threat passed through a Catholic Action linked to the ecclesiastical hierarchy, the papacy, and the bishops: neither the temptations of autonomy of the Catholics' political party nor the theology of the reform movements had any room in the Church between the First and Second World War. The chosen option was the one represented by an organized group of laypeople, heirs of the Catholic movement that originated in the late nineteenth century.

1. Movement and Society during Pius XI's Pontificate

In a Catholic Church whose leadership was still essentially European, that had interpreted the First World War as the painful evidence of the catastrophic consequences of abandoning the Catholic faith on the part of European societies, and that had taken from modernity the tools[1] but not the modern thought, "movement" and "mobilization" shared more than just the same etymological root.

At the time of his election (February 6, 1922), Pius XI faced a number of different Catholic organizations, the offspring of the nineteenth-century Catholic associations, which responded to the need for mobilization launched by the Church as a response to the mass and youth mobilization instigated by the authoritarian and totalitarian regimes in Europe. In the years immediately following the end of the Great War, the Catholic world was characterized by the impulse to mobilization, organization, and militancy. It was widely believed that the war, from which mass social phenomena had sprung, disrupted the balance of the political-religious structures of the liberal age, thus establishing the conditions of a profound change in the public role of religion in Europe.

But the profound change that the Catholic hierarchies hoped for was certainly not going toward a movement aiming to reform the Church at the hands of lay groups interested in exploring a new type of relationship between Church and society, between clergy and laity. In the thought of the ecclesiastical hierarchy between the two world wars, a priority objective was the preservation of a social and political

---

[1] The first Code of Canon Law was issued in 1917 and was modeled on the civil codes of the nineteenth-century liberal states.

order aiming to preserve the "freedom of the Church" in its teaching role exercised by the pope and the bishops and some of the principles of natural law and Christian ethics pertaining to Catholic marriage, education, and youth formation.

With these specific goals in mind, the socio-political organizations of lay Catholics would soon be put to shame and then sacrificed. If it is true that the tone of Pius XI's pontificate undergoes a certain change in the 1930s, following the confrontation with the totalitarian regimes,[2] it is also true that the ecclesiology of the papacy remained tied to the notion of the "Kingship of Christ."[3] In what has been called the "theology of Catholic Action" enunciated by the encyclical *Ubi Arcano Dei Consilio* (1922), Pope Pius XI declared that Christ reigns when "His Church is recognized, for He bestowed on the Church the status and the constitution of a society which, by reason of the perfect ends which it is called upon to attain, must be held to be supreme in its own sphere; He also made her the depository and interpreter of His divine teachings, and, by consequence, the teacher and guide of every other society."[4]

Catholic Action became an active part of the Church's plan, aiming at the "restoration of the Kingdom of Christ" in a modern society viewed as corrupt and lacerated in the struggle between classes, between political parties, and within families. The restoration of peace had to go through the reestablishment of the *societas Christiana* under the guidance of the papal and episcopal ecclesiastical authority.

The Roman Catholic Church as *societas perfecta* neither created nor left room for attempts at reform and renewal from the bottom up. The imperative of political confrontation with the regimes, the rejection of modernity, the tradition of neoscholastic theology, and the recent codification of the Code of Canon Law certainly did not constitute a fertile ground for the creation of new ecclesial groups, creating instead a heavy atmosphere against the theologies and spirituality that escaped this framework. In 1928, the encyclical *Mortalium Animos* was an abrupt awakening from the dream of some Catholics

---

[2] See Emma Fattorini, *Pio XI, Hitler e Mussolini. La solitudine di un papa* (Turin: Einaudi, 2007); English translation on: *Hitler, Mussolini and the Vatican: Pope Pius XI and the Speech That Was Never Made*, trans. Carl Ipsen (Cambridge, UK: Polity, 2011).

[3] See Daniele Menozzi, *Sacro Cuore. Un culto tra devozione interiore e restaurazione cristiana della società* (Rome: Viella, 2001).

[4] Pius XI, encyclical *Ubi arcano*, December 23, 1922, no. 48.

of an ecumenical movement that would restore the visible unity of Christians;[5] the Catholic thought projected toward the opening to the modern world continued to remain on the margins of the official theology;[6] the biblical renewal movement suffered disappointments until the end of Pius XI's pontificate and became part of the language of the Church well after the disappearance of its first advocates.[7]

2. Pius XI's Catholic Action

The negative reading of modern times on the part of the Catholic magisterium was not without consequences on the structure of the organizations of the Catholic laity and especially on the balance between "social action" (inspired and guided by the ecclesiastical hierarchy) and "political action" (led by Catholic laypeople with limited spaces of autonomy, which, however, in the eyes of the ecclesiastical hierarchy, were already dangerously increasing). The Catholic movement culture that originated in the 1920s suffered from the decision, taken in the period between the two world wars, to bring the laity under the control of the papacy and the bishops, with the idea of saving them—as far as possible—from the violence of totalitarian regimes but also from the exercise of lay autonomy regarding modern freedoms.

At the dawn of fascism in Italy, the tension between what would become the apple of Pius XI's eye, Catholic Action, and the Italian Partito Popolare would soon be resolved with the Holy See's repudiation of the party in October 1922. Rome decided to bet on Catholic Action as an appropriate force to put a stop to the hegemonic claims of fascism, not only with regard to youth formation. The Church still put up with fascism, however, to preserve the political and social order already under socialist and Communist threat. Between December 1922 and the end of 1923, that is, during the first year of his pontificate, Pope Pius XI not only imparted his directives for Catholic Action but also ordered its

---

[5] See Étienne Fouilloux, *Les catholiques et l'unité chrétienne du XIXe au XXe siècle. Itinéraires européens d'expression francaise* (Paris: Le Centurion, 1982).

[6] See Étienne Fouilloux, *Une Église en quête de liberté. La pensée catholique française entre modernisme et Vatican II (1914–1962)* (Paris: Desclée de Brouwer, 1998); Yves Congar, *Journal d'un theologien (1946–1956)*, ed. Étienne Fouilloux (Paris: Cerf, 2001).

[7] See François Laplanche, *La crise de l'origine. La science catholique des Evangiles et l'histoire au XXe siècle* (Paris: Michel, 2006).

reorganization.[8] A central board was established, its highest governing body, consisting of members appointed by the pope and by the presidents of the Italian Catholic Youth Organization (Gioventù Cattolica Italiana, GCI), the Italian Catholic Federation of University Students (Federazione Universitaria Cattolici Italiani, FUCI), the Union of Italian Catholic Women (Unione Femminile Cattolica Italiana, founded in 1908), and the Federation of Catholic Men (Federazione degli Uomini Cattolici, created by Pope Pius XI in November 1922).

Inside the new Catholic Action, which was formed by a series of organizations, GCI and FUCI were the two more institutional ones, which not surprisingly manifested strong resistance to the new unitary model of the Catholic movement, centered on the principle of the "ecclesiastical mandate of the Church," under the guidance of the pope and the bishops. On October 2, 1923—the conventional date for Catholic Action's birth—Pius XI approved the new structure, which transformed Catholic Action into an organization showing signs of innovation compared to the Catholic movement of the past.

The Italian situation had clear peculiarities that nevertheless had particular significance when considering that Pius XI's model for Italy was also exported and applied to other European countries, such as France and Belgium. Pius XI's plan was to bring about the unity of the different organizations of the Catholic laity under the umbrella of Catholic Action, which would then occupy a central role in the Catholic "militant" world, under strict ecclesiastical control, instead of being led by the autonomous initiatives of a laity exposed to the influence of the ideologies of the modern world.

Described as a "form of apostolate" and a "collaboration of the laity in the hierarchical apostolate," Catholic Action was defined as "participation of the laity in the mission of the Church" and "totally dependent on the ecclesiastical authority." Thus, the Catholic laity was somewhat removed from the social and political sphere, was absorbed by the ecclesiastical one, and had an ancillary function only. The Church itself

---

[8] See Mario Casella, "L'Azione Cattolica del tempo di Pio XI e di Pio XII (1922–1958)," in *Dizionario storico del movimento cattolico in Italia, 1860–1980*, ed. Francesco Traniello and Giorgio Campanini, vol. 1/1 (Genova: Marietti, 1981), 84–101; Guido Formigoni, *L'Azione Cattolica Italiana* (Milan: Ancora, 1988), 53–73. See also John Pollard, "Pius XI's Promotion of the Italian Model of Catholic Action in the World-Wide Church," *Journal of Ecclesiastical History* 63 (October 2012): 758–84.

determined the Church's competences and the limits of its interference, as well as those of Catholic Action. The responsibility for defining the attitude of Catholics toward the regime was left to the Holy See, while Catholic Action was entrusted to perform an action of spiritual and cultural influence, according to a model that excluded elements of particularism or sectarianism. There was no possibility of dividing the members on the basis of specific professional interests or social commitments that could lead to internal factions or, worse, echo the ongoing class struggle—as the specialized movement of Catholic Action and the international "specialized movements" (including Jeunesse Ouvrière Chrétienne [JOC]) in France and Belgium attempted to do in the 1920s. In these two countries, the "lay apostolic" organizations such as the Legion of Mary (founded in 1921), which were not part of Catholic Action's structure, were nevertheless still organized on the model of the military legion and used a military type of vocabulary, albeit guided by laypeople and nourished by Marian spirituality.[9]

The "general mobilization" of the Catholic laity at the orders of the Church hierarchy did not contemplate the possibility of a laity committed to reflect or discuss the theological or pastoral choices of a Church involved in a confrontation with modernity. The condition for membership in Catholic Action was to act according to the teachings of the Church, the Holy See's directives, and under the dependence upon the competent ecclesiastical authority. Unlike tertiary orders and fraternities, Catholic Action was not included in the text of the Code of Canon Law. But centralism was the key element of the new Catholic Action; according to the decree approved in October 1923, the diocesan associations and parish councils were dependent on the central board, which imparted directives to Catholic Action as a whole, "as blood reaches the extreme capillaries," as Pius XI reminded attendants at the diocesan council on May 16, 1926. The selection of leaders was no longer by election (which in the early twentieth century was the model chosen by most of the Catholic circles and which from now on was kept only at the local level) but was entrusted to the ecclesiastical authority, which was thus in direct control of the leadership of Catholic Action. As a result, the assembly form of participation

---

[9] On the founder of *Legio Mariae*, see Hilde Firtel, *Ein Leben für Christus. Frank Duff und die Legion Mariens* (Sankt Ottilien: EOS, 1983).

gradually disappeared from the new Catholic Action, surviving only in branch associations and diocesan assemblies but without the power to influence the direction of a system governed by the directives of the central board. Catholic Action's widespread presence in all dioceses and the centralism of the organization were two complementary elements: uniformity and compliance under the control of the diocesan councils.

Moreover, ecclesiastical control was made tangible by the presence at every level of a priest responsible for monitoring the compliance of Catholic Action's activities with the directives of the ecclesiastical authority. The pope appointed the central ecclesiastical assistant, while the bishops appointed the ones at the diocesan level. As "representatives of the ecclesiastical authority," the ecclesiastical assistants had to carry on the business of moral and religious education and monitor the suitability of the members, but on a level of "separateness" from the lay members of the leadership, which exempted the ecclesiastical assistant from voting.[10] Catholic Action's obligation to be loyal to the directives of the ecclesiastical authority had, as the other side of the coin, the obligation on the part of the clergy to consider Catholic Action as an integral part of the pastoral ministry of bishops and parish priests.

Much of the Catholic movement of the late nineteenth century was formed and led by clerics and religious. Pius XI's Catholic Action acknowledged the need to swell the Catholic ranks with the laity but regularized and systematized the prominent position of the ecclesiastical authority, its representatives, and the ecclesiastical assistants within the new Catholic Action. Obedience to the pope and his representatives, an integral part of the nineteenth-century intransigent Catholic culture, converged and was maintained in the ecclesiology for much of the twentieth-century Catholic Action. Other players in the relationship between Catholicism and regime were soon eliminated: in exchange for the survival of Catholic Action, the only remaining Catholic organization left to confront the Fascist Opera Nazionale Balilla, Pius XI decided to suppress, between 1927 and 1928, the Italian Catholic Scout Association (ASCI, with twenty-eight thousand subscribers), established on January 16, 1916, by Count Mario di Carpegna, one of the pope's noble guards.[11]

---

[10] See Liliana Ferrari, *L'Azione Cattolica in Italia dalle origini al pontificato di Paolo VI* (Brescia: Queriniana, 1982), 56.

[11] See Mario Sica, *Storia dello scautismo in Italia*, 4th ed. (Rome: Fiordaliso, 2006); Paola Dal Toso, *Nascita e diffusione dell'ASCI 1916–1928* (Milan: Franco Angeli, 2007).

It was a confirmation of Catholic Action's special and privileged position in the relationship dynamics between Catholics, the Catholic Church, and the Fascist regime.

After the crisis of 1931 in the relationship between the Church and the Fascist regime, Catholic Action's new decree, dated December 30, 1931, reinforced the dependence on the ecclesiastical authority by way of further clericalization, to the detriment of its lay component at the leadership level, while limiting the autonomy of the individual organizations (especially of the GCI) from Catholic Action. But the 1931 decree also meant a certain degree of "diocesanization," which did not lead to a loosening of the integrated link with the hierarchy in Rome but was rather emblematic of the effort to involve Catholic Action more closely at the peripheral level by granting more room to the diocesan councils.

Between Pope Pius XI's intentions, the "letter" of the associative statutes, and the reality of the Catholic movements, there was a distance not easily quantifiable. For example, Catholic Action did not reach the quorum needed in every diocese. In any case, by 1930 Catholic Action's 250,000 members became almost 400,000 in 1939. The centralized organizational structure of Catholic life implemented through Catholic Action's reorganization led to a centralization of the cultural life of the entire Catholic laity, with lasting consequences not only on the papal and Roman orientation given to Catholic culture but also on the balance of the ecclesiological powers between clergy and laity.[12]

3. Between Catholic Action and the *Reconquista*: Opus Dei, the Legionaries of Christ, and the Cursillos de Cristianidad

Undoubtedly, Pius XI and "his" Catholic Action represented, within the history of Catholic movements, a central phase of connection between two different periods: "on the one hand, the epic of the nineteenth-century intransigentism in its different variants, . . . on the other, the history of the great mass organizations of the 1930s and 1940s, solid in their strict centralism."[13]

---

[12] See Renato Moro, *La formazione della classe dirigente cattolica (1929–1937)* (Bologna: Il Mulino, 1979), 53.

[13] Ferrari, *L'Azione Cattolica in Italia*, 12.

Even the history of Catholic movements is part of the atmosphere inspired by the "literature of the crisis" of civilization of the 1930s.[14] Among medieval nostalgia and modernizing impulses (an intellectual itinerary exemplified by Jacques Maritain), a first "leverage" of movements, organizations, and institutions emerged in the 1930s in response to the need to react, on the level of action of the Catholic faithful in the "world," to the epochal crisis aiming at a Christian "reconquest" of society. Under the sign and as a response to this "crisis," between the 1920s and 1940s there was an uninterrupted materialization of new religious institutions and so-called secular institutes for consecrated lay Catholics.[15]

An important "cradle" of the new ecclesial movements can certainly be located in the Spain of Franco's "national Catholicism," animated by the spirit of *reconquista* (in the ideal footsteps of the reconquest accomplished by Ferdinand and Isabella of Castile in 1492 at the expense of Muslims and Jews) against modern and liberal culture—a spirit opposed to any idea of internal reform of the Catholic Church but rather a staunch advocate of integral Catholic identity, more nationalistic and revanchist than traditional and Tridentine. In this cultural and political environment, two realities emerged, Opus Dei and the Cursillos de Cristianidad, which can be considered identifying models for a trend of twentieth-century ecclesial movements.

Founded in Madrid by the Spanish priest Escrivà de Balaguer—the male branch on October 2, 1928, and the female branch in February 1930—Opus Dei had been slowed in its development by the Spanish Civil War, which, however, had provided some confirmations to the founder's reading of the modern times in line with the approach of the intransigent culture. In 1941, at the time of its first legal recognition on the part of the Diocese of Madrid, Opus Dei had already acquired its fundamental features: a base consisting of a group of laypeople and some priests, privacy and secrecy as its main traits, and the apostolate among intellectuals.

[14] See *Cattolicesimo e totalitarismo. Chiese e culture religiose tra le due guerre mondiali: Italia, Spagna, Francia*, ed. Daniele Menozzi and Renato Moro (Brescia: Morcelliana, 2004).

[15] See Jerzy Kwiatkowski, *Gli istituti secolari nei documenti precodiciali e nella legislazione canonica attuale* (Rome: Pontificium Athenaeum Antonianum, 1994).

Devoted to the training of university students and the country's elite, who were charged with the responsibility for the outbreak of the Civil War, Opus Dei responded with these features to "the intellectuals' desertion" of Christian teachings.[16] In a Catholicism such as the Spanish one, particularly committed to elite religious associations (starting from the Jesuits) in the service of the *reconquista*, Opus Dei embodied a reactionary spirit rooted in a desire for a structured defense against the spirit of the time.[17] At the basis of Opus Dei, there was a clerical vision in which the priests were to exhort, inspire, and direct the laity in the fulfillment of their Christian and professional duties, as Escrivà de Balaguer wrote in his book *The Way*, thus supporting the priests' authority and the unchanging role of the laity as "disciples."[18] Subsequent developments of Opus Dei as to its place in canon law and its role at the summit of the Catholic Church provide confirmation of its initial genetic traits. On the path to the legal creation of its "personal prelature," Opus Dei would experience a rising integration within the national ecclesial structure and the Vatican, through a modernization that nevertheless would remain disconnected from the modernizing trends visible in the theological and political culture of the time.

In this sense, Opus Dei represented the perfectly ideal-typical example of the relationship between the organizational model and the ecclesial awareness present in many other ecclesial movements of the late twentieth century. Escrivà de Balaguer's creation was not, however, the only response to the political and religious crisis of the 1920s and the clash between the nationalist-political culture and the Catholics' designs of social reconquest. After living through the armed conflict of the late 1920s between insurgents shouting "Viva Cristo Rey!" and the anticlerical government, Mexico became the ideal scenario for the

---

[16] In addition to numerous works on Opus Dei with an apologetic slant, see Giancarlo Rocca, *L'Opus Dei. Appunti e documenti per una storia* (Milan: Paoline, 1985); John Allen Jr., *Opus Dei: An Objective Look behind the Myths and Reality of the Most Controversial Force in the Catholic Church* (New York: Doubleday, 2005).

[17] See Guy Hermet, *Les catholiques dans l'Espagne franquiste*, 2 vols. (Paris: Presses de la Fondation Nationale des Sciences Politiques, 1980–81), 1:231–46. For an accurate (and "official") history of Opus Dei, see Amadeo de Fuenmayor, Valentin Gomez Iglesias, José Luis Illanes, *El itinerario juridico del Opus Dei. Historia y defensa de un carisma* (Pamplona: Universidad de Navarra, 1989).

[18] Completed between 1934 and 1939, *Camino* by Escrivà de Balagueris a best seller, translated into more than forty languages.

birth, in 1941, of Father Marcial Maciel's Congregation of the Legionaries of Christ, which would be followed, in 1959, by the apostolate movement Regnum Christi.[19]

What Opus Dei and the Legionaries undertook "from the top down," namely, a re-catholicization through the formation of the religious elites first and then of the laity, other movements during the twentieth century continued "from the bottom up." Pursuing a project that saw the historical and social situation as equally negative, the element of difference was in the selection and formation of a "missionary proletariat": from the socially and intellectually lower classes, that is, the ones more willing and eager to embark on a new life path of belonging to the Catholic Church, under the banner of a program of evangelization carried out through a combination of mysticism and slogans typical of phenomena of religious enthusiasm.

Among the movements that were inspired by this strategy, there was, in a Spain that had come out of the Civil War, the Cursillos de Cristianidad.[20] The *cursillo*—meaning a "short course" designed to help to grasp "certain fundamental truths of our holy Catholic religion"—was intended to develop a strategy for evangelization.[21] Emerging from the youth branch of Catholic Action among priests and laypeople of the Diocese of Mallorca and started during the pilgrimage made by the youth of Catholic Action to Santiago de Compostela in August 1948, the movement spread around the world. Animated by the desire to restore medieval Christianity in Spain under the umbrella of Franco's National Catholicism, the *cursillos* had already started in Mallorca in 1941 and saw, between 1944 and 1945, the founding of a "school for leaders and propagandists" aiming to disseminate good religious culture. Consisting of a spiritual director, a secular rector and various "teachers" and assistants, the courses, which made use of group

---

[19] See Jason Berry and Gerald Renner, *Vows of Silence: The Abuse of Power in the Papacy of John Paul II* (New York: Free Press, 2004).

[20] See Joan Josep Matas Pastor, "Origen y desarrollo de los Cursillos de Cristianidad (1949–1975)," *Hispania sacra* 52, no. 106 (2000): 719–42, which includes a bibliographic review. About the Cursillo in America, see Kristy Nabhan-Warren, *The Cursillo Movement in America: Catholics, Protestants, and Fourth-Day Spirituality* (Chapel Hill: University of North Carolina Press, 2013).

[21] See Juan Hervàs y Benet, *Los Cursillos de Cristiandad, instrumento de renovación cristiana* (Madrid: Euramérica, 1957).

psychology techniques together with slogans and mottos, were centered on the themes of the theology of grace and strategies of apostolate in different social environments (comparable to the French *pastoral d'ensemble* but without the background element of renewal of French theological culture). Between 1949 and 1953, the movement experienced a phase of development within the diocese. In 1955, the Cursillos were already widespread in twenty different groups: in 1956 they arrived in Bolivia; in 1957 in the United States (in Waco, Texas); between 1958 and 1962 they were present throughout the entire American continent. Already in May 1966 the first world conference of a movement among the least "media-friendly"—but no less emblematic of the path of twentieth-century Catholic lay movement culture and its deep roots—was celebrated in Rome.

4. Catholic Movements between War and Reconstruction: Focolare and Gioventù Studentesca

If the twentieth century was the century of ideologies, we cannot assume that the Catholic Church was impervious—both from the point of view of a political culture and from an organizational culture of mobilization—to the winds of conflict between different ideological visions of the world. The Italian Catholic Action, which in 1948 had two million members, emerged under Pius XI's pontificate, with its own structure and its own theology, even as a reaction to the pitfalls that the Fascist regimes and Communist ideology posed to the Catholic Church. The militant and rigidly hierarchical model of that Catholic Action was indebted to a political and religious culture alien to the spirit of modernity, both the modernity of the "modern freedoms" and the modernity of totalitarian regimes that subjected the Church to a "statolatric" ideology.

In this mix of repulsion and attraction toward the authoritarian and controlling culture lies one of the ambiguities—but also the European origin and the political and cultural versatility—of the phenomenon of "Catholic movements" in the twentieth century. The case of Spain plays a central role in the creation of different paths of Catholic movements in the twentieth century. The Spanish Civil War broke out at a crucial time for the incubation of some agents of contemporary Catholicism and played an important role in defining the characteristics of Spanish Catholicism. Certainly not inspired by *contemptu mundi*, a detachment from worldly concerns, Spanish-speaking Catholicism is a focal point for the understanding of the difficult relationship between Church and modernity in the twentieth century, especially in terms of the relationship between Church and politics, the Catholic tradition of religious freedom, and the crowning achievement of the Concordat as a strategic device to deal with the nation-states.

The Spanish Civil War and the role of Catholics in that conflict provided French Catholics in the 1930s and 1940s the chance to gain awareness of the real political and anthropological nature of fascism and the urgency for Catholics to accept democracy. For Italian Catholics, weighed down by the anticommunist policy of the Vatican, the Spanish conflict did not have a similar impact. Franco-Belgian Catholicism was instead able to translate this awareness even in the theological culture and pastoral models necessary to readdress social issues, according to different theological lines, but not entirely incompatible with those that animated Dorothy Day and the Catholic Worker in response to the economic and social crisis of the 1930s in the United States.[22] But only gradually, with the Second Vatican Council and during the postconciliar period, were revealed the cultural ties between European Catholic social movements and the radicalism of the Catholic Worker in a new Church that was the fruit of the innovations introduced by those movements in the decades prior to the convening of the council.

During the pontificate of Pius XII (1939–58), France and Belgium were at the forefront of Catholic theological reflection. In these countries, which had already awakened from the dream of a Christianity removed from secularization, the *nouvelle théologie* was an element in the development not only of the action of the laity but also of the reflection on the position of the laity within the mission of the Church. Additionally, such experiments as the joint pastoral action (the Teams of Our Lady, a new movement focusing on married couples' experiences, created by the French priest Henri Caffarel, on December 8, 1947) and the new forms of priestly life (the worker priests movement) developed. These were clear elements of a movement culture in Pius XII's Church. Beyond the Alps, the new ecclesiology of the Church as the "mystical body of Christ" (Pius XII's encyclical *Mystici Corporis*, June 29, 1943)

---

[22] See Mark Massa, *Catholics and American Culture: Fulton Sheen, Dorothy Day, and the Notre Dame Football Team* (New York: Crossroad, 1999), 102–27.

found a particular version of the response of European Catholicism to the crucial point of the relationship between Church and world, namely, the French response, which "took on" the reality of the laity in a positive way and which later would become one of the sources of conciliar renewal and thus, indirectly, of the development of Catholic movements.

In this sense, the path followed in France by the Catholic movements originating from specialized Catholic Action was directed toward de-confessionalization and political action. The path of the lay Catholic movement in Italy followed instead a different direction. Faced with the consequences of the catastrophe of the Second World War and the compromise between the Church and the Fascist regime, the Italian laity of Catholic Action did not move in the direction of politicization or de-confessionalization, instead tightening further its relations with the Holy See and the Church hierarchy and collaborating with the political party of Catholics in a "collateralism" that would survive until the first few years of the postconciliar period.

The role of Catholicism in the reconstruction of postwar Europe was much more complex than what the slogans of the early 2000s on the "Christian roots of Europe" would want to admit. Even during a pontificate like that of Pius XII—characterized by distinctive traits on the relationship between the Church, society, and politics and between the clergy and the laity—the history of the different paths of the Catholic movements in Europe reveals the uniqueness of the responses of the Catholic laity and its theological and political culture in facing a crisis triggered by the two world wars. The response of the Catholic movements was only one of the responses: in Italy and Spain—albeit in a nonidentical fashion—it found expression through a differentiation between "mass action" and "research of intellectual groups," and a political osmosis with elite Catholic leadership. In Francophone countries, it followed the path of a specialized Catholic Action, which eventually resulted in a movement of Marxist-inspired political action disavowed by the French bishops in 1949. In Germany, an association of chivalric, aristocratic elites was succeeded, after the Second World War, by a Catholic Action closer to the principle of local ties with parish priests and bishops than to the principle of personal *Verbandkatholizismus*.[23]

---

[23] See *Verbandskatholizismus? Verbände, Organisationen und Gruppen im deutschen Katholizismus*, ed. Heinrich Krauss and Heinrich Ostermann (Kevelaer: Butzon & Bercker, 1968).

It is no exaggeration to say that in Italy during Pius XII's pontificate all Catholic movements were reincorporated in Catholic Action. Catholic Action was, for a long time, the organization *par excellence* of the Catholic laity; it was more closely tied to the person of the pope than to the Italian bishops or the political Catholicism led by Alcide De Gasperi. An interesting internal split occurred between an interventionist political line alongside or in opposition to the Christian Democratic party and another line more inclined to respect the autonomy of the Catholic movement from the Christian Democrats.[24]

But during the postwar period, some entities, which were destined to become some of the most original and eloquent movements of the contemporary Catholic Church, took shape independently from Catholic Action in Italy. In 1944, the Christian Revival Movement came to light: a lay reality originating from a historical-political situation that posed serious questions regarding the final days of the war and reconstruction. In 1946, Father Marcial Maciel from Mexico came to Rome seeking recognition for the congregation of the Legionaries of Christ, and in 1950, during the Holy Year, the Legionaries of Christ established themselves for the first time in Rome. In 1947, the Opera di Maria (later known as the Focolare movement)—founded by Chiara Lubich, an elementary school teacher who grew up in the Catholic circles of Trent's Catholic Action and the Franciscan Third Order—obtained recognition from the diocesan bishop of Trent. In 1948, the first Focolare group of men was established in Trent; Chiara Lubich met in Rome the Member of Parliament Igino Giordani, who became the first married Focolarino; in 1954, the branch of diocesan priests and religious members was founded; in 1956, the first issue of *Città nuova* was released.[25]

---

[24] See Mario Casella, *L'Azione Cattolica alla caduta del fascismo. Attività e progetti per il dopoguerra, 1942–45* (Rome: Studium, 1984); and Mario Casella, *L'Azione Cattolica nell'Italia contemporanea, 1919–1969* (Rome: AVE, 1992).

[25] See Enzo Maria Fondi and Michele Zanzucchi, *Un popolo nato dal Vangelo. Chiara Lubich e i Focolari* (Cinisello B.: San Paolo, 2003), largely based on Igino Giordani, *Storia del movimento dei Focolari*, cyclostyled, 3 vols. (Rocca di Papa, 1977); Chiara Lubich and Igino Giordani, *"Erano i tempi di guerra . . ." Agli albori dell'ideale dell'unità* (Rome: Città Nuova, 2007), which includes a section dedicated to the "history of the nascent Focolare movement" (pp. 41–228). For the history of the Focolare movement in the United States, see Thomas Masters and Amy Uelmen,

In addition, another relevant experience among the movements within the Catholic Church emerged in the Northern Italian region of Lombardy. In 1954, a young priest from Desio and a teacher at the Giovanni Berchet high school in Milan, Luigi Giussani, founded a new group within Milan's Catholic Action called Gioventù Studentesca (Student Youth); in 1969, it would become Communion and Liberation.[26] Contrary to the Focolare movement, which in its official history has only marginally dealt with the link between Catholic Action's situation and the new foundation, Fr. Giussani's group did put emphasis (and still does) on the connection between the birth of Communion and Liberation and Catholic Action's crisis. In January 1954, the resignation from office of Mario Rossi, who was at odds with both the movement's activism and Luigi Gedda's organizational militant choices, marked the most critical point of the evolution of the largest organization of lay Catholics.

Focolare: Living a Spirituality of Unity in the United States (Hyde Park, NY: New City Press, 2011).

   [26] See Massimo Camisasca, *Comunione e Liberazione. Le origini (1954–1968)*, introduction by Cardinal Joseph Ratzinger (Cinisello B.: San Paolo, 2001). See also Davide Rondoni, *Communion and Liberation: A Movement in the Church* (Montreal and Ithaca, NY: Cooperativa Editoriale Nuovo Mondo by McGill-Queen's University Press, 2000).

CHAPTER 5

Beyond Catholic Action: The Second Vatican Council and the Birth of the Movements

1. Pius XII's Militant Church

The diaspora of the Catholic laity from the "one size fits all" model of Roman and European Catholic Action—a diaspora that began with the Second Vatican Council if not a few years earlier—was an epochal phenomenon, if we consider not only the origin of that particular form of "Catholic action" (lowercase) but also the situation of the Catholic Church in the 1950s. As with all historical and social phenomena, the factors and causes of this transformation are multiple and complex. In order to explain this metamorphosis of the Catholic laity, however, we can assume the convergence of a triad of different movements—in the sense of dynamic elements—that have accompanied the Catholic laity from Pius XII's pontificate through the 1950s until the Second Vatican Council.

The first element was represented by the *developments in Roman Catholic ecclesiology*. Even before Vatican II, Pius XII's encyclical *Mystici Corporis* (June 29, 1943) created an opening for a more "dynamic" idea of Church (even though certainly no less institutional, social, and visible), conceived as a "mystical body" composed of various members. In Pius XII's Church, where theology and ecclesial practice designated the pope as the key reference point, and papal magisterium was simply *the* magisterium of the Church, the Church as a whole was placed under the banner of mobilization. But the outcome of these different signals given by Pius XII to the ecclesial body favored the organized laity; the bishops and the clergy were in a sense "restrained" compared to both the papacy and the laity, and the emphasis of Vatican II on the theology of the episcopate would only relatively avert the decline of the diocesan bishops' authority. The bishops, who were deprived of the opportunity to give voice to a strong and authoritative magisterium by the mega-papacy (originating more from a Catholic "interpretation" of the modern state and modern political systems than from Catholic theology before the Counter-Reformation), were left with the pastoral care of the faithful; compared to the parish priests, the bishops had different powers, but more in terms of quantity than quality. In the age of mobilization, it was the Church's "new" laity instead that was asked to "collaborate" with the ministry of the hierarchy in the conflict between Church and modern world, a struggle in which secularization and materialism were identified by the Catholic magisterium as the sources of all evil. Positioned at the intersection between Church and world, the laity was deemed capable of working and collaborating in various ways with the Church hierarchy. The protagonism of the laity already emerged during Pius XII's pontificate, under the influence of two different (in origin and intent) yet convergent trends: on the one hand, the papal magisterium and the crisis of the bishops and clergy's authority and, on the other hand, the theology of the laity.

The second element, deriving from the first, was an increasing *diversification of Catholic action* (lowercase) in its various forms. Several new experiences emerged from Catholic Action, such as the Cursillos de Cristianidad in Spain and the Opera di Maria (the Focolare movement) in Italy. The diversification of experiences went on, without following the path of the "specialized" apostolate (based on different environments or social and professional sectors) but following in the footsteps and the individual charisms of new founders and leaders. Considering also the "new position" of the laity between the Church and the secular world and the theology of the laity—emerging between the 1940s and 1950s and supported by the work of first-rate theologians, such as the French Dominican theologian Yves Congar—the Catholic concept of lay apostolate and collaboration between laity and hierarchy gradually became more diversified. It developed into a multifaceted and versatile reality of the Catholic laity, which, according to Pius XII's wishes, had to be not only subject to the ecclesiastical hierarchy but also capable of confronting other mass organizations.[1] Throughout the 1950s, the *Manual of Catholic Action* by Monsignor Luigi Civardi not only continued to be reprinted but represented also the guide for Catholic laity organized under the umbrella of Catholic Action.[2] Gradually, however, other "mobilization" initiatives took off that did not fit in either the established pattern of Catholic Action or the specialized apostolic movements typical of the Franco-Belgian experience. Rather, they fell—just like the calls for "a better world" and Fr. Riccardo Lombardi's "crusade of kindness"—within the idea of conquest of public space, in tune with Pius XII's message and in direct ideological contrast with the political propaganda of socialists and Communists.[3]

The third element was represented by the *contribution of the reform movements*. The movements for biblical, liturgical, ecumenical, and patristic reform were able to preserve the core elements of their theological and historical reflections together with their proposals for the renewal and reform of the Church. These movements for reform originated mostly in France, Belgium, and Germany in the nineteenth century thanks to the work of some scholars—mainly theologians and monks—and survived both the first modernist crisis at the beginning of the century and, afterward, the condemnations of Pius XII's magisterium. The *biblical movement* helped to introduce, albeit gradually and not without difficulty, the principle of access to the Bible for all the faithful, even laypeople, thus breaking with the tradition (typically southern European) of a Catholic spirituality removed from a direct and daily contact with the biblical text read and meditated on in the common language. The *liturgical movement*, which emerged in the nineteenth century from the need to recenter the life of faith on the liturgy, contributed in the 1950s to Pius XII's first liturgical reforms, to the preparation of theologians and bishops for the conciliar

---

[1] See Yves Congar, *Jalons pour une théologie du laïcat* (Paris: Cerf, 1953). English edition: *Lay People in the Church: A Study for a Theology of the Laity*, trans. Donald Attwater (Westminster, MD: Newman Press, 1957).

[2] See Luigi Civardi, *Manuale di azione cattolica secondo gli ultimi ordinamenti* (Pavia: Artigianelli, 1924).

[3] See Giancarlo Zizola, *Il microfono di Dio: Pio XII, padre Lombardi e i cattolici italiani* (Milan: Mondadori, 1990).

debate on the role of the liturgy in the life of the Church and Christians, and to the necessary reforms for a healthy relationship between liturgy and spiritual life. The *ecumenical movement* had greatly benefited from the first spontaneous and embryonic North European experiences of encounter between Christians of different confessions and had broken the taboo of relations with Lutherans, Reformed, and Orthodox, who for centuries had been labeled by the Catholic magisterium as "heretics" and "schismatics." The *patristic movement* had supported the cause for a return to the great tradition of the Church, preserved in the writings of the fathers of the Church more than in the recent theological tradition of the Church of Rome.[4]

Thus, the Catholic Church and its laity were, as Vatican II approached, in a situation characterized by different trends that were, to a certain extent, at odds with one another (such as between the "papolatric" devotion, typical of the Catholic laity between Vatican I and Vatican II on the one side and the search for an ecumenical common ground between different Churches on the other). But all of these forces had to address the ecclesiological question that at Vatican II would become *the* fundamental question—one that did not yet include, from a theological, canonical, or sociological point of view, the notion of Catholic movements (in the plural).

2. The Event of Vatican II and Ecclesial Movements

Ecclesial movements identify themselves or are usually identified as the offspring, if not as the offspring *par excellence*, of the Second Vatican Council. In reality, if the epochal break of the council had a relation to the genesis of the movements, the role played by the council in the history of the movements is neither so obvious nor univocal.[5] The Second Vatican Council, called in January 1959 by Pope John XXIII (1958–63), came after Pius XII's pontificate, which

---

[4] See *La théologie catholique entre intransigeance et renouveau. La réception des mouvements préconciliaires à Vatican II*, ed. Gilles Routhier, Philippe Roy, and Karim Schelkens (Louvain-la-Neuve: Bibliothèque de la Revue d'Histoire Ecclésiastique, 2011).

[5] See Massimo Faggioli, "Between Documents and the Spirit: The Case of the New Catholic Movements," in *After Vatican II: Trajectories and Hermeneutics*, ed. James L. Heft with John O'Malley (Grand Rapids, MI, and Cambridge, UK: Eerdmans, 2012), 1–22.

had confirmed and promoted the privileges given by his predecessor, Pius XI, to Catholic Action.

In the wake of the developments within the theology of the laity, which since the late 1940s in Europe had been focusing on the relationship among the role of the laity, the Church's mission, and ecclesiology, the council influenced the birth and development of some of the ecclesial movements that today, at the beginning of the twenty-first century, are among the most visible and recognized. Yet the link between the council and the movements is oblique and complex. In fact, the conciliar sessions did not address directly the phenomenon of ecclesial movements, which had not yet emerged in all the variety and strength so evident beginning in the 1970s and 1980s. Vatican II tackled questions dealing with certain aspects of the life of the movements in relation to the theology of the laity and the lay apostolate. Nevertheless, the rich experience of the preconciliar theological-spiritual movements for biblical, liturgical, ecumenical, and patristic reform remained in the background of the conciliar reflections and nourished the movements born in the postconciliar period to a lesser degree than usually claimed.

The documents of Vatican II, approved by more than two thousand conciliar fathers, represent a broad-based theological legitimacy for the movements, especially *Apostolicam Actuositatem* (Decree on the Apostolate of the Laity; November 18, 1965); chapter 4, on the laity, in *Lumen Gentium* (Dogmatic Constitution on the Church; November 21, 1964); paragraph 43, on the duties of Christians, in *Gaudium et Spes* (Dogmatic Constitution on the Church in the Modern World; December 7, 1965); and paragraph 8, on associations, in *Presbyterorum Ordinis* (Decree on the Ministry and Life of Priests; December 7, 1965). But it was only the Decree on the Apostolate of the Laity that dealt with legitimacy, without, however, directly touching on the phenomenon of ecclesial movements that were not part of Catholic Action and that, until then, had only appeared in an embryonic and semi-clandestine form.

The council's approach to the question of the lay apostolate was purely theological and did not dwell on the legal, canonical, or institutional solutions that were necessary to the new protagonism of the laity organized under different names. The conciliar debate on the structure of the laity focused, in its final stages, on the opportunity to offer a more theological reading of the laity, namely, the need for a precise statement on the rights, duties, and areas of intervention of the laity in the Church yet always within a reading of the organized apostolate called to "renewthe temporal order" in communion with the Church hierarchy.[6] Chapter 4 of *Apostolicam Actuositatem*, paragraphs 18–21, especially paragraph 20, tackle the question of the multiplicity of forms of the organized apostolate, its fundamental role, and the danger inherent in scattering the forces of the lay apostolate. Paragraph 18 of *Apostolicam Actuositatem* states the possibility of being apostles "both in their families and in the parishes and dioceses, which express the communitarian character of the apostolate; apostles too in the free associations they will have decided to form among themselves." Paragraph 20 refers specifically to Catholic Action, presenting it as a typical example of the organized lay apostolate, without explicitly mentioning other associative possibilities, but at the same time pointing to a plurality of organizational forms based on a diversity of purposes. Perhaps more important, *Apostolicam Actuositatem* already tried to bring under the umbrella of Catholic Action a whole series of associations, groups, and movements that escaped the parameters planned in the 1920s:

> These types of apostolate, whether or not they go by the name of Catholic Action, are today doing a work of great value. They are constituted by the combination of all the following characteristics:
>
> (a) The immediate aim of organizations of this sort is the church's apostolic purpose. In other words, the evangelization and sanctification of men and women and the christian formation of their consciences, so as to enable them to imbue with the Gospel spirit the various social groups and environments.
>
> (b) The laity, cooperating in their own particular way with the hierarchy, contribute their experience and assume responsibility for the direction of these organizations, for the investigation of the conditions in which the church's pastoral work is to be carried on, for the elaboration and execution of their plan of action.
>
> (c) The laity act in unison after the manner of an organic body, to display more strikingly the community aspect of the church and to render the apostolate more productive.

[6] See *History of Vatican II*, vols. 1–5, ed. Giuseppe Alberigo; English edition edited by Joseph A. Komonchak (Maryknoll, NY: Orbis, 1995–2006), esp. vol. 4; Barbara Zadra, *I movimenti ecclesiali e i loro statuti* (Rome: Pontificia Università Gregoriana, 1997), 7–21.

(d) The laity, whether coming of their own accord or in response to an invitation to action and direct cooperation with the hierarchical apostolate, act under the higher direction of the hierarchy, which can authorize this cooperation, besides, with an explicit mandate.

Organizations which, in the judgment of the hierarchy, combine all these elements should be regarded as Catholic Action, even if they have forms and names that vary according to the requirements of localities and peoples. (AA 20)

Apostolic aim, cooperation with the hierarchy, unity of the lay apostolate, mandate of the Church hierarchy: these four "criteria" will then be resumed and developed by Pope John Paul II's apostolic exhortation *Christifideles Laici* in 1988.[7] But the "prudence" (or delay) of the magisterium (first of Vatican II and then of the popes of the post–Vatican II period) to deal with the phenomenon of movements is also demonstrated by the fact that, until John Paul II's pontificate, the main point of the directives of the magisterium would be aiming more to complete and return to the conciliar texts than to regulate and theologically and normatively address a phenomenon that escaped the control of the local hierarchy (the bishops) and was clearly tolerated in Rome—more by the pope, less by the Roman Curia.

In effect, the documents of Vatican II maintained a typology of lay apostolate as Catholic action (lowercase), which, even if it started to emancipate itself from the direct subordination to the ecclesiastical hierarchy, still indirectly maintained a binding "mandate" with regard to the indications of the magisterium. This ecclesiological angle of Vatican II about the ecclesial movements was amply disputed in the following postconciliar experience and became, in terms of the relationship between hierarchy and movements, one of the elements of tension (for the hierarchy) and vitality (for the movements).

Similarly, even the constitution *Lumen Gentium*, which, finally, opened with a section dedicated to the Church as "people of God" (which since the late 1960s had played a central role in the Catholic consciousness of being Church), in chapter 4 reserves to the mission of the laity a very "internal" sense of Catholic action in society:

Besides this apostolate which belongs to absolutely every Christian, the laity can be called in different ways to more immediate cooperation

---

[7] John Paul II, apostolic exhortation *Christifideles Laici*, December 30, 1988.

in the apostolate of the hierarchy, like those men and women who helped the apostle Paul in the Gospel, working hard in the Lord (see Phil 4:3; Rom 16:3ff.). They may, moreover, be appointed by the hierarchy to certain ecclesiastical offices which have a spiritual aim. (LG 33)

On the basis of a specific reading—more institutional than movement oriented—of the history of early Christianity as attested by the New Testament, in *Lumen Gentium* the role of the laity was seen as closely linked to the hierarchy in its purposes and structures, almost in a complementary position with respect to the ministry of the hierarchy. The question of an institutional and canonical configuration of the laity and its ministry, whether individual or in an associative form, was not taken into account, nor was the need to embody "the ecclesiology of the People of God," as enunciated by *Lumen Gentium*, with a new regime of relations between clergy and the organized laity, that is, a new regime different from Catholic Action's institutionalized subordination to the "Church of the Piuses" (Pius X, Pius XI, and Pius XII).

During the conciliar debate in St. Peter's Basilica, the indication of the subsequent postconciliar codification of the new Code of Canon Law (which would end only in 1983) served as an expedient (in this as in other cases during Vatican II) to postpone indefinitely the legal solution to a theological question that the council had formulated in an embryonic form only, but without the strength to change the ecclesiastical set of rules and practices. In effect, the Code of Canon Law of 1983 would eventually deal with the movements, but not exactly in the direction wished for by the proponents of the apostolate of the laity within ecclesial movements.[8]

The text of *Gaudium et Spes* restated the concept of the laity called to "animate the world," but without developing further on the sphere of the responsibilities of the organized lay Christians toward the Church and the world and, conversely, the Church's responsibilities toward the laity engaged in the world: "The laity are called to participate actively in the entire life of the church; not only are they to animate the world

---

[8] See Eugenio Corecco, "Aspects of the Reception of Vatican II in the Code of Canon Law," in *The Reception of Vatican II*, ed. Giuseppe Alberigo, Jean-Pierre Jossua, and Joseph Komonchak (Washington, DC: The Catholic University of America Press, 1985), 249–96.

with the spirit of Christianity, they are to be witnesses to Christ in all circumstances and at the very heart of the human community" (GS 43). It was a classic division of responsibilities, echoed by the immediately preceding passage, which stated: "It is to the laity, though not exclusively to them, that secular duties and activity properly belong. . . . It is their task to cultivate a properly informed conscience and to impress the divine law on the affairs of the earthly city. For guidance and spiritual strength let them turn to the clergy" (GS 43).

Compared to the postconciliar developments, where the roles of the clergy and the laity, whether in ecclesial movements or not, would become more and more combined and interconnected, the definition in *Gaudium et Spes*, leaving to the laity the "secular duties" and to clerics the "guidance and spiritual strength," belongs to the category of those fruits of the council largely superseded by the reception of Vatican II and subsequent developments. In effect, since the 1970s, and especially in Catholic Churches outside the Vatican and Italian borders (in France, Germany, the United States, Latin America), the active laity has assumed ecclesial ministries until then exclusively reserved to the clergy (preaching, the teaching of theology), and, conversely, the clergy has stepped forward in areas openly "secular" in the sense of "worldly" (in Catholic schools and universities, vocational institutions, and higher education; private health enterprises, social welfare activities; mass media production and publishing).

If it is true that the conciliar documents have prepared the ground for subsequent developments, however, it is more accurate to say that subsequent developments may find legitimacy in some insights present in the conciliar instructions.[9] Nevertheless, it should be noted that the conciliar documents on the laity were firmly grounded in the historical context of the pre–Vatican II "theology of the laity" and that a literal interpretation or application of them would never have allowed the development of such a wide and variegated galaxy of Church movements, such as the ones identified today with "the rise of the movements."

Compared to the real praxis of ecclesial movements, the theology of the laity of Vatican II was still centered on Catholic Action siding with the hierarchy. In other words, its theology of the laity was not only

[9] See Franco Giulio Brambilla, "Le aggregazioni ecclesiali nei documenti del magistero dal concilio fino ad oggi," in *La Scuola Cattolica* 116 (1988): 461–511.

the offspring of the separation between clergy and laity but also fundamentally against any commitment to reform or develop new forms of Christian life involving a spiritual, catechumenal, liturgical, and educational dimension. Nor did the theology of the laity formulated before and during the council make room for the Catholic "vanguards" in the field of interreligious dialogue for peace, contact with non-believers, or the reception of the "other" (the poor, the handicapped, the immigrant, the foreigner, or even the non-Christian) within a community of faith that was still conceived, even by Vatican II, as merely local, diocesan, parochial, and within the conceptual basis provided by the Council of Trent.

The documents of Vatican II on the apostolate of the laity should, therefore, still be read in terms of the dualism of hierarchy/laity, which will be largely superseded—in a peaceful and nonconfrontational way—by the postconciliar development of the movements, especially starting from the early 1980s.[10] The two meetings of the World Congress for the Lay Apostolate in 1951 and 1957 were still marked by the "classic" view that to a large extent characterized the conciliar magisterium as well.[11] Within the teachings of Vatican II there was no reference to an inspirational factor leading the faithful to express their communion in associative form; the goal instead was the affirmation of the right within the Church to form or join an association and that this right must be exerted in communion with the hierarchy.

True, paragraphs 15–22 of *Apostolicam Actuositatem* affirm, in magisterial form, the historical reality of mobilization as a political idea typical of the twentieth century—but still under the strict control of the ecclesiastical hierarchy. In addition, from an institutional perspective, the scenario known to the conciliar fathers was that of Catholic Action, with its public and official role, deemed capable of integrating, under the direct control of the papacy and the episcopate, all the movement-oriented forces inside a Catholic Church still perceived as led by the pope and bishops.

---

[10] See Bruno Forte, "Associazioni, movimenti e missione nella chiesa locale," *Il Regno Documenti* 1 (1983): 29–34; Juan José Etxeberría, "Los movimentos eclesiales en los albores del siglo XXI," *Revista Española de Derecho Canonico* 58 (2001): 577–616.

[11] See Bernard Minvielle, *L'apostolat des laïcs à la veille du Concile (1949–1959). Histoire des congrès mondiaux de 1951 et 1957* (Fribourg: Editions Universitaires, 2001).

The conciliar documents, therefore, were grounded in a different, if not antithetical, perspective from that of the postconciliar movements: on the one hand, they affirmed the individual character of the apostolate and the importance of organizations, thus leaning toward a lay apostolate in a missionary perspective and within a context dominated by Catholic Action. On the other, Vatican II opened the way for the multiplicity of ecclesial groups, but only thanks to an ecclesiological vision of renewed emphasis on the individual local church, the episcopal ministry in the dioceses, and the creation of structures for dialogue and co-responsibility of the people of God within the canonical territory of the local churches.

From the point of view of the documents of Vatican II, the support given by the council to the new movements can be defined as an argument from silence grounded more in the spirit of the council than in its documents. The opening of Vatican II toward the movements was only oblique and related to factors distinct not only from its final documents but also from the conciliar debates. The path of one of the greatest leading figures of the council, the Belgian Cardinal Leo Jozef Suenens, exemplifies the complexity of the relationship between Vatican II and the movements: Suenens's lucid and courageous commitment to Church reform in the years of the council was replaced, in the postconciliar period, only by his support of charismatic renewal, a movement in which the spiritual and charismatic dimensions appear stronger when free from any attempt to reform the ecclesiastical institution.[12]

3. From the Council to the Postconciliar Period: The "Rise of the Movements"

The Second Vatican Council is, in the "authorized autobiography" of most Catholic movements, a watershed moment: a birth certificate, a proof of orthodoxy, a guarantee against objections coming from critics of the Catholic pro-movement phenomenon. And yet, the organized movements had no role to play at the council, neither among its leading figures, nor in relation to the topics discussed. As the most important historical event in the Catholic Church of the modern era,

---

[12] See Leo Jozef Suenens, *A New Pentecost?*, trans. Francis Martin (New York: Seabury Press, 1975).

the council had been prepared and was conducted with a view to updating the institution, according to theological and legal coordinates
that soon showed their limits.

We can therefore conclude that the first birth of ecclesial movements, at least on the European continent, was anticipated by twenty
years, during the period between 1948 and 1968 that saw, as a result of
the balance of forces within the Catholic Church, a favorable outcome
for the new laity. Relatively organized and in line with the single model
represented by Catholic Action, this new laity, in the years between
World War II and the 1960s, had common roots that transcended the
differences of names and denominations. Both the drive to preserve
and reshape society and the Church on the strength of a model of
militant commitment, not without a tinge of political and ideological
colorings,[13] and the communitarian dream of a palingenesis of ecclesial
praxis[14] derived not only from a Catholic spirituality removed from
the Tridentine model, which was strongly regional, but also from the
intellectual approach of the reform movements of the early twentieth
century. It was just the early stages of a communitarian-evangelical
turning point of the new Christian movements, Catholic or not, that
would eventually take over at the end of the twentieth century.

The rise of postconciliar movements was a result of the climate
of the council and the postconciliar period rather than a direct effect
of the debates and documents of Vatican II. One of the first factors
was the paradigm shift in Catholic ecclesiology. The emphasis placed
by the council on the laity had put an end to the separation within
the Church between the *duo genera christianorum*, the hierarchical
separation between clergy and laity. A new vision of authority in the
Church, according to the model of "Church as communion," made
room for the emergence of different experiences outside (if not *against*)
the verticality of the "faithful–priest–bishop" relationship. Even the
attempt to further establish the core of Catholicism in the "local" or

---

[13] Catholic Action, Catholic Scout Association, and the movement led by Christian Democrat Giuseppe Dossetti in Italy; the experiences from Spanish-speaking
countries; the JOC movements in France and Belgium; the Catholic Worker in the
United States.

[14] The movements of Catholic dissent of the first postconciliar period, the communities in Latin America, the catechumenal and Pentecostal groups in Europe and
North America.

"individual" churches contributed to the renewal of an ecclesiological-hierarchical and universalist model that was against the formulation of new ecclesial experiences articulated more in a communal dimension than on the adherence to a standard model in terms of liturgical content, spiritual foundation, and institutional structure.

A second factor, different but always dependent on the ecclesiological turn of Vatican II, was the crisis of Catholic Action and the model it represented of a unique container and collector of all the experiences of the laity under the direct control of the papacy and bishops. Conceived at the beginning of the twentieth century by the Catholic hierarchy as the response to and mobilization against the attacks of the political cultures perceived as hostile to Catholicism, Catholic Action lost much of its meaning and its mission when the ideological enmity between "Church and the modern world" and its ideological and political setbacks faded away.[15] The crisis of this model not only helped to open new paths for the Catholic laity but also contributed to the crisis of authority of the Catholic bishops in the postconciliar years.

Between the beginning of the 1960s and the end of Paul VI's pontificate (1978), the rise of ecclesial movements had the characteristics of a slow progression of individual phenomena independent from one another, but all linked to a cultural, social, and political climate rather than a theological school or devotional style. Each one of them had its own trajectory dependent not only on the founder's charism and the underlying theological choices but also on the conditions of the local churches of origin.

The movements that survived that rushing phase of the emergence of new communities and associations, in search of new forms of a life of faith, soon had to deal with the difficulty of obtaining from the ecclesiastical institution—the bishops first and then Rome—the recognition of new models of faith communities, essentially *extra legem* ("outside the law") in terms of canonical regulations. The "passion of the movements," which was the result of the Vatican's misunderstanding and became a distinctive trait of these new realities, originated between the time of Vatican II and the 1970s and later became one of the identifying traits of the movements and the source of their lack

---

[15] See Giuseppe Ruggieri, "Chiesa e mondo," in *Cristianesimo, chiese e Vangelo* (Bologna: Il Mulino, 2002), 307–38.

of scruples today, now that their suffering has been translated, by the popes and the bishops, into their exaltation and celebration.

The transition from the council to the postconciliar period coincided with the stabilization and institutionalization of some entities that originated many years before. Between 1960 and January 1962, Escrivà de Balaguer petitioned the Holy See to transform Opus Dei's canonical designation from a secular institute to a "prelature *nullius*," assuming as model the structure of Mission de France; certainly a risky model, considering that Mission de France was conceived in 1954 with a very specific goal within the French Church and with a clergy prepared for the purpose. Opus Dei's decision to take such a step stemmed from the misunderstanding suffered by the founder at the hands of the Vatican Congregation for Religious Life and for juridical controversies concerning the development impressed on the structure of secular institutes. Neither John XXIII nor Paul VI accepted Opus Dei's petition. In 1969, Paul VI invited Opus Dei to convoke a general congress in order to study issues relating to the nature of the institution's work. The request for institutionalization, however, was revived only in 1979, that is, after the end of Pope Paul VI's pontificate. A major obstacle had to do with Opus Dei's identity as an organization: was it a secular or lay institution, or something else? Ultimately, Opus Dei's problem in the eyes of the Holy See was not just its secrecy and the difficult relationship between its leadership and the congregations of the Roman Curia but also the ambiguity and discrepancy between the secular soul that the founder claimed to have given to his creature and the reality of it as an institution, where priests could be ordained even without going through seminary and could have a secular profession outside the institution.[16]

Not all movements met with the same obstacles encountered by Opus Dei, as not all of them had the extraordinary and rapid success of Escrivà de Balaguer's institution during John Paul II's pontificate.[17] Other movements followed different paths, less spectacular but no less rooted in contemporary Catholicism. In 1964, the ecclesiastical authority approved the Schoenstatt movement. This movement was

---

[16] See Giancarlo Rocca, *L'Opus Dei. Appunti e documenti per una storia* (Milan: Edizioni Paoline, 1985).

[17] See Giancarlo Zizola, *Quale papa? Analisi delle strutture elettorali e governative del papato romano* (Rome: Borla, 1977).

founded in 1914 in Germany by the priest Joseph Kentenich, who survived not only Nazi persecutions but later also misunderstandings on the part of the Vatican, especially at the hands of the Holy Office and the most important ecclesiologist in the Vatican of the early postwar period, Sebastian Tromp, SJ (who sent Kentenich into "exile" in the United States after the apostolic visit to Schoenstatt between 1951 and 1953).[18] In 1962, Pope John XXIII approved *ad experimentum* ("as an experiment/temporarily") the Opera di Maria, which in the summer of 1959 had brought together near Trent (Northern Italy) more than ten thousand people from twenty-seven different countries. In 1963, the first Mariapoli was held at Rocca di Papa, near Rome, a center for the formation of the members of the movement; in 1966, the youth branch of the society was created, and in the same year Chiara Lubich was received by the archbishop of Canterbury, Michael Ramsey, who encouraged her to spread the spirituality of the Focolare movement in the Anglican Church of England. The following year the ecumenical patriarch of Constantinople, Athenagoras, made a similar request. In October 1965, Pope Paul VI approved the statutes of Focolare's general council.[19]

Moreover, it was not in Italy alone that these new movements were coming to life. After Opus Dei and the Cursillos, Spain had seen the birth of the Neocatechumenal Way in 1964 in a shantytown on the outskirts of Madrid. This group was founded by Francisco "Kiko" Argüello, an artist and layman, and Carmen Hernández, the daughter of an entrepreneur and educated at the Institute Misioneras de Cristo Jesús. Founded as a path of adult faith formation, this new experience was centered on a postbaptismal catechumenate, based on the "tripod" of "Word of God–liturgy–community," with different stages (kerygmatic, pre-catechumenate, catechumenate, election). The parish was conceived as a "community of communities," and the

---

[18] See Engelbert Monnerjahn, *Pater Joseph Kentenich. Ein Leben für die Kirche* (Vallendar: Patris, 1975); English edition: *Joseph Kentenich: A Life for the Church* (Cape Town: Schoenstatt Publications, 1985); *Schönstatt-Lexikon: Fakten–Ideen–Leben*, ed. Hubertus Brantzen (Vallendar: Patris, 1996); Josef Maria Klein, *Albert Eise: aus der Gründungszeit der Schönstatt-Bewegung* (Vallendar: Patris, 1995).

[19] See Enzo Maria Fondi and Michele Zanzucchi, *Un popolo nato dal Vangelo. Chiara Lubich e i Focolari* (Cinisello B.: San Paolo, 2003); Edwin Robertson, *The Fire of Love: A Life of Igino Giordani, 'Foco', 1894–1980* (London: New City, 1989).

internal structure of the catechumenal community was centered on different services, albeit all entrusted to laypeople (supervisors, local and itinerant catechists, cantors, readers, altar servers).[20] Following a highly successful model for the institutional grounding of new ecclesial groups, Kiko Argüello and Carmen Hernández arrived in Rome in 1968 to open a center of the Way in the Martyred Canadian Saints parish. The expansion in Rome of the new movement led the Way to an early recognition, which was accompanied by the recommendation to adopt a more appropriate name—"neocatechumenate"—for the catechetical formation of adults already baptized, in line with the *Ordo Initiationis Christianae Adultorum* (Order of Adult Christian Initiation) of 1972.

The Neocatechumenal Way was the most noticeable example, but not the only one, of the vitality of evangelical and deinstitutionalizing communitarian currents even within the post–Vatican II Catholic Church. There was another movement that emerged in the United States during that period, which was also uninterested in issues relating to institutional reform of the Church as structure. In 1967 there emerged the Renewal in the Spirit movement (or Catholic charismatic renewal), which spread from the East Coast of the United States and its industrial and agricultural Midwest—that is, from Pennsylvania, Indiana, and Michigan (Pittsburgh's Duquesne University, University of Notre Dame, Michigan State University)—between Iowa and Oregon. It was based on the need to accommodate a "renewed outpouring of the Holy Spirit" and the rediscovery of baptismal grace and Christian identity.[21] Charismatic Catholicism had found in the Second Vatican Council an opportunity to exist within the Church:

---

[20] See Bernard Sven Anuth, *Der Neokatechumenale Weg: Geschichte, Erscheinungsbild, Rechtscharakter* (Würzburg: Echter, 2006); Ricardo Blazquez, *Le comunità neocatecumenali. Discernimento teologico*, ed. Ezechiele Pasotti (Cinisello B.: San Paolo,1995); English edition: *Neo-Catechumenal Communities: A Theological Discernment* (St. Paul Publications, 1987); Paolo Sorci, "Ermeneutica della Parola nel cammino neocatecumenale," *Rivista liturgica* 6, no. 84 (1997): 867–80. See also Ezekiel Pasotti, *Il Cammino Neocatecumenale secondo Paolo VI e Giovanni Paolo II* (Milan: San Paolo, 1993); English edition: *The Neocatechumenal Way According to Paul VI and John Paul II* (Maynooth, Ireland: St. Pauls, 1996).

[21] See Paolo Maino, *Il post-moderno nella Chiesa? Il Rinnovamento carismatico* (Cinisello B.: San Paolo, 2004); Mario Panciera, *Il Rinnovamento nello spirito in Italia: una realtà ecclesiale* (Rome: RnS, 1992); Francis A. Sullivan, *Charisms and*

Today the dichotomy between institution and charism is being gradually healed over. . . . In the Second Vatican Council we have a remarkable instance of a reform council equally concerned about the authentic faith-life of persons and correct church order. In this prevailing atmosphere it is to be hoped that a movement such as charismatic renewal will be able to exist fruitfully within the institutional structure while at the same time serving and contributing to the renewal of the church.[22]

In a movement where the founder is identified with the Holy Spirit and the charisms are manifold (outreach, prophecy, intercession, healing, liberation, evangelization, and government), members adhere to the charismatic spirituality rather than to a specific charism. In 1970, a magazine (*The New Covenant*) appeared, and in 1973 the first *Directory of Catholic Prayer Groups*; in 1976, the movement's International Liaison Office moved to Belgium, where it found Cardinal Suenens's support. The movement reached Rome in 1971, thanks to Fr. Valerian Gaudet, at the Pontifical Gregorian University. A year later, the Renewal in the Spirit movement spread throughout Italy, away from the spotlight but not without the interference of the Church hierarchy along its path. Born in the Unites States against the backdrop of the American Protestant neo-Pentecostalism in an informal ecumenical context (unmediated by bilateral official commissions chaired by clerics of particular churches), once Renewal arrived in Europe its nondenominational character faded away, not so much for specific choices on the part of the movement as for the impact with a confessional geography radically different from that of North America. A "normalization" of the movement (the founders of the Blessed Virgin Mary's Prayer Group left the movement in 1976) found support in the recognition accorded by Paul VI's two speeches at the meetings of the movement's leaders on October 10, 1973, and May 19, 1975.

Charismatic Renewal: A Biblical and Theological Study (Ann Arbor, MI: Servant Books, 1982). See also Kilian McDonnell, *The Charismatic Renewal and Ecumenism* (New York: Paulist Press, 1978); Randy R. McGuire, *Catholic Charismatic Renewal: The Struggle for Affirmation (1967–1975)* (PhD diss., Saint Louis University, 1998); Kilian McDonnell, ed., *Presence, Power, Praise: Documents on the Charismatic Renewal*, 3 vols. (Collegeville, MN: Liturgical Press, 1980).

[22] Kevin and Dorothy Ranaghan, *Catholic Pentecostals Today* (South Bend, IN: Charismatic Renewal Services, 1983), 189.

The immediate postconciliar period and the climate of the 1960s represented not only a hotbed but also a filter and a dividing line for the development of many ecclesial groups and associations, especially around the question of the relationship between communities of faith and political commitment. All the movements that emerged at this time were characterized by the revival of collective and communal religious experiences; the ones characterized instead by a strong political stance were short-lived and left little trace of themselves on the identityof the contemporary Catholic Church. When these "radical" political choices infiltrated existing ecclesial groups and were approved by the hierarchy, they marked the beginning of a crisis. In the crucial Italian scenario, the Christian Associations of Italian Workers (ACLI) claimed greater autonomy from the ecclesiastical hierarchy at the conventions in Turin (1969) and Vallombrosa (1970). Similar choices were made by the Italian Catholic Federation of University Students at the Congress of Verona (1969). The birth of the base ecclesial communities and the Christians for Socialism group (1973) was accompanied by a shift toward the left of the Italian Catholic youth.[23] The most lasting and less ephemeral legacy of the movements emerging within Catholicism, however, would come from those groups that addressed social and political issues in a nonideological and nonorganic manner compared to those of the political left.

In the aftermath of Vatican II and at the height of the climate of the 1960s, a new movement, which would later take the name of Community of Sant'Egidio, was founded in Rome by a group of students at the Virgilio high school and led by the eighteen-year-old Andrea Riccardi. Focusing on the reading of the gospels, the example of St. Francis of Assisi, and the service to the poor and marginalized, in 1970 the Community of Sant'Egidio established its center in a church in the area of Santa Maria in Trastevere, where it began its ritual of daily prayer and laid its institutional foundation.[24] The Roman identity of the community was related not only to the founder and other leaders' provenance but also to the choice of creating a bond with "the bishop

---

[23] See Massimo Faggioli, "The New Elites of Italian Catholicism: 1968 and the New Catholic Movements," *The Catholic Historical Review* 98, no. 1 (January 2012): 18–40.

[24] See Andrea Riccardi, *Sant'Egidio, Roma e il mondo. Colloquio con Jean-Dominique Durand e Régis Ladous* (Cinisello B.: San Paolo, 1997); Hanspeter Oschwald, *Bibel, Mystik und Politik. Die Gemeinschaft Sant'Egidio* (Freiburg i.B.: Herder, 1998).

of Rome" (that is, the pope) in his role (that had been forgotten by the modern papacy until the pontificate of John XXIII) of diocesan bishop. That choice, which led to the official recognition of the group only ten years later with John Paul II in 1978, was founded on ecclesiological motivations but had also to do with the need to establish relations with the Roman, Italian, and Vatican political and institutional world, considered important in matters pertaining to the welfare activities conducted by the members of the Community. Sant'Egidio's "Roman" choice was one of the counter-tendencies of the group founded by the "self-taught theologian" Riccardi in light of the climate of the 1960s and even within the Catholic Church. Sant'Egidio pursued this path of service to men and women in the spirit of juvenile rebellion and in a period in which the ecclesial groups were elaborating—arduously and not independently from the wave of anti-institutional protest that affected Catholicism as well—their choice of independence from Catholic political influence and the control exerted by the papacy over the organizations of the Catholic laity. Contrary to Catholic Action, the Community of Sant'Egidio emerged differently: without being anchored to a parish or particular district but rather to the city of Rome. Its organizational structure was "lightweight" and not canonically normalized, yet clear, well-defined, and ritualized in an unwritten form and more dependent on the founder's charism and its ruling elite than on new formulas or unique institutional arrangements. This type of structure protected the Community of Sant'Egidio from ideological degenerations (certainly not alien to the political culture of the time) and represented in the eyes of ecclesial (and political) interlocutors a warrantee of the stable identity of the community. Between 1968 and the 1970s, the Community of Sant'Egidio represented one of the exceptions to a politically engaged Catholicism, which was trying to move past its previous institutional and political culture, namely, from its antiliberal and anticommunist stance, to a modernizing socio-political culture closer to Marxist, socialist, Third Worldist and anti-imperialist views.[25] In fact, the first half of the 1970s saw not only the "religious choice" of Italian Catholic Action—a choice challenged by the Holy See because it was perceived as a move toward the left of the Italian

---

[25] See Agostino Giovagnoli, ed., *1968 fra utopia e Vangelo. Contestazione e mondo cattolico* (Rome: AVE, 2000).

political spectrum—but also the retaliation against the Italian Christian Workers Associations, from which the ecclesiastical assistants were removed in 1971.[26]

The "Franciscan" choice of the Community of Sant'Egidio—both in the sense of its spirituality, founded on the reception of the poor, and "institutionalization" through public recognition by the pope—differed even from the more radical postconciliar choice and the more explicitly political one of the Italian Catholic Scout Association, which in 1974 saw the merging of the women's Italian Guide Association (AGI) with the men's Association of Italian Catholic Scouts (ASCI) to form the new Association of Italian Catholic Guides and Scouts (AGESCI). Marked by a progressive, democratic, and clearly "anti-Fascist" and antiauthoritarian political culture, and by a relationship of freedom but also loyalty to the Catholic Church—but without Catholic Action's direct hierarchical obedience—the AGESCI statutes shaped an "association movement" that translated its political choices into educational policy. Fidelity to the Second Vatican Council was, in Italy and in France, at the origin of a long-lasting split between the more anticonciliar wing (close to the anticonciliarism of Monsignor Marcel Lefebvre) of the Catholic Scout movement and the one more determined to translate, at the educational, social, and liturgical level, the new theological orientations of the conciliar culture rather than of the council as such.[27] Based on a methodology in part indebted to the intuition of the founder of the World Scout Movement, the British General Lord Robert Baden-Powell (1857–1941), and the language of the Franco-Belgian Youth Christian Workers (YCW), AGESCI gave rise to an Italian form of scoutism unique in its ecclesiology and "rivalry" with Catholic Action, with the latter remaining, until the conciliar period and beyond, dominant in matters regarding

---

[26] See Alberto Scarpitti and Carlo Felice Casula, eds., *L'ipotesi socialista. Trent'anni dopo: 1970–2000* (Rome: Aesse, 2001); Valentino Marcon and Tino Mariani, *Storia del Movimento lavoratori di Azione cattolica* (Rome: AVE, 2005).

[27] See Gerard Cholvy, *Histoire des organisations et mouvements chrétiens de jeunesse en France, XIXe–XXe siècle* (Paris: Cerf, 1999), 338–68. See also Marie-Thérèse Cheroutre, *Le Scoutisme au féminin. Les Guides de France, 1923–1998* (Paris: Cerf, 2002); Christian Guérin, *L'utopie Scouts de France. Histoire d'une identité collective, catholique et sociale 1920–1995* (Paris: Fayard, 1997); Philippe Laneyrie, *Les Scouts de France. L'évolution du Mouvement des origines aux annés 80* (Paris: Cerf, 1985).

the privileged relationship with the bishops and the Holy See. Since the first half of the 1970s, AGESCI's autonomy from the ecclesiastical hierarchy translated not only into the unabashed aloofness of the Catholic scout world against the bishops' "call to arms" and in a clear resistance to their every other call to the "political unity of Italian Catholics" during elections, but also into a relationship with the local church marked by greater independence from the bishops and parish priests, compared to the umbilical relationship of Catholic Action and other postconciliar realities.[28]

The most obvious difference between experiences such as that of the scouts and Catholic Action, on the one hand, and Opus Dei, the Neocatechumenal Way, and the Community of Sant'Egidio, on the other, is in sheer numbers. If there were associations-movements such as Catholic Action and AGESCI, on the one side, which included many tens of thousands of members, both adults and children, on the other there were organizations with a lower level of institutionalization that not only chose much "lighter" associative and organizational structures (or much less formal and visible ones) but were directed to a Catholic elite made of cultural, intellectual, and spiritual groups and vanguards.

From this perspective, in the period between Pope Paul VI's pontificate and that of John Paul II, the ability of the new religious movements to influence the complex machine of the Catholic Church and accompany it in its postconciliar journey was inversely proportional to their mass, the level of democracy of their political culture, and the level of their institutionalization and bureaucratization.

---

[28] See Mario Sica, *Storia dello scautismo in Italia*, 4th ed. (Rome: Fiordaliso, 2006); Vincenzo Schirripa, *Giovani sulla frontiera. Guide e Scout cattolici nell'Italia repubblicana (1943–1974)* (Rome: Studium, 2006).

Ecclesial Movements and the Postconciliar Period: "Culture of Presence," Catholic Dissent, and Monastic Communities

1. The Movements and Paul VI: Between the Council and the Postconciliar Period

Steering the council at a crucial time, after the death of John XXIII on June 3, 1963, Paul VI long remained faithful to the letter and the spirit of Vatican II in matters relating to ecclesial organizations and the role of the laity in the Catholic Church. Paul VI's pontificate represented, at the height of the conciliar reception, a critical moment, if not yet a paradigm shift in the history of the relations between the Catholic Church and the organized laity.

The long fifteen years of Paul VI's pontificate can be divided, in light of his attitude toward the movements, into three periods based on the tone of his teaching about this new reality of the Church: an initial period of "exegesis" of the Second Vatican Council (1963–68); a second period dictated by prudence and uncertainties with regard to the development of ecclesial movements, influenced as they were also by the more general anti-institutional protest (1968–74); and a third period of revival of the conciliar project and of overcoming the traditional "ecclesiocentrism" related to the Vatican policy toward the movements (1974–78).[1]

---

[1] See Franco Giulio Brambilla, "*Le aggregazioni ecclesiali nei documenti del magistero dal concilio fino ad oggi*," *La Scuola Cattolica* 116 (1988): 461–511.

In effect, the first decade of Paul VI's pontificate with regard to the movements must be examined more in light of the force of external events than in terms of the Church's initiatives. A few actions led to a pontifical recognition of the movements during Vatican II. In 1962, John XXIII had already approved *ad experimentum* the statutes of the Opera di Maria–Focolare's general council. On December 14, 1963, a few months after his election to the papacy, Paul VI approved the Cursillos de Cristianidad. In 1964, the Neocatechumenal Way emerged from the outskirts of Madrid, and in 1968 it reached Rome, with its founders Kiko Argüello and Carmen Hernández opening a center of the Way in the Martyred Canadian Saints parish. On February 6, 1965, Paul VI granted the Legionaries of Christ the *Decretum Laudis*, thus recognizing the Legion as a congregation of pontifical right.

Regardless of Vatican recognition, and inspired by the opening to the global community typical of the Catholicism of the 1960s, during these years several new experiences came to life. In Rome, in 1965 Father Anastasio Gutiérrez founded the community (defined by him as "typically atypical") Seguimi (Follow Me), an association of singles, married couples, and priests engaged in "promoting human and Christian life, centered on the person of Christ and the centrality of man in a secular lifestyle that values interpersonal relationships."[2] The Community of Sant'Egidio emerged between 1968 and 1969 in Rome and was founded by the young layman Andrea Riccardi. During the same years and following those groups emerging from Protestant circles in the early twentieth century, the first groups of the Renewal in the Spirit movement came to light in the United States (Pennsylvania, Indiana, and Michigan) and spread to Italy in 1972.

The bishops and the papacy, during the first postconciliar period, were more like distant spectators of the flourishing of these various experiences and ecclesial organizations and were waiting for their maturation before granting their recognition or rejection, but they were spectators with very different roles and moving in opposite

---

[2] See Anastasio Gutiérrez, *Cristiani senza sconto. Anatomia di un gruppo ecclesiale* (Rome: Pontificia Università Lateranense, 1980); 2nd ed., ed. Gruppo Laico Seguimi (Rome, 2001); Anastasio Gutiérrez, "Seguimi," in *Dizionario degli Istituti di perfezione*, ed. Guerrino Pelliccia and Giancarlo Rocca, vol. 8 (Rome: Paoline, 1988), coll. 1255–61; Paola Majocchi, Vittoria Prisciandaro, *In cordata. La storia del gruppo Seguimi* (Padova: Messaggero, 2005).

directions with regard to power relations inside the Church. If Pope Paul VI's encyclical *Populorum Progressio* (1967) went much further in recognizing the legitimacy of some social and political movements aiming at the rebalancing of wealth between rich and poor—movements that in Latin America had their roots in the reception of Vatican II—nonetheless, the papal document affirmed what would, during John Paul II's pontificate, later be forbidden to the Latin American clergy to admit while reaffirming the centrality of the figure of the pope in the power structure of the Catholic Church.[3]

While the episcopate in theory emerged strengthened by Vatican II from a theological point of view but weakened in its "political" and social power over the universal Church and the individual local Churches, the papacy remained—even after Vatican II—the strongest "point of confessional identity" for Catholicism. It was the place to go to for recognition, or from which to create distance in order to advance an agenda of criticism against the forms of ecclesiastical power and the Vatican's doctrinal politics of the first postconciliar period. At the same time, at the end of the honeymoon between Paul VI and large sections of the Church, disappointed by the process of reception and application of Vatican II, and especially by the encyclical *Humanae Vitae* (1968), the episcopate was gradually renewed and transformed by Paul VI. He did this quickly, albeit without being able to avoid the initial contrasts with those sections of the Church that rejected the council (such as the numerically small but strong following of the French bishop Marcel Lefebvre, who became the founder of the schismatic ultraconservative group, Society of Saint Pius X).

Between the 1970s and 1980s, the movements that chose the path of loyalty to the pope and the Holy See came out strengthened and corroborated by the Vatican recognition, but not by virtue of the mere protections guaranteed by the Holy See to these new groups. Rather, their integration with and material and symbolic attachment to Rome (a relationship not always easy to manage or devoid of humiliating moments experienced by the *status quo* of the established ecclesiastical power) was emblematic of an unscrupulous and pragmatic reading of the epochal moment experienced by the Church of Rome. It was pragmatic mainly because completely removed from the conciliar dream to renew the Church "from the head" (the pope, the curia, the hierarchy, the clergy), even before its "members" (the faithful). The loyalty to the

---

[3] Paul VI, encyclical, *Populorum Progressio*, March 26, 1967.

ecclesiastical institution of these new Catholic movements was the most successful attempt to translate the message of Vatican II into a line of strengthening the ecclesial structure rather than in the direction of a radical restructuring of the institutional Church.

Paul VI's relationship with the movements should be seen in a perspective of conflicting forces, more complex and contradictory than today's propaganda of the postconciliar "rise of the movements" and John Paul II's enthusiasm for the phenomenon. During the first postconciliar decade, until the mid-1970s, the caution and diffidence shown by Pope Paul VI were attributable to the spirit of autonomy or "dissidence" (and sometimes open dissent) of some Catholic associations. But for this autonomy, Catholic Action, Associazioni Cristiane Lavoratori Italiani (ACLI), and Catholic scout groups experienced a period of difficult relations with the Church hierarchy toward the end of Paul VI's pontificate.

In effect, even toward movements of proven loyalty to the ecclesiastical hierarchy, the attitude of the Holy See was marked by wary caution. Following in the footsteps of his predecessor John XXIII, Paul VI rejected the petition made in 1960 and in 1962 by Josemaría Escrivá de Balaguer to give the status of prelature to the institution he founded in Spain in 1928. The suspension of Opus Dei's case would last until the period following the end of Paul VI's pontificate, that is, in 1979, when it was resumed by Cardinal Sebastiano Baggio (the same cardinal who had worked for the recognition of the Catholic scout association, AGESCI, granted by the Italian Episcopal Conference in 1976).

In 1972 and 1973, there were some cautious openings from the Vatican toward the new associations that developed in the first postconciliar period. In 1972, the publication of the *Ordo Initiationis Christianae Adultorum* (the Order of Christian Initiation of Adults)—which suggested in chapter 4 to adapt the contents of the *Ordo* to baptized adults who had not been catechized—did convey to the leaders of the Neocatechumenal Way a first endorsement from the Holy See. Rome made it clear, however, through the Congregation for Divine Worship and the Discipline of the Sacraments, that the *Ordo* could not be applied to those who had been baptized.[4] The Neocatechumenal Way received a public acknowledgment the following year by the Congregation

---

[4] See *Ordo Initiationis Christianae Adultorum* (Civitas Vaticana: Typis Polyglottis Vaticanis, 1972).

for Divine Worship.[5] A reaffirmation of the separation between clergy and laity in ecclesial ministries came from Pope Paul VI's motu proprio *Ministeria Quaedam*, which presented a condensed theology of ecclesial ministries and stated that the revision of the "minor orders" (offices of reader and acolyte) "will bring out more clearly the distinction between clergy and laity, between what is proper and reserved to the clergy and what can be entrusted to the laity. This will also bring out more clearly that mutuality by which 'though they differ essentially and not only in degree, the common priesthood of the faithful and the ministerial or hierarchical priesthood are none the less interrelated; each in its own way shares in the one priesthood of Christ' (*Lumen Gentium*, 10)."[6]

Starting from 1974 and 1975, there was a change in Paul VI's line of action inspired more by the reading of the ecclesial situation—and above all by the crisis of Catholic Action—and less by the perception of the reliability of this or that movement. The reading of the situation, at a time that coincided chronologically with the decline of the papacy and the climax of the postconciliar crisis, was negative and even gloomy with its denouncing of the infiltration of evil in the Church. Ten years after the conclusion of Vatican II, the perception of the "state of ecclesial communion" was far away from the optimistic atmosphere of the "golden 1960s." The golden era of the *Ostpolitik* of John XXIII was gone, the hopes for decolonization were worn out, the brief period between the late 1960s and early 1970s of détente between East and West had been dismissed, and even the agenda of the Catholic Church suffered from this change of scenarios.

The paradigm shift that the postconciliar papacy was trying to steer left Paul VI exposed to criticism from both the "right," nostalgic for the past, and the "left," dissatisfied by his caution in attempts of reform. On the European continent and in North America, the participation in the sacraments collapsed after 1968, especially in France, Germany, and Holland. The collective efforts of the bishops in these countries showed the vitality of postconciliar Catholicism, but in ways that did not always meet with Rome's approval and that could not guarantee a quick recovery of control of the situation. In Italy, the referendum

---

[5] See Paolo Sorci, "Ermeneutica della Parola nel cammino neocatecumenale," *Rivista liturgica* 6 (1997): 867–80.

[6] Paul VI, apostolic letter, *Ministeria Quaedam*, August 15, 1972; Introduction.

that confirmed the law legalizing divorce (May 1974) represented a momentous defeat for the Italian church and the Christian Democratic party. In Spain, the presence in Francisco Franco's dictatorial government of ministers who were members of Opus Dei did not improve the relationship between a moribund Catholic nationalist regime and the Holy See. The liberationist thrusts coming from the South American continent collided with a Christianity still strongly linked to military and technocratic regimes that if, on one side, were able to maintain order, so important to the Catholic hierarchy, on the other, showed the dark side of the relationship between Catholicism and politics in the twentieth century. The Medellín conference of 1968 represented a bold experiment, destined to be blocked and then dismissed by Rome, as would happen with the "liberation theology" of the mid-1970s and mid-1980s.[7] The developing world presented, even for Catholicism as a world force, enormous problems in the face of the hopes aroused by decolonization. Caught between a long missionary tradition, the demands for the inculturation of theology in the local churches, and the challenge of dialogue, the situation presented more uncertainties than assurances. In North America, some "conservative" episcopal appointments were not able to hide the rift between the hierarchy and the base, or stop the trend toward secularization, even within American Catholicism. The Italian situation, characterized by an unstable political and social scenario and exposed to legislative initiatives that represented also a break with a "lost Christendom," was not any more encouraging.

One of the elements that helps us to locate between 1974 and 1975 a turning point in Paul VI's attitude toward the movements was the section on evangelization of the 1974 Synod of Bishops and the apostolic exhortation following the synod, *Evangelii Nuntiandi* (December 8, 1975). In this document, Pope Paul VI still listed the "apostolic movements" under the heading of the "diversified ministries" of the laity, but in a missionary perspective he called them "valuable for the establishment, life, and growth of the Church, and for her capacity to influence her surroundings and to reach those who are remote

---

[7] See Alicia Puente Lutteroth, ed., *Actores y dimensión religiosa en los movimientos sociales latinoamericanos 1960–1992* (México: Porrúa-Uaem, 2006); Silvia Scatena, *In popolo pauperum. La chiesa latinoamericana dal concilio a Medellín (1962–1968)* (Bologna: Il Mulino, 2008).

from her."[8] Loyal to the main directives of Vatican II, Pope Paul VI also opened the way to a variety of ministries in collaboration with the hierarchy, not just for the animation of the temporal order, but also in the service of the ecclesial communion by exercising ministries in the Church: "The laity can also feel themselves called, or be called, to work with their pastors in the service of the ecclesial community for its growth and life, by exercising a great variety of ministries according to the grace and charisms which the Lord is pleased to give them."[9]

In December 1976, Paul VI also reorganized the structure of the Consilium de laicis, which he founded in 1967 on an experimental basis, renaming it Pontificium Consilium pro laicis (Pontifical Council for the Laity). In the motu proprio *Apostolatus Peragendi* were evident some of the underlying aspects of the Vatican position on the new ecclesial movements and lay associations.[10] In terms of understanding the phenomenon and the aspirations of the Church of Rome, on the one hand, it was stated: "Different forms of the apostolate or 'varieties of service' [1 Cor 12:5] that help to build up the Mystical Body of Christ, which is the Church, belong by full right also to the laity. The Second Vatican Ecumenical Council has taught this in our times, setting forth the traditional teaching on this matter in a new light." On the other hand, it was noted, according to a tormented reading of the modern times and the postconciliar period, that "the present time clearly calls for a more earnest and more widespread apostolate on the part of the laity; indeed, 'A sign of this urgent and many-faceted need is the manifest action of the holy Spirit making lay people nowadays increasingly aware of their responsibility and encouraging them everywhere to serve Christ and the church' (*Apostolicam Actuositatem*, 1)."[11]

In terms of classification of the phenomenon, the papal document attempted to include, albeit synthetically and without any suggestion of a greater systematization, everything under the sun of Catholic (and Roman) associationism, whether lay or not, well-established or not:

---

[8] Paul VI, apostolic exhortation, *Evangelii Nuntiandi*, December 8, 1975, no. 73. Translation from http://www.vatican.va/holy_father/paul_vi/apost_exhortations /documents/hf_p-vi_exh_19751208_evangelii-nuntiandi_en.html; accessed May 30, 2014.

[9] Ibid.

[10] Paul VI, apostolic letter, *Apostolatus Peragendi*, December 10, 1976.

[11] Ibid.

In particular, the Pontifical Council for the Laity has the tasks of:

1. encouraging the laity to participate in the Church's life and mission, both—and this is the principal way—as members of associations for the apostolate and as individual Christians;

2. evaluating, guiding, and, if necessary, fostering initiatives regarding the apostolate of laypeople in the various spheres of society, with due regard for the competence of other bodies of the Roman Curia in this matter;

3. dealing with all questions concerning:
   — international and national organizations of the lay apostolate, with due regard for the competence of the Secretariat of State or Papal Secretariat;
   — Catholic societies for the promotion of the apostolate and the spiritual life and activity of the laity, without interference in the rights of the Sacred Congregation for the Evangelization of Peoples regarding societies fostering missionary cooperation exclusively;
   — pious associations (i.e., archconfraternities, confraternities, pious unions, sodalities of all kinds), in consultation with the Sacred Congregation for Religious and Secular Institutes whenever it is a case of an association erected by a Religious Family or a Secular Institute;
   — lay third orders, with regard only to questions concerning the activity of their apostolate, and thus without interference in the competence of the Sacred Congregation for Religious and Secular Institutes for other questions;
   — associations of both clerics and laypeople, with due regard for the competence of the Sacred Congregation for the Clergy in the matter of the observance of the general laws of the Church (cf. the norms of the Apostolic Signatura).[12]

Thus, international and national organizations of laypeople, pious associations, lay third orders and regular associations fell under one Vatican "jurisdiction," in a clear acknowledgment of an extremely fluid and mobile situation with regard to the canonical status of the new ecclesial organizations. A similar fluidity emerged also in relation to the functional configuration of the new Vatican dicastery, and

---

[12] Ibid., no. 6.

therefore of the other bodies subject to that dicastery as well. The new Council for the Laity had the task of:

4. fostering on its own initiative active participation by the laity in such fields as catechetics, liturgy, the sacraments, and education, in collaboration with the various departments of the Roman Curia dealing with these matters;

5. seeing that the Church's laws regarding the laity are strictly observed and examining by administrative means disputes involving laypeople;

6. in agreement with the Sacred Congregation for the Clergy, dealing with questions concerning pastoral councils, whether on the parish or diocesan level, in order to encourage laypeople to take part in joint pastoral action.[13]

On the one hand, this papal document showed the will to implement and develop the "theology of the laity" as it was explicated by the council, which in turn incorporated that theology from the best transalpine theological developments of the 1940s and 1950s and used it in relation to the ecclesiology of the "people of God," without going much further.

On the other hand, Paul VI expressed the effort to support the rise of the new movements in a similar "practical-pastoral" context but not directly in "legislative" and defining terms. Paul VI's attempt to bring together the phenomenon of lay communities under the control of one dicastery—an attempt that did not meet with significant results until the end of John Paul II's pontificate—also showed a desire to unify a reality that over the years would reveal its centripetal character with regard to its course of action and pastoral purposes: besides its unwavering loyalty to the pope, the true figure and ultimate synthesis of the catholicity of contemporary ecclesial movements. The reference to the "*pastorale d'ensemble*" recalled the pioneering experiences of the French school in the 1950s and, at the same time, the first concerns for the dispersion of the forces of the Catholic laity over many distinct projects, spiritualities, messages, devotional styles, intellectual trends, and communal experiences. In short, facing the most varied and diverse alternatives, the experience of a Church led by parish clergy and bishops and guided by uniform pastoral programs risked becoming the memory of a past time.

---

[13] Ibid.

2. High Fidelity: From Catholic Action
to Communion and Liberation

The second period of Paul VI's pontificate saw two gestures that symbolically marked a watershed moment: the unofficial recognition granted by the Holy See to Communion and Liberation and the meeting of charismatics in Rome.

After the congress of leaders held in 1973 at Grottaferrata near Rome, in symbolic proximity to the Holy See, in 1975 the charismatics were able to overcome the obstacle represented by the curial entourage. On the feast of Pentecost in 1975, ten thousand charismatics gathered in Rome at the catacombs of Saint Callixtus, led by Cardinal Suenens, to be received only later by Paul VI during a special audience (granted not without doubts and precautions on the part of the Roman Curia, whose concerns were fueled both by the secretary of state, Cardinal Villot, and by sections of the Catholic Church in the United States). During the audience, the pope's speech offered Vatican recognition for the charismatic renewal, in appreciation of its witness "to this secularized world." In 1976, the charismatic-oriented Communauté de l'Emmanuel was founded in France; in the galaxy of charismatic groups, it was the one that was most supported by Rome and the first to be recognized.[14]

Of greater public and political impact was the episode of Communion and Liberation. On April 23, 1975, for the celebration of the holy year, Pope Paul VI granted the use of an auditorium for an assembly and spoke to the fifteen thousand young people led by Fr. Luigi Giussani, a gesture that from the front pages of the news passed directly into the foundational mythology of the movement that originated in Milan.[15] The decision to speak to Communion and Liberation had consequences for Fr. Giussani's movement and, by extension, for the entire Catholic world, not just for young people, in the throes of an epochal crisis.

After Vatican II, Catholic Action had tried to refashion itself, but it was lagging behind in terms of both the development of a theology of the

---

[14] See Olivier Landron, *Les Communautés nouvelles. Nouveaux visages du catholicisme français* (Paris: Cerf, 2004).

[15] See Massimo Camisasca, *Comunione e Liberazione. La ripresa (1969–1976)* (Cinisello B.: San Paolo, 2003), 305–12.

laity and the cultural evolution of society and the Catholic laity. Its new statutes of 1969 marked this acute delay, which was due not so much to lack of responsiveness with respect to Vatican II but to the slowness in adapting to an institutional and ecclesial model in line with the transformations of the 1960s. The consultation of the base did nothing to bring fresh air into the genetic code of the organization founded by Pius XI.[16]

Catholic Action's decision, led by Vittorio Bachelet, to bring the association into the local churches was in line with the ecclesiology of Vatican II.[17] The movements relating directly to the Holy See and the person of the pope had better luck, however, in asserting their "ecclesiality." In this perspective, it was not the difference between "associations" and "movements" that weighed down Catholic Action. The drastic decline in enrollment was accompanied by the perplexity of the Holy See and the Italian bishops in dealing with an association that, in the debate over its renewal between 1966 and 1969, split between a radically innovative line and another that did not intend to bury the legacy of the glorious Catholic Action. Additionally, its presidency (Vittorio Bachelet and Monsignor Franco Costa) was engaged in an exhausting mediation between these two positions. In the foreword to the new statutes (approved by the Italian bishops in September 1969 and by Pope Paul VI on October 10, 1969), Catholic Action testified to the decision to remain faithful to the idea of proposing the co-responsibility of the laity in building the edifice and mission of the Church.

In a Church experiencing a general crisis of consensus and participation, from a political point of view the decline of members penalized Catholic Action, which had been created half a century ago as the organization of the laity *par excellence*. It was a punishment more severe than a careful reading of the numbers suggests, if compared with the new movements born at the same time. Catholic Action's weakness was in its embodiment of a model of the laity and the Church under attack from the right and left: From the right, it was criticized for not cultivating a strong obedience to the papacy and for not taking a stand regarding the cultural trends of the time that were infiltrating the Catholic Church. From the left, accusations

---

[16] See Ernesto Preziosi, *Obbedienti in piedi. La vicenda dell'Azione Cattolica in Italia* (Turin: SEI, 1996), 313–25.

[17] Vittorio Bachelet, a professor of law at the University of Rome, was assassinated by the Red Brigades in 1980.

were made of "clericalization of the laity," which was the result of the more general anti-institutional thrust and claims—more political than theological—of the possibility of participation in the pastoral bodies within the hierarchical structure of the Church.

Catholic Action's difficult position, in a Catholicism stuck between opposing forces, became apparent in Italy on the occasion of the divorce referendum in May 1974, during which the council of Catholic Action committed the association to "avoid demonstrations for or against the referendum." Adherence to the Italian bishops' pastoral plan, "Evangelization and Human Promotion" (from the title of the pastoral conference of the Italian Episcopal Conference of 1976), meant embracing the best teachings the bishops had to offer in the postconciliar period, but it did not help to stop the political crisis of Catholic Action facing new and more belligerent movements, which grew slowly but suddenly burst on the scene in the mid-1970s. This split between the teaching of the bishops and Italian Catholic laity was confirmed between 1978 and 1981 with the law legalizing abortion and the referendum that confirmed it.

If it is true that Paul VI had a "special concern" for Catholic Action, offering throughout his pontificate an integrated magisterium on the association and following its difficult path toward renewal, it is no less true that at the end of his pontificate we witness his first openings toward "other" movements. "Other" movements not only because they were different from Catholic Action but also because they had their own spirituality, their own reading of the ecclesial situation, and a political ruthlessness in sharp contrast to Catholic Action's troubled prudence (in any direction). Paul VI's attitude toward Communion and Liberation was paradigmatic of a shift, not only on the part of the pope, but also of the bishops, in the direction of recognition—wary until the end but increasingly more unequivocal—of the charism of the new association. The initial caution of the Italian bishops and their leadership toward Fr. Giussani's movement, whom they considered exposed to the "disease of integrism," was replaced, especially after Paul VI's pontificate, by increasingly unconditional support and harmony between the Holy See and the movement.[18]

---

[18] See Massimo Faggioli, "Tra referendum sul divorzio e revisione del Concordato. Enrico Bartoletti segretario della CEI (1972–1976)," *Contemporanea* (2001/2): 255–80.

Undoubtedly, the attitude toward Communion and Liberation assumed the significance of a milestone in the relationship of the Church and the papacy with Catholic "movementism."[19] The movement founded by the Milanese priest Luigi Giussani in 1954 under the name of "Gioventù Studentesca" (GS) at this time took the first step on its historical path from the margins to the center of the Catholic world.[20] Having experienced the growth crisis of 1964 to 1968, Communion and Liberation was one of the few Italian Catholic forces in the early 1970s that tried to restore life to a Catholic movement politically not disengaged but rather very present in the board rooms of political and economic power.[21] Communion and Liberation not only accepted the invitation of the Church hierarchy to get involved in the 1974 referendum campaign against the divorce law but also, after forming the Popular Catholics in universities in 1973, founded its own political branch in 1975. This branch was in a dialectical relationship with the political party of the Christian Democrats, called Movimento Popolare (The People's Movement), and held its first public demonstration on November 16, 1975.

The following year, Communion and Liberation, which at the time never ceased to arouse the suspicion of the highest authorities and was not invited to the national ecclesial congress, "Evangelization and Human Promotion," petitioned for the Holy See's recognition, which eventually came in 1981, only after Paul VI's pontificate. Communion and Liberation was later reorganized to include, together with the main movement, the Fraternity of Communion and Liberation (established in 1980 by the abbot of Monte Cassino and recognized by the Holy See in 1982) and an association, Memores Domini, where members take private vows but live a monastic spirituality, in small groups, active in the world. The rise of Communion and Liberation

---

[19] See Camisasca, *Comunione e Liberazione*, 287–316.

[20] See Salvatore Abbruzzese, *Comunione e Liberazione. Identité catholique et disqualification du monde* (Paris: Cerf, 1989); Salvatore Abbruzzese, *Comunione e Liberazione* (Bologna: Il Mulino, 2001); Anke M. Dadder, *Comunione e Liberazione. Phänomenologie einer neuen geistlichen Bewegung* (Konstanz: UVK, 2002), esp. 97–142.

[21] See *Gli estremisti di centro. Il neo-integralismo cattolico degli anni '70: Comunione e liberazione*, ed. Sandro Bianchi and Angelo Turchini (Rimini-Firenze: Guaraldi, 1975); and *Il caso CL nella chiesa e nella società italiana. Spunti per una discussione* (Trent: Margine, 2014).

in the eyes of the Holy See would culminate with the Extraordinary Synod of Bishops in the autumn of 1985; a decade after Pope Paul VI's laborious and unofficial recognition, Communion and Liberation was invited with other organizations (excluding Catholic Action) to attend the synod convened for the assessment of Vatican II, twenty years after its conclusion.

The early life of Communion and Liberation in the 1970s was challenging, but with John Paul II, many of the difficulties disappeared. The attitude of the pope and of the episcopate toward other movements, however, was much more cautious and distant. For some of movements, the difficulty in obtaining support and attention from the Church hierarchy revealed an explicit suspicion of new ecclesial associations, as in the case of the Italian Catholic Scouts (AGESCI), whose statutes were an expression not only of the transition from an elitist to a more participative form of organization but also of a profound reception of the conciliar *aggiornamento*. (This was evidenced, in Italy as well as in France, from the split of the factions more unreceptive to Vatican II, the contemporary pedagogical innovations, and the emergence of an associative model and a democratic political culture openly anti-Fascist and socially inclusive in terms of gender and class.[22])

If it is true that only with John Paul II would Communion and Liberation enter the world of the Catholic laity from the front door, it is undeniable that already with Paul VI we see the beginning of a preference for a certain type of Catholic movement and an indifference toward other types of experience. Contrary to what the apologists or some members of the movements claim, in some cases (including Communion and Liberation) the Vatican endorsement was not intended to confirm the loyalty of the movements to the teachings of Vatican II, its ecclesiology, and its theology of the laity. Rather, during those difficult postconciliar years, the Vatican's recognition went to an organized laity that, besides the existentialist type of theological language, was the continuation of a much earlier line of "Catholic movement," closer to the nineteenth century than to what came from Vatican II. The same decision to create a network of cooperatives linked to Communion and Liberation in the context of universities, services, and formation

---

[22] See Philippe Laneyrie, *Les Scouts de France. L'évolution du Mouvement des origines aux annés 80* (Paris: Cerf, 1985).

brought to mind the beginnings of the late nineteenth-century Catholic movement with the creation of a network of economic and social solidarity that not only was a source of income but also tended to deny the legitimacy of the Italian state in the creation of the civil community (through state schools, for example) and of Catholics active within the democratic political framework. Communion and Liberation's ecclesiocentrism was not far from a "communitarian" spirituality typical of other contemporary (and not only Catholic) Christian movements: a close community as the ideal community in the world, even better than the outside world—a world that for Communion and Liberation does not constitute a universe of values worth engaging.

Detached from the party of Italian Catholics,[23] Communion and Liberation aimed to revive in Italy the "culture of presence" (against the dreaded "culture of mediation," more typical of liberals) of Catholics on the cultural and social scene, within a liberal society considered unable to deal with the perverse effects of the industrial revolution.[24] Founded by, and revolving around, a charismatic personality like Fr. Giussani, Communion and Liberation combined this "modern" feature with another one, typical of the earlier Catholic movements, namely, the visceral rejection of the liberal political culture—even before the rejection, in the best Roman Catholic tradition, of socialist and Communist stances.[25]

The political culture and theology of Communion and Liberation has lived through the Cold War and its end because it is rooted in a reading of the present and the antiliberal history (not surprisingly emerging from a country like Italy, where the presence of "liberal Catholicism" has always struggled to leave a trace of itself, both intellectually and politically). This antiliberal core explains well the true affinity between certain claims of Communion and Liberation and those of the protest movement of the 1960s, as well as certain exchanges of activists from one side to the other (even after the end of the contestation period).[26]

---

[23] Certainly not because it was against the idea of the "political unity of Italian Catholics" but because of the political mediation carried out by the Christian Democrat party since Vatican II.

[24] See Italo Mancini, "Forme di cristianesimo," in *Tornino i volti* (Genova: Marietti, 1989), 3–31.

[25] Cf. Danièle Hervieu-Léger, *Vers un nouveau christianisme* (Paris: Cerf, 1986).

[26] See Massimo Faggioli, "The New Elites of Italian Catholicism: 1968 and the New Catholic Movements," *The Catholic Historical Review* 98, no. 1 (January 2012): 18–40.

In Giussani's first book, *Traces of Christian Experience*, the key elements were experience and community as a self-sufficient entity, which were able to offer a *Christian experience as a comprehensive human and social experience*, in a gesture of enduring protest against the modern world and critique of Jacques Maritain's distinction between the temporal and spiritual dimensions, considered the cause of the decline of the Catholic presence in society.[27] It was a return to Giussani's positions of the early 1960s: offer "Christ as the solution of all things"; promote an educational effort aimed to engage young people "in a Christian way to act"; combine universal responsibilities with a "deep sense of community" as the sphere of human liberation; and reading modern and contemporary history as a progression of laicism, starting from the French Revolution, destined to make the "Church as phenomenon" unintelligible.

In this sense, it is easy to understand the problematic (to say the least) reception of the texts of Vatican II within Communion and Liberation, especially with regard to the relationship between the Church and the world as it is presented in the pastoral constitution *Gaudium et Spes*. Beyond the three dimensions of the Christian life—"culture, charity, and mission"—Communion and Liberation refused to define a clear political or religious project but aimed rather at an immediate "liberation" based on the recognition of the presence of Christ in the world. As a result, within the movement emerged a "culture of presence," a mode of disillusioned social action and a radical disqualification of the political sphere, which from a theological perspective led Fr. Giussani to embrace Henri de Lubac and Hans Urs von Balthasar while drastically opposing those positions of Karl Rahner.

The rejection of modernity by Giussani's movement took the form not so much of a rejection of the democratic political culture in the structures of Communion and Liberation, in which, as in most contemporary Catholic movements, the internal power is based neither on rational rules of democratic power nor on right of assembly but instead originates from the founder's charism, the sole arbiter of internal dissent and true spiritual guide. Within the universe of Communion and Liberation, the revulsion for modernity and the rejection

---

[27] See Luigi Giussani, *Tracce di esperienza cristiana e altri scritti* (Milan: Jaca Book, 1977).

of the conciliar theology (two alternatives that are not equivalent but have much in common) were evident in the negative perception of the *Aufklärung* (Enlightenment, which included the Catholic *Aufklärung*), ecumenism, and the alterity of Judaism as potential threats to the Christian and Catholic identity.

3. Catholic Dissent

Of opposite tendencies to those of Communion and Liberation was the short but intense experience of groups of the so-called Catholic dissent, a label that encapsulates a wide range of heterogeneous experiences of criticism and protest but also of participation in the Catholic Church in the postconciliar period until the end of the 1970s.

This stage—which was particularly discernible in Italy, with the Isolotto community in Florence, Fr. Ernesto Balducci, and the Christians for Socialism—developed in three phases: a first phase linked to the council and the years immediately following, characterized by a focus on issues of ecclesial praxis (e.g., the role of the laity in the Church and democracy, celibacy of the clergy); a second phase, from 1968 onward, more politicized and sensitive to the consequences of the Catholic Church's political attitude (the Concordat policy and relations with modern states); and a third phase, starting in 1973, during which the "basic ecclesial communities" and the Christians for Socialism became prominent.[28] The vast galaxy of dissent is hardly noticeable without considering the role of magazines and newsletters, in an environment where the culture of discussion was the true, almost liturgical, or para-liturgical, foundation of the dissenting communities.[29] A Marxist reading of the Bible, the "choice of social class" and new "ecclesiogenesis," opening the role of women in the ecclesial community, and acceleration in the ecumenical journey: these were the key themes of this experience. A brief but intense one indeed, which

---

[28] See Mario Cuminetti, *Il dissenso cattolico in Italia, 1965–1980* (Milan: Rizzoli, 1983); Daniela Saresella, *Dal Concilio alla contestazione. Riviste cattoliche negli anni del cambiamento (1958–1968)* (Brescia: Morcelliana, 2005); Daniela Saresella, *Cattolici a sinistra. Dal modernismo ai giorni nostri* (Rome-Bari: Laterza, 2011).

[29] Among these reviews: "Com" and "Com-Nuovi Tempi" (Rome); "Il Gallo" (Genova); "Aggiornamenti sociali" (Milan); "Testimonianze" (Florence); "Il Tetto" (Naples); "Idoc-internazionale" (Rome); "Lettere" (Fontanella di Sotto il Monte Giovanni XXIII); "Bozze" (Rome).

in Europe remains only a vague memory in today's Catholic Church, linked as it was to the Catholic lay leaders of the time, while in North America these Catholic dissent movements have become part of the wider experience of so-called *liberal Catholicism.*

Established not only in Europe, these movements found fertile ground in Latin America, where liberation theology had helped to call into question not only the economic and social order but also its ecclesial and theological representation. The complex interplay between preferential option for the poor and the politicization of the clergy, between indigenous theology and base communities would ultimately be simplified, separated but not completely removed from the fight about liberation theology.

The movements of dissent played a role in the selection mechanism of Catholic movements in the bustling postconciliar period, even if they are difficult to define as "ecclesial movements" in the full sense, if only for their choice to operate from the outside, without the need or the desire for any kind of recognition from the Vatican. Their strong political imprint led them to the center of the debate on the occasion of specific battles (like the divorce law in Italy, between 1970 and 1974, and abortion, between 1978 and 1981 in Italy and in France in 1975). That was also the cause of their premature decline, however, at the end of a specific political-ideological season. In this sense, the interdiction to which the institutional Church condemned them was only one element of the crisis they experienced at the end of the 1970s— together with a changed political situation. The politicization of these Catholic base movements and the protest movement was one of the elements that emerged only to disappear soon after in the short span of twenty years. Already in the mid-1980s, the socio-political horizon had completely disappeared from the vocabulary of the new Catholic movements, creating room for aspirations of a different type.

4. Neo-Monastic Communities: Taizé and Bose

Realities that cannot be considered fully part of the movement phenomenon but that do have common roots with it, both from a chronological perspective and from a theological and ideal one, are the communities of life and prayer that emerged and developed in the postconciliar period, in search of a way to interpret the conciliar aspirations as well as those of postwar European churches.

The ecumenical community of Taizé, founded in France during the Second World War by the young Swiss Protestant Roger Schutz, became a center of attraction for young Christians from all over the world beginning in the 1960s. Engaged in the ecumenical journey—intended as aspiration toward reconciliation between Christians and centered on biblical spirituality and the service to others—the Taizé community has in time assumed the character of an ecumenical monastic community. A meeting place for Christians of various denominations, and therefore also of several generations of young Catholics, Taizé has implemented Vatican II's message in an original way, as evidenced from the opening of the "Council of Youth" on August 30, 1974, which was announced and convoked four years earlier and which brought together forty thousand young people from all over the world. This "parable of community" (as John Paul II called Taizé during his visit to the community on October 5, 1986) did not become an organized "ecclesial movement" in the sense of an association within a particular Church committed to have its demands—the ones relevant to its founder, its members, and the social network it has built—recognized and supported by the Church by means of infiltrating its structure at an official and institutional level.[30]

As with Taizé, the community of Bose, founded in Piedmont, Italy, by a young layman, Enzo Bianchi, at the end of the Second Vatican Council in December 1965, has developed its influential power from the decision not to become an organized and ramified movement. Rather, a monastic community was established as a center of ecumenical prayer, reflection, and meeting open to the world and the media, while at the same time remaining rooted in the patristic theological tradition. After encountering in the first few years of its life a strong hostility from the local church—suspicious of a community founded by a layman and the coming and going of non-Catholics in that farmhouse of theirs in the hills surrounding Turin in Northern Italy—in 1968 the community of Bose saw a first recognition by the cardinal of Turin, Archbishop Michele Pellegrino, and the entry in the original community of non-Catholic brothers and sisters. The

---

[30] See José Luis Gonzales-Balado, *The Story of Taizé* (London: Mowbray, 1978); Rex Brico, *Frère Roger e Taizé: una primavera nella Chiesa* (Brescia: Morcelliana, 1982); Jason Brian Santos, *A Community Called Taizé. A Story of Prayer, Worship, and Reconciliation* (Downers Grove, IL: IVP Books, 2008)

ecumenical character of the community did not end with the presence of non-Catholic brothers and sisters but was constantly kept alive throughout the history of the community through the search for "pneumatophores," both men and women (not only monks, nuns, and theologians), belonging to other churches and Christian denominations.[31]

The cases of Taizé and Bose are worth mentioning because they represent the two most fruitful examples of a radical "re-conversion," in a spiritual, ecumenical, and intellectual sense, of the aspirations that spread throughout Christian Europe between John XXIII's pontificate, the end of Vatican II, and the mid-1970s. The striving for a more compassionate and less institutional Church; the search for a more biblical and less disembodied spirituality and the abandonment of devotionalism; the welcoming of the end of the "Constantinian era" and the centuries-old "co-belligerence" of Church and State against the openness to modernity; the service to the poor and others in need as a true form of charity and sharing; ecumenical hope as a response to the scandal of the division among Christians of different denominations: all these aspirations were channeled neither in a movement where socio-political demands are expressed in a religious language nor in an ecclesial-humanitarian agency. Instead, they became the fabric of a monastic community, consistent with the strongest sources of the conciliar *aggiornamento* and *ressourcement*: the rediscovery of the Bible, the return to the theology of the fathers of the Church, and the full reception of the monastic liturgical movement. These characteristics have given rise in the Church to a non-movement mode for creating a stream of innovations. In such instances, the power to influence the ecclesial praxis is entrusted neither to the official recognition granted by the ecclesiastical institution nor to the social and political network within the institution. Rather, it comes through the cultural and spiritual authority deriving from the ability to grasp—through a dynamism not attainable by an institution and with an aesthetic sensibility closer to Eastern and Protestant Christianity rather than the Catholic tradition—the "signs of the times" of postconciliar Christianity.[32]

---

[31] See Mario Torcivia, *Il segno di Bose. Con un'intervista a Enzo Bianchi* (Casale Monferrato: Piemme, 2003).

[32] See Mario Torcivia, *Guida alle nuove comunità monastiche italiane* (Casale Monferrato: Piemme, 2001).

5. The Last "Pope of Catholic Action": Paul VI

Paul VI steered the Church not only from Vatican II to the post-conciliar period but also from one model of laity to another. The model of laity shaped on Catholic Action's structure within a few years was replaced by a more active, pluralistic, and internally divided laity, in which the ecclesial movements (whether organized or not) had a role in shaping, even at the level of public debate, the reception of Vatican II.

Paul VI's attitude toward the movements was accompanied by a magisterial teaching that grasped the historical urgency of an associated lay apostolate, without excluding associative forms different from Catholic Action, but still reserving for Catholic Action—indicated, because of its ties with the hierarchy, as the model of associative forms of apostolate—special favors and attention. This magisterium, set within a framework of increasing difficulty and frustration experienced by the papacy over the development of the postconciliar directives, gradually assumed the tone of concern for the fragmentation of Catholic groups, the loss of cohesion, the anti-institutional spirit, and the lack of ecclesial unity. Paul VI's theoretical reflection on the laity and associations remained faithful to the context of the theology of the laity of Vatican II, without adding any substantial innovations from an ecclesiological perspective and in keeping with the close unity between the institutional and charismatic aspects of the ecclesial reality. The only exception, with regard to Paul VI's caution toward the movements, was the case of Communion and Liberation, with its semiofficial and wary recognition.

The discussion on ecclesial organizations was tainted by the indeterminacy of the theological framework; alongside a cautious openness on the part of the Holy See to the pluralism of associative forms, Paul VI intended to revive Catholic Action as the distinctive and normative model. Despite Paul VI's insistence on this particular mode of mobilization and union of the Catholic laity to the ecclesiastical hierarchy, Catholic Action would never again recover its glorious past, in part because of the dwindling number of registered members in Catholic Action's organizations.

The insistence of a pope close to Catholic Action for generational and biographical reasons, but also for the deeply rooted conviction of Catholic Action's greater capacity for the reception of Vatican II (compared with the liturgical, theological, and political peculiarities of other groups led by a single charism rather than by a Catholic sense of the whole) eventually gave way to his successor's greater openness to the phenomenon of the movements. John Paul II gave a new centrality to the phenomenon, seen as linked more to the challenge of the New Evangelization than to the necessity of turning the movements into the cradle of the laity of the Church of Vatican II.

The risks of fragmentation of the ecclesial structure, feared by the observers of ecclesial movements during the years of John Paul II's pontificate, were still far away. It was during the mid-1970s, however, that the first cracks emerged within the postconciliar ecclesial structure, divided not only along the different lines of the various receptions, or rejections, of the Second Vatican Council but also along the many possible choices—liturgical, spiritual, devotional, sociopolitical—interpreted by the different movements.

CHAPTER 7

John Paul II
and the Global Pontificate as Movement

1. The Pope of the Movements

A decisive change in the Vatican policy and papal magisterium on the ecclesial movements took place with John Paul II's pontificate. From the early years of his pontificate, John Paul II's reflections on the movements evolved, in part as a result of his being a former collaborator of the Consilium de Laicis and one of the members of the Council of the Synod of Bishops, which proposed to Pope Paul VI the theme of evangelization for 1974. Wojtyla was also one of the speakers at that same synod on evangelization.

John Paul II's vision on the role of lay groups in the Church of the modern world was frequently formulated in the course of his apostolic journeys, his meetings with the laity, especially on the feast of Christ the King, and during the *ad limina* visits of bishops. In light of the inheritance received from the Second Vatican Council and his predecessors, John Paul II observed, beginning with his programmatic encyclical, *Redemptor Hominis* (March 4, 1979), that a "spirit of collaboration and shared responsibility" had spread even among laypeople, "not only strengthening the already existing organizations for lay apostolate but also creating new ones that often have a different outline and excellent dynamism."[1]

---

[1] John Paul II, encyclical letter, *Redemptor Hominis*, March 4, 1979, no. 5. Translation from http://www.vatican.va/holy_father/john_paul_ii/encyclicals/documents /hf_jp-ii_enc_04031979_redemptor-hominis_en.html.

With John Paul II, there was a substantial expansion of the papal magisterium, which embraced a series of acts and events of extraordinary importance for the future of ecclesial movements. During John Paul II's pontificate, we can identify two main shifts in policy toward ecclesial groups: the first consisting in the "launch" of the movements in the early years of his pontificate (1981–82) and the second represented by their "tribute" during the period of preparation and celebration of the jubilee (1998–2000).

An increased activism was evident from the early years of John Paul II's pontificate: in April 1980, the first meeting of the movements was held, promoted by the Pontifical Council for the Laity. A few months later, the pope's first hearing with the Renewal in the Spirit movement in Italy took place. In May 1981, John Paul II addressed a message to the Fourth International Congress of the Charismatic Renewal, and the Italian Episcopal Conference (CEI) published the pastoral note of the Episcopal Commission for the Apostolate of the Laity, *Criteria of Ecclesiality for Groups, Movements, and Associations of the Faithful in the Church*.[2] A few months later, in September 1981, the first international conference of the movements was held at Rocca di Papa (near Rome), promoted by Vita e Luce and Communion and Liberation.[3] On this occasion, marked by the contrast with Catholic Action's "religious choice" and its more dialogical approach to the world and secular culture, the pope stated in his brief welcome speech, "The church itself is a movement."[4]

In the early 1980s, John Paul II gave great attention to Communion and Liberation, which in 1980 celebrated its first Meeting for Friendship among the Peoples at Rimini (now taking place every year in August), and Communion and Liberation in 1982 proposed through its weekly newspaper, *Il Sabato*, the appointment of a bishop in charge

---

[2] See *Enchiridion della Conferenza episcopale italiana, 3 (1980–1985)* (Bologna, 1986), 309–30.

[3] See *I movimenti della Chiesa negli anni Ottanta. Atti del Convegno (Rome, 23–27 September 1981)*, ed. Massimo Camisasca and Maurizio Vitali (Milan: Jaca Book, 1982). Other meetings were held between February 28 and March 4, 1987, at Rocca di Papa (see *I movimenti nella chiesa. Atti del II colloquio internazionale: Vocazione e missione dei laici nella chiesa oggi* [Milan, 1987]); in Bratislava from April 1–4, 1991; and in Rome on Pentecost in 1998.

[4] Homily, September 27, 1981, in *Insegnamenti di Giovanni Paolo II*, vol. 4/2 (Vatican City, 1982), 305.

of all the Italian ecclesial movements.[5] That same year, on February 11, 1982, the Fraternity of Communion and Liberation (established in 1980 by the abbot of Monte Cassino with Fr. Luigi Giussani as president for life) received by the pope (and not by the Italian Episcopal Conference) recognition as a lay association of pontifical right. In September 1982, the pope, as a special gift to Communion and Liberation, made a visit to the Rimini meeting. The special relationship between John Paul II and Fr. Giussani's movement continued in the following years, and in October 1985, Communion and Liberation was invited to participate in the Extraordinary Synod of Bishops.

This interest in new movements also involved Opus Dei, which did not enjoy particular favors from the Holy See during the pontificates of John XXIII and Paul VI. With John Paul II's pontificate beginning in the 1970s, the redefinition of Opus Dei's external mission and activities, in terms of a return to its origins in developing education projects, was followed by the highest recognition. In 1982, after an investigation of the Congregation for Bishops that lasted three and a half years, with the apostolic constitution *Ut Sit Validum*, Opus Dei, better known as the Prelature of the Holy Cross and Opus Dei, became a "personal prelature," and the Holy See appointed Monsignor Alvaro del Portillo as the first prelate of the institution.[6] On June 29, 1983, John Paul II also approved the final text of the constitutions of the Legionaries of Christ congregation, thus revealing a clear line of support for Spanish-speaking movements (Opus Dei of Spanish origin and the Legionaries from Mexico) of the *reconquista* of the modern world. Undoubtedly, the anticommunist cultural background of these two movements, born in two key countries (Spain and Mexico) for the clash between Church and secularism in the twentieth century, played an important role in their official recognition.

In conjunction with this activism in favor of the movements, the work of reform of the Code of Canon Law—which was announced by Pope John XXIII in 1959, carried out by Pope Paul VI during the 1970s, and ended in 1983 during John Paul II's pontificate—did not give the same attention to the canonical aspects of the ecclesial role of charisms and movements. In light of the positive opinion of their

---

[5] See "Un vescovo per i movimenti?," *Il regno-attualitá* 22 (1982): 507.
[6] John Paul II, apostolic constitution, *Ut Sit Validum*, November 28, 1982.

role in the New Evangelization, Pope John Paul II's attitude in dealing with the movements was not particularly attentive to their various institutional configurations, with their most varied and ever-changing combination of lay, religious, and clerical elements within them. In the 1980 schema of the revised Code of Canon Law, the codes regarding the movements were not included; instead, they were in the concepts of the previous *Lex Ecclesiae Fundamentalis*.

Pope John Paul II had decided not to promulgate the *Lex Ecclesiae Fundamentalis*, in response to the mounting opposition throughout the world that had spread since the early 1970s against a project perceived as contrary to the spirit of Vatican II. Yet the schema of the revised Code of 1982 included the rules of canon 15 of the *Lex Ecclesiae Fundamentalis* on the rights and duties of the faithful, from which derived canon 215 of the 1983 Code, included in book 2, "People of God" (part 1, "The Christ's Faithful"; title 1, "Obligations and Rights of Christ's Faithful").[7] In canons 298–313 (book 2, "People of God"; part 1, "The Christ's Faithful"; title 5, "Associations of Christ's Faithful"), the distinction between private and public associations, which comes from civil law, was also introduced. The Code of 1983 did not, however, want to create a rigid classification of associations, as did the Code of 1917. In effect, in contrast to the case of "personal prelatures"—the communities of faithful excluded from the ordinary jurisdiction of bishops that were included in the Code (cc. 294–97)—in the new codification the expression *motus ecclesiales* does not appear. The expression "ecclesial movements" was not even present in the preparatory phase of the new Code, being by definition not easily expressible in legal terms. Similarly, the term "charism," cited seven times in the schema of 1982, had been rejected and did not appear in the revised Code.[8]

During the 1980s, the growth of movements and associations in the consideration of papal policy had been steady and full of significant events. Even the frequent apostolic journeys during John Paul II's itinerant pontificate and the beginnings of the World Youth Days,

[7] See Barbara Zadra, *I movimenti ecclesiali e i loro statuti* (Rome, 1997); Velasio De Paolis, "Diritto dei fedeli di associarsi e la normativa che lo regola," in *Fedeli Associazioni Movimenti*. 18 Incontro di Studio (July 2–6, 2001), ed. Gruppo Italiano di Docenti di Diritto Canonico, Quaderni della Mendola, 10 (Milan, 2002), 127–62.

[8] See Eugenio Corecco, "Die kulturellen und ekklesiologischen Voraussetzungen des neuen CIC," *Archiv für katholisches Kirchenrecht* 152 (1983): 3–30.

organized since 1984 every three years and then every two, became an unparalleled spotlight for ecclesial movements. Such events were capable of concentrating in the figure of the pope the legitimizing reference of movements and ecclesial groups often in difficult relations (when not in open conflict) with each other and with the local hierarchies, bishops, and episcopal conferences.

At the second Congress of the Italian Church, held in Loreto in April 1985, the pope called the movements the "privileged channel for the formation and promotion of an active laity that is aware of its role in the Church and in the world" and pointed to the fundamental and necessary role of bishops. Also thanks to the new attention given to the movements by this pontificate, Loreto 1985 was a fundamental moment in the change brought by John Paul II to the Italian Church in the sense of a less dialogical and more confrontational approach to secularism. At the second meeting of the movements at Rocca di Papa, in February and March 1987, Pope John Paul II stated: "The great blossoming of these movements and the manifestations of energy and ecclesial vitality which characterize them are certainly to be considered one of the most precious fruits of the vast and profound spiritual renewal promoted by the last Council."[9] In calling attention to the role of the movements, the pope's statement implicitly revealed a clear preference for movements (such as Communion and Liberation) that were more willing to bring a "Polish model" of relationship between Church and modern society, not only on the Italian scene, but for the whole Church. The preference for this model led John Paul II's pontificate to support the phenomenon of the movements, to the relative neglect of the problems of the relationship within the Church between the movements and the bishops and between the movements and an active Catholic laity not associated with any particular group.

John Paul II essentially reduced the complex issue of "communion" of the movements with the Church to the question of the movements' obedience to the pope and the Holy See. The post-synodal apostolic exhortation *Christifideles Laici*, published on January 30, 1989, defined the group apostolate as a "sign . . . that must be manifested in relation to 'communion' both in the internal and external aspects of the various

---

[9] John Paul II, speech of March 2, 1987, in *Insegnamenti di Giovanni Paolo II* 10, no. 1 (1987): 476.

group forms and in the wider context of the Christian community."[10] This wish was linked to a reading of the moment:

> In recent days the phenomenon of laypeople associating among themselves has taken on a character of particular variety and vitality. In some ways lay associations have always been present throughout the Church's history as various confraternities, third orders and sodalities testify even today. However, in modern times such lay groups have received a special stimulus, resulting in the birth and spread of a multiplicity of group forms: associations, groups, communities, movements. We can speak of a *new era of group endeavours* of the lay faithful.[11]

The pope pointed to, in a perspective that largely took note of the existing reality, the five "ecclesiological criteria" for the movements' inclusion in the ecclesial communion: (1) the primacy given to the call of every Christian to holiness, (2) the responsibility of professing the Catholic faith, (3) the witness to a strong and authentic communion, (4) conformity to and participation in the Church's apostolic goals, and (5) a commitment to a presence in human society.

The presence of the theme of the movements in John Paul II's magisterium never faded during the 1990s, when it became increasingly clear that the pope saw the movements as a specialized and more advanced vanguard of the New Evangelization. In addition to this role, the internal development of the movements in the Church posed some questions of coexistence with the traditional structures of recruitment and training of the clergy. Even the statement of the Special Assembly for Europe of the Synod of Bishops in 1991, and the following post-synodal apostolic exhortation *Pastores Dabo Vobis* of 1992, tackled the issue of the new traits of the priest-members of movements, emphasizing the positive role of these new groups for the vocation of pastoral care and giving a positive assessment of the link between the seminarians and priests and their communities or associations of origin:

> Associations and youth movements, which are a sign and confirmation of the vitality which the Spirit guarantees to the Church, can

---

[10] John Paul II, post-synodal apostolic exhortation, *Christifideles Laici*, December 30, 1988, no. 30. Translation from http://www.vatican.va/holy_father/john_paul_ii /apost_exhortations/documents/hf_jp-ii_exh_30121988_christifideles-laici_en.html.

[11] Ibid., no. 29.

and should contribute also to the formation of candidates for the priesthood, in particular of those who are the product of the Christian, spiritual and apostolic experience of these groups. Young people who have received their basic formation in such groups and look to them for their experience of the Church should not feel they are being asked to uproot themselves from their past or to break their links with the environment which has contributed to their decision to respond to their vocation, nor should they erase the characteristic traits of the spirituality which they have learned and lived there in all that they contain is good, edifying and rich. For them too, this environment from which they come continues to be a source of help and support on the path of formation toward the priesthood.[12]

John Paul II's pontificate helped to welcome and include the movements within the bodies of the Roman Curia and Catholic Rome: particularly successful were the exploits of the groups of Spanish-speaking origin. For the Neocatechumenals, the first recognition by John Paul II of the movement "as an itinerary of Catholic formation, valid for our society and for our times . . . for the new evangelization," came on August 30, 1990. That same year, John Paul II granted recognition to the Focolare movement as an "international association of the faithful of Pontifical Right." Between 1991 and 1992, the Legionaries of Christ inaugurated their new center of higher studies in Rome and created a novitiate in Northern Italy; the pope approved their statutes on November 26, 2004. The support given by John Paul II to Opus Dei, since the beginning of his pontificate, was confirmed by further recognition given to the Opus Dei prelature, through the beatification of the founder Josemaría Escrivá de Balaguer in 1992 and his rapid canonization in 2002. All these initiatives contributed to the firm and permanent establishment of Opus Dei in Rome and in the Roman Curia, while consolidating its Pontifical University of the Holy Cross in open and increasing competition with other pontifical universities in Rome.[13]

The line of John Paul II's papacy with regard to the movements was not tied to a particular ideology, even though some movements

---

[12] John Paul II, post-synodal apostolic exhortation, *Pastores Dabo Vobis*, March 25, 1992, no. 68. Translation from http://www.vatican.va/holy_father/john_paul_ii /apost_exhortations/documents/hf_jp-ii_exh_25031992_pastores-dabo-vobis_en.html.

[13] See John L. Allen Jr., *Opus Dei: An Objective Look behind the Myths and Reality of the Most Controversial Force in the Catholic Church* (New York: Doubleday, 2005).

were obviously closer than others to his vision of the Church and modernity. On April 29, 1993 the Episcopal Commission for the Laity of
the Italian Episcopal Conference issued a new pastoral note titled *Lay
Associations in the Church*, which represented a significant opening
toward the movements, a reception of *Christifideles Laici* with regard
to certain criteria of ecclesiality, but also a warning to the movements
not to consider themselves *the* Church.[14] The role of the movements
for the New Evangelization was also mentioned in the apostolic letter
Tertio Millennio Adveniente of November 10, 1994, in which, among
the signs of hope for the New Evangelization, the pope emphasized: "*In
the Church*, they include a greater attention to the voice of the Spirit
through the acceptance of charisms and the promotion of the laity, a
deeper commitment to the cause of Christian unity and the increased
interest in dialogue with other religions and with contemporary culture. The reflection of the faithful in the second year of preparation
ought to focus particularly *on the value of unity* within the Church, to
which the various gifts and charisms bestowed upon her by the Spirit
are directed."[15]

Even in the post-synodal apostolic exhortation *Vita Consecrata*
of 1996, John Paul II stressed, in more problematic terms, the role of
movements with regard to the membership of consecrated people in
ecclesial movements:

> In recent years, many consecrated persons have become members
> of one or other of the *ecclesial movements* which have spread in our
> time. From these experiences, those involved usually draw benefit,
> especially in the area of spiritual renewal. Nonetheless, it cannot be
> denied that in certain cases this involvement causes uneasiness and
> disorientation at the personal or community level, especially when
> these experiences come into conflict with the demands of the com-
> mon life or of the Institute's spirituality. It is therefore necessary to

[14] Episcopal Commission for the Laity of the CEI, *Le aggregazioni laicali nella
chiesa*, April 29, 1993, in *Enchiridion della Conferenza episcopale italiana: decreti,
dichiarazioni, documenti pastorali per la Chiesa italiana, 5 (1991–1995)* (Bologna,
1996), 697–739.

[15] John Paul II, apostolic letter, *Tertio Millennio Adveniente*, November 10,
1994, nos. 46–47. Translation from http://www.vatican.va/holy_father/john_paul
_ii/apost_letters/1994/documents/hf_jp-ii_apl_19941110_tertio-millennio-adveniente
_en.html.

take care that membership in these ecclesial movements does not
endanger the charism or discipline of the Institute of origin, and
that all is done with the permission of Superiors and with the full
intention of accepting their decisions.[16]

The Vatican recognition policy toward the movements grew significantly in the 1990s, up to the crucial hour of preparation and management of the 2000 Jubilee Year. In May 1998, the Fourth World Congress
of movements and new communities was held in Rome: the approxi-
mately 300,000 members of sixty movements and new communities
were received by the pope, who in his speech on the eve of Pentecost
(May 27, 1998) called those gathered "the answer" to the challenge of
secularization.[17] In that same speech, the movements were described
as "one of the most significant fruits of that springtime in the Church
that was foretold by the Second Vatican Council but unfortunately
has often been hampered by the spread of secularization."[18] The pope
also highlighted an open agenda on the path of the movements toward
"ecclesial maturity," exhorting the movements to offer the Church
"mature fruits of communion and commitment."[19] A seminar held
in Rome in June 1999, organized by the Roman Curia (the Pontifical
Council for the Laity and the Congregation for the Doctrine of the
Faith), assembled a hundred bishops and cardinals and the main "communities and movements" in order to take stock of the relationship
between bishops and movements. In his message, Pope John Paul II
focused on the existing problems and asked the movements to take the
next step toward "ecclesial maturity" and an "effort of communion";

---

[16] John Paul II, post-synodal apostolic exhortation, *Vita Consecrata*, March
25, 1996, no. 56. Translation from http://www.vatican.va/holy_father/john_paul_ii
/apost_exhortations/documents/hf_jp-ii_exh_25031996_vita-consecrata_en.html.

[17] Among those present at the Congress of 1998, the most well-known move-
ments included the Neocatechumenal Way, Communauté de l'Arche, Emmanuel
Community, Communion and Liberation, the Community of St. Giles, Cursillos de
Cristianidad, Foyers de Charité, Legion of Mary, the Focolare Movement (Work of
Mary), Schoenstatt, and Renewal in the Holy Spirit.

[18] Pontifical Council for the Laity, *Movements in the Church* (Vatican City: Libreria
Editrice Vaticana, 1999); Pontifical Council for the Laity, *I Movimenti ecclesiali nella
sollecitudine pastorale dei Vescovi* (Vatican City: Libreria Editrice Vaticana, 2000).

[19] Address of John Paul II to the Fourth World Congress of Ecclesial Movements,
May 30, 1998, in *I movimenti nella chiesa*, 222.

from the bishops, he asked for "magnanimity" in a spirit of "fatherhood and charity."

Between 1999 and 2001, in the wake of the spur given by the pope to these new movements, new meetings (promoted by Renewal in the Spirit, Community of Sant'Egidio, the Focolare movement, the Neocatechumenal Way, and Communion and Liberation) were held at Speyer, Germany, and at Castel Gandolfo near Rome. But it was the Great Jubilee of 2000 that represented an important step in terms of the movements' recognition and consecration. In his homily of the Mass for Pentecost, on Sunday, May 31, 2000, John Paul II stated: "The movements and new communities, providential expressions of the new springtime brought forth by the Spirit with the Second Vatican Council, announce the power of God's love which in overcoming divisions and barriers of every kind, renews the face of the earth to build the civilization of love." During the Pentecost vigil, about 300,000 people from sixty different ecclesial movements inaugurated the first World Congress. Before the speech of John Paul II, those gathered listened to the testimony brought by Chiara Lubich (foundress of the Focolare movement), Kiko Argüello (co-founder of the Neocatechumenal Way), by Jean Vanier (founder of L'Arche), and Fr. Luigi Giussani (founder of Communion and Liberation).

In some cases, the event of the Jubilee of 2000 meant a special "indulgence" for movements that had required long scrutiny or had momentarily fallen into disgrace for excesses in the liturgy or caused tensions in their relationship with the local churches. At the meeting on September 20–23, 1999, the Italian Episcopal Conference approved the statutes of the Cursillos de Cristianidad. Even for the Neocatechumenals the new millennium brought the approval *ad experimentum* for five years of their statutes, which were published on June 29, 2002. The pope had expressly urged the drafting of the statutes in the audience granted to the initiators and directors of the Neocatechumenal Way from around the world on January 24, 1997. In 2008, the Neocatechumenal Way received final approval by a decree of the Pontifical Council for the Laity. On March 14, 2002, the Renewal in the Spirit movement received from the Italian Episcopal Conference approval of the statutes of the association, which was announced by Cardinal Camillo Ruini in his homily in St. John Lateran on the occasion of the thirtieth anniversary of the presence of the movement in Italy.

All these movements received from John Paul II's pontificate substantial support that silenced every objection raised by the bishops and by most of the laity. But the transition of the pontificate from John Paul II to Benedict XVI in April 2005 put the continuation of Vatican support after John Paul II's death into question. Already during John Paul II's papacy, there were clear voices that were less enthusiastic about the role of movements in the Church.

2. John Paul II's and Other Views of the Ecclesial Movements

The growth of the influence of the ecclesial movements and associations during John Paul II's pontificate (and as a result of his pontificate) was not equally welcomed by all theologians, bishops, pastors of local churches, and other forces within the Catholic Church. At the Synod of Bishops in 1987 on the role of the laity in the Church—attended (as auditors only) by many representatives of the movements of various countries—some senior leaders of the Church hierarchy expressed evaluations that were, to say the least, problematic: Cardinals Carlo Maria Martini, Aloisio Lorscheider, and Frantisek Tomasek spoke of the movements as "parallel churches."[20] If the end result of the synod did not seem to take into account the concerns raised with regard to the ecclesiology of the movements and the pastoral problems related to their activities in dioceses and parishes, it was evident that the Holy See and the pope's approval of the movements' activism was not shared at all levels.

Despite the rumors and recurring accusations of elitism and sectarianism raised against the movements (accusations frequently not unfounded but often initiated and raised by critics, who are not always impartial), critics of the phenomenon were essentially moved by two types of arguments: on the one hand, concerns rising from theological and ecclesiological considerations, and, on the other, from more "institutional" matters.

On the theological side, the legacy of Vatican II brought the Church's unhindered support of the movement phenomena into ques-

---

[20] See Marco Garzonio, *Il Cardinale. Il valore per la Chiesa e per il mondo dell'episcopato di Carlo Maria Martini* (Milan: Mondadori, 2002), 37–39. See Robert Moynihan, "At Synod, a Split on Lay Movements?," *National Catholic Register* 63 (October 25, 1987), 1.

tion because of the manner in which these new groups implemented the council's teachings and its theology. Reiterating the repeated accusations of sectarianism, it was shown that, in the transition from a "local church" to a "personal church" made of small communities, the social mechanisms in force in these new movements led to self-managed forms of inquisitorial control of the members' Christian life (and sometimes even in relatively spontaneous endogamous practices within the communities). From an ecclesiological viewpoint, it was observed that the analogy between the new movements and the medieval mendicant orders, often reiterated for apologetic purposes, implied a dismissal of Vatican II, its ecclesiology, and its overall vision of the baptized as "people of God." In an uncommonly clear fashion, the Italian ecclesiologist Severino Dianich observed that "the new Christian associations arise from a constant spur, that is, the feeling of a fundamental inadequacy of the local church with regard to its mission and the demands of an authentic evangelical existence. The question is, how far can we go with this verdict of inadequacy?"[21]

Another bishop in line with the conciliar teachings, Karl Lehmann, a German theologian and bishop (appointed cardinal in 2001), also exposed the risks of one-sidedness inherent in community life, the feeling of being *the* Church, thus becoming either a shelter or a ghetto, with eyes and ears shut to the needs of the world. His critique reveals the sensitivity of the German church, characterized by a "local" model (contrary to the majority of other Catholic Churches) in which bishops have a clear role as leaders of the Church and where the movement's "communitarian" approach is less typical.[22]

Among the charges brought against the movements were the "spirituality of conquest" typical of some groups, a clear sign of lacking interest in "the modern world," a substantial indifference or distrust of ecumenism, a reaffirmation of a clerical sense of Catholic identity, and a nostalgia for one's origins—a *regressus ad uterum*, searching for the "pure roots" in the period before the Second Vatican Council,

---

[21] See Severino Dianich, "Le nuove comunità e la "grande chiesa": un problema ecclesiologico," *La Scuola Cattolica* 116 (1988): 512–29; see also, Piero Coda, "Movimenti ecclesiali e chiesa in Italia. Spunti ecclesiologici," *Communio* 149 (September–October 1996): 64–73.

[22] See Karl Lehmann, "I nuovi movimenti ecclesiali," *Il Regno-Documenti* 1 (1987): 27–31.

namely, in the Council of Trent, the first millennium, the fathers of the Church, the desert fathers, the period before the birth of canon law, and so on.[23] Behind these cultural and theological preferences aiming to regain a place in the world for the *true* Church, some noticed an "apologetics of enmity"[24] and an experiential element almost bordering "on apophacy . . . essentially not representable outside experiential revelation."[25]

The "institutional" arguments against the movements focused instead on the fact that these new associations represented, in the organization of the government of the universal Catholic Church, an element not only new but also alien to both the efforts of the conciliar ecclesiology to limit the centralism of Roman Catholicism and the attempts of canonical standardization to provide a proper legal status for the movements. Of particular concern were a number of issues related to the substantial freedom enjoyed by the movements in their development: the role of priests within the movements; the question of "double" memberships, that is, the membership of consecrated people; the participation of non-Catholics in Catholic movements; and the rivalry between local Churches and movements (with regard to the management of priestly vocations and seminaries).[26]

The two different but complementary criticisms (the theological and the institutional) of the movements emphasized a substantial contradiction between the explicit and the implicit ecclesiology carried out by the movements. On the one hand, the movements supported and lived a "community" model of Church, which was the fruit of a new understanding of the laity disengaged from institutional structures and processes. On the other, their quest (in a regime of fierce competition with other movements) for support and recognition from the Holy See and the pope encouraged the already strong clerical and centripetal

---

[23] See Domenico Sartore, "Nuove forme di aggregazione nella chiesa. Tra il particolare e l'universale," *Rivista liturgica* 6 (1997): 841–51, and the whole index of that issue of the magazine.

[24] See Giuseppe Ruggieri, "Chiesa e mondo," in *Cristianesimo, chiese e vangelo* (Bologna: Il Mulino, 2002), 307–38.

[25] See Alberto Melloni, "Movimenti. De significatione verborum," *Concilium: "Movimenti" in the Church*, ed. Alberto Melloni (2003/3): 13–35.

[26] See Gabriele De Rosa, "I movimenti ecclesiali oggi," *La Civiltà Cattolica* 3696 (June 19, 2004): 523–36.

mechanisms of Roman Catholicism, in contrast with conciliar aspirations and postconciliar theology. The preconciliar theological vision of some movements and the logic of integration within the organization of Catholicism led some observers to see a dangerous lack of scruples in some movements, ever at the service of themselves, in an integralist and clerical attitude.[27]

3. A Pontificate of Movement Predilection

Looking at the history of John Paul II's papacy, it can be said that the criticism against the movements proved incapable of opposing, from the standpoint of both theology and church politics, their impact within the Catholic Church. As a result, Benedict XVI inherited a cluster of movements largely forged by John Paul II's pontificate.

John Paul II's pontificate was able to select and filter the vast world of the movements that were the protagonists of the blossoming of new experiences within the Catholic Church between the first postconciliar period and the 1970s. It is difficult to say whether and how the protagonism of the movements at the end of his pontificate was substantially different from that of 1978.[28] But it is certain that at the beginning of the twenty-first century, the protagonism of Catholic movements is such that any opposition is increasingly less audible and ever more marginalized in a Church that had pushed aside the culture of mediation while reviving identity-based distinctions and the return to a form of clericalism typical of the *duo genera christianorum*.

In fact, alongside John Paul II's undeniable emphasis on the phenomenon of the ecclesial movements and associations as such, a clear preference based on specific criteria was given to a number of groups and associations. With the fading of many Catholic dissent and Christian base movements and groups (along with the repression of liberation theology in the 1980s, which was the strongest theological reference points for these types of movements), there was a clear revitalization of a series of movements with specific connotations.

---

[27] See *A colloquio con Dossetti e Lazzati. Intervista di Leopoldo Elia e Pietro Scoppola (19 novembre 1984)* (Bologna: Il Mulino, 2003), 98–113.

[28] See *Lebenswege des Glaubens: Berichte über Mönchtum heute, Gemeinschaften Charles de Foucaulds, Fokolar-Bewegung, Gemeinschaften christlichen Lebens, Schönstatt-Bewegung, Équipes Notre-Dame*, ed. Joseph Sauer (Freiburg i.B.: Herder, 1978).

To begin with, significant papal support was granted to those circles and groups (difficult to define as "movements" in the strict sense but they still had an effect on the ecclesial structure similar to that of real movements) inspired by a devotional and anti-intellectual Catholicism. The groups revolving around the figure of Padre Pio (who was beatified in 1999 and canonized in 2002)[29] and Marian devotion (carried out by a powerful international network like that of Radio Maria)[30] succeeded with John Paul II and were exempt from the theological judgment issued by the council and postconciliar Catholicism on devotional practices. Despite the conciliar theologians and bishops, devotional Catholicism was again proposed to the whole Church—by means of technological modernization but in rejection of modernity—through a conventional and nineteenth-century type of theology, yet modern in its means. Likewise, devotions were reintroduced in open competition with the bishops' teachings and sometimes clearly aligned, in some European countries such as Poland's "Radio Maryja," with revanchist, anti-Semitic, and extreme right-wing ideologies and political parties.

Further, Pope John Paul II's anticommunist predisposition limited and eventually rejected those movements (especially in Latin America) more linked to certain strands of liberation theology and hopes for a Christian socialist revitalization while clearly giving the green light to new orders, institutions, and movements—such as Opus Dei and Legionaries of Christ—strongly tied to the antiliberal and anticommunist culture of the 1930s and 1940s. The support given by John Paul II to the Legionaries of Christ and its conservative ideology would later become a controversial topic of debate within the Church between 2009 and 2010 when the double life of the founder Marcial Maciel came to light and the Legionaries were disciplined (but not suppressed) by Benedict XVI in 2010.

In this sense, an emblematic aspect of Vatican policy on the movements, from John Paul II onward, was the culture of *revanche* ("revenge") or reconquest of the modern world, a culture that since the end of the

[29] See Sergio Luzzatto, *Padre Pio. Miracoli e politica nell'Italia del Novecento* (Turin: Einaudi, 2007), 393–97; English edition: *Padre Pio: Miracles and Politics in a Secular Age*, trans. Frederika Randall (New York: Henry Holt and Co., 2010).

[30] See Livio Fanzaga, *Tra cielo e terra. Radio Maria: un miracolo di volontariato* (Cinisello B.: San Paolo, 2004); Marco Politi, *Il ritorno di Dio. Viaggio tra i cattolici d'Italia* (Milan: Mondadori, 2004), 144–62.

1970s has affected Catholicism as much as other world religions.[31] Very keen on the use of the instruments of modern culture, John Paul II's pontificate granted substantial support to movements inspired by religious ideologies against modernity per se and that were committed to returning to an idealized "regime of Christendom," distrustful of political mediation but open to an unscrupulous use of politics.

Typical of John Paul II's pontificate, and in contradiction with the culture of *revanche*, was the support granted to movements that had made ecumenical dialogue with other Christians and interreligious dialogue with Judaism their main mission. During the time between the interreligious meeting in Assisi in 1986 and the 1990s, the Community of Sant'Egidio expanded its presence in the media, in the Vatican, and also in its "earthly mission" far from Rome.[32] Such development was based not only on the clever creation of a network of political and ecclesiastical partnerships in Rome, the "pope's diocese," but also on having grasped, before and better than others, the central role, in John Paul II's policy, of developing connections between the Church's response to Western secularization, the mission of world religions, and peace-building among civilizations and religions.

As is evident from the case of Sant'Egidio, the transition from Paul VI's pontificate to John Paul II's also meant the stabilization of a system for the Holy See to grant recognition to the movements, based not so much on a formal act from the pope as on the pope's approval of the initiatives of the movements and their leaders. Hence, the increasing "Romanization" of the new movements became apparent, substantiated by a clear ability of their leaders, their governing bodies, and their "corporate" culture to infiltrate the Catholic and papal Rome and the Roman Curia. At the end of John Paul II's pontificate,

---

[31] See Gilles Kepel, *La Revanche de Dieu. Chrétiens, juifs et musulmans à la reconquête du monde* (Paris: Seuil, 1991); English edition: *The Revenge of God: The Resurgence of Islam, Christianity, and Judaism in the Modern World*, trans. Alan Braley (University Park: Pennsylvania State University Press, 1994); *Ai quattro angoli del fondamentalismo. Movimenti politico-religiosi nella loro tradizione, epifania, protesta, regressione*, ed. R. Giammanco (Scandicci: La Nuova Italia, 1993); *Religion and Politics in Comparative Perspective: The One, The Few, and The Many*, ed. T. Gerard Jelen and Clyde Wilcox (Cambridge: Cambridge University Press, 2002).

[32] About the Community of Sant'Egidio's engagement in diplomacy and social work, see Robert Calderisi, *Earthly Mission: The Catholic Church and World Development* (New Haven, CT, and London: Yale University Press, 2013), 227–30.

these new movements were able to create and maintain a social and political network favorable to the demands of the movements' highly charismatic leaders.

4. The Rise and Reality of a Phenomenon

This case study of the most well-known movements in the media's eye is also useful to reflect on the relations with the various groups that were less popular and less present in the public eye. In fact, to a certain extent, John Paul II's pontificate, true to his personal and actorial style in managing papal public speeches and appearances, transmitted the same style to the movements that had made their way inside the Catholic Church during the last quarter of the twentieth century. The movements that most benefited from John Paul II's pontificate were both the preconciliar ones (such as Opus Dei and the Legionaries of Christ), which managed their visibility in a prudent and cautious way, and the ones closer to Vatican II (such as the Community of Sant'Egidio), adept at managing the political-national and international Catholic news cycle through annual meetings for members and observers and through events created for the interaction between senior members of the hierarchy and the clergy of different churches involved in ecumenical and interreligious dialogue for peace.

In such cases, the impact of the events and their media coverage should not be reduced to bare figures about the numerical strength of single movements promoting this or that event. It is clear that the movements' relevance has to do less with their numerical strength and more with their ability to mobilize communities into action while offering strong interpretations of the present time. The mass events organized by movements in recent years, therefore, do not constitute a proof of the movements' numerical consistency, nor are they representative of the true identity of this new form of Catholic base communities.

Similarly, focusing on the most well-known cases is likely to distort the overall assessment of a phenomenon that, during John Paul II's pontificate, found a development path that goes beyond the public sanction of the position of some of the movements. If we consider community-movements involved in service to others, such as the John XXIII Community of Fr. Oreste Benzi or Jean Vanier's L'Arche,[33]

---

[33] See Kathryn Spink, *Una vita di comunione: Jean Vanier e l'Arca* (Cinisello B.: San Paolo, 2007).

we understand how movement culture has become, in the contemporary Church, a way of being Catholic that has expanded beyond the institutional limits in which the Church has kept its members and has grown despite the lack of sympathy toward movements from people not in the movements. This incomprehension often turns (though certainly not in the case of Fr. Benzi and Jean Vanier) into silent hostility, which evokes one of the historical precedents to which the movements often refer themselves, namely, that of the medieval mendicant orders.

Often there is a greater distance between the Church and the "individual" Catholic layperson, who does not belong to any association, movement, or community, than between the Church and non-Catholics or non-Christians, who at times share with certain movements similar apostolates or occupations. This new "practical" ecumenism, along the lines of "life and work," brings types of activism closer together, but at the cost of the erosion of communion within the Catholic Church.

Until a few decades ago, the "committed layperson in the Church" was the individual who was dedicated to translating his or her Christian vocation within the political sphere in the wider world, along the narrow tracks of autonomy granted by the Church. With John Paul II, the laity engaged in ecclesial movements and associations created—alongside clerics, monks, and religious and according to the most diverse and contradictory variations among them in terms of the relationship with the clergy and Church hierarchy—a mode of living existentially the Church in the concrete situation of a small community. In light of an experience of faith, typical of John Paul II's pontificate, that is mainly given, lived, and, in extreme cases, only instinctive, membership in a movement, in the vast majority of cases, means to ignore ecclesiological consideration, the legacy of Vatican II, the theological discourse on the role of the laity, or the movements' conservative or liberal identity and to focus instead on pragmatic results in terms of community, service, and mobilization. It is no coincidence that the problems related to the phenomenon of movements is perceived almost exclusively by those who do not belong to one, or who have left one, because in most cases they have experienced the return to the neglected "third class" of Catholics not belonging to any group—apart from their parish as local church.

But this tension has not found a resolution in the postconciliar period. One of the unchanged polarities during John Paul II's pontificate was that between the sense of belonging to a parish and the engagement in a movement. The wish expressed by the final document of the Synod for Europe of 1999 signaled the existence of a tension that had already been expressed at the synod of 1987, which, twenty years after the beginning of John Paul II's pontificate, still seemed unresolved between two separate souls of Catholicism:

> The Gospel continues to bear fruit in parish communities, among consecrated persons, in lay associations, in groups devoted to prayer and the apostolate and in various youth communities, as well as through the presence and growth of new movements and ecclesial realities. In each of them the one Spirit finds ways of awakening renewed dedication to the Gospel, generous openness to the service of others, and a Christian life marked by Gospel radicalism and missionary zeal.
>
> In today's Europe too, both in the post-Communist countries and in the West, *the parish*, while in need of constant renewal, continues to maintain and to carry out its particular mission, which is indispensable and of great relevance for pastoral care and the life of the Church. The parish is still a setting where the faithful are offered opportunities for genuine Christian living and a place for authentic human interaction and socialization, whether in the situations of dispersion and anonymity typical of large modern cities or in areas which are rural and sparsely populated.
>
> At the same time, together with the Synod Fathers, I express my great esteem for the presence and activity of the different apostolic associations and organizations, and for Catholic Action in particular. I also wish to note the significant contribution that, in fellowship with other ecclesial realities and never in isolation from them, they can offer to *new movements and to new ecclesial communities*. Such groups, in fact, "help Christians to live a more radically evangelical life. They are a cradle for different vocations, and they generate new forms of consecration. Above all, they promote the vocation of the laity, and they help it to find expression in different spheres of life. They favour the holiness of the people. They are able to be both the messenger and the message for people who otherwise would not encounter the Church. Frequently they promote the journey of ecumenism and they open the ways to interreligious dialogue. They are an antidote to the spread of sects and an invaluable aid to the spread of joy and life in the Church."[34]

---

[34] John Paul II, post-synodal apostolic exhortation, *Ecclesia in Europa*, June 28, 2003, nos. 15–16. Translation from http://www.vatican.va/holy_father/john_paul_ii /apost_exhortations/documents/hf_jp-ii_exh_20030628_ecclesia-in-europa_en.html.

A similar dualism permeated also the Apostolic Exhortation *Ecclesia in America* of 1999, with its juxtaposition of parishes and movements:

> The parish is a privileged place where the faithful concretely experience the Church. Today in America as elsewhere in the world the parish is facing certain difficulties in fulfilling its mission. The parish needs to be constantly renewed on the basis of the principle that "the parish must continue to be above all a Eucharistic community." This principle implies that "parishes are called to be welcoming and fraternal, places of Christian initiation, of education in and celebration of the faith, open to the full range of charisms, services and ministries, organized in a communal and responsible way, capable of utilizing existing movements of the apostolate, attentive to the cultural diversity of the people, open to pastoral projects which go beyond the individual parish, and alert to the world in which they live."[35]

New associative realities and Catholic Action were thus put all on the same level, in the realization of the loss of supremacy of Catholic Action, the "cradle" of the Catholic laity forged by the Church of the Piuses in the first half of the twentieth century. John Paul II did not hide the problems created by the coexistence of different Catholic lay movements. But in *Ecclesia in Europa* the call to order was addressed both to the movements and to the bishops: the two antagonists were treated equally by John Paul II, who as bishop had attended the Second Vatican Council, during which the reality of ecclesial movements was not mentioned at all:

> In this regard, the new movements and the new ecclesial communities must "abandon every temptation to claim rights of primogeniture and every mutual incomprehension," advance along the path of more authentic communion between themselves and with all other ecclesial realities, and "live with love in full obedience to the Bishops." But it is also necessary for the Bishops 'to show them that fatherhood and that love which are proper to Pastors' and to acknowledge, maximize and coordinate their charisms and their presence for the building up of the one Church.[36]

---

[35] See John Paul II, post-synodal apostolic exhortation, *Ecclesia in America*, January 22, 1999, no. 41. Translation from http://www.vatican.va/holy_father /john_paul_ii/apost_exhortations/documents/hf_jp-ii_exh_22011999_ecclesia-in -america_en.html.

[36] John Paul II, *Ecclesia in Europa*, no. 29.

Despite the unresolved tension between parishes (including bishops) and movements, the papal document concluding the work of the Synod for Europe effectively offered one of the interpretive keys for the phenomenon of movements: their essentially European origin. In a Church at loggerheads with modernity, the movements of John Paul II's Church represented a response of European Catholicism to the very European phenomenon of secularization and de-confessionalization: the crisis of a socio-religious system based on a normative framework inspired by the traditions of the *societas christiana*. Under John Paul II, the movements intensified their distinctive programs, namely, the regaining of spaces of action, in the face of the epochal crisis of participation experienced on the continent by parishes and diocesan churches. The new European ecclesial associations do not seem to be entirely an effect of secularization *tout court* (which in concrete terms affects members of movements just like all other European Catholics), nor of the de-privatization of religion (which is not a very European phenomenon), but rather an effect of *de-confessionalization* intended as neutralization of spaces of sociality—schools, assistance, mutual aid, and welfare networks; educational projects; and agencies of moral-ethical education—which until the early to mid-twentieth century were in Europe managed by Catholicism and the Church.

In this perspective, to question the lay character of and loyalty to the conciliar teachings of the movements of John Paul II's Church is beside the point. The base movements involved in the field of education and social assistance chose the path of creating *social* spaces of new confessionalization, being less interested in projecting their message on a political level, or along the theological-pastoral lines of the entire Church. The groups more animated by the "spirituality of the *reconquista*" or by the "culture of presence" began instead to build *ecclesial* spaces of new confessionalization, aiming to climb the ladder of the Catholic Church (the episcopal hierarchy, the Roman Curia, the Holy See's political and media agencies) to influence the most important issues of the postconciliar Church (liturgical reform, ecumenical and interreligious dialogue, secularism, and Church-state relations).

In the last thirty years, the lay members of these "community-movements" have increasingly combined vocational choices with professional paths along lines no less totalizing than those of clerics, monks, and religious. Therefore, without trying to create theological vanguards with which the postconciliar period abounded, lay Catholics engaged in movements have taken in the full sense and have far exceeded the narrow theological debate focused on the question: "Who is the layperson?"

5. Lay Identities and Clerical Tendencies

The activism of the laity engaged in movements (both in exclusively lay and "mixed" ones) certainly did not "declericalize" the Catholic Church under John Paul II. The pursuit of Vatican recognition and media attention by the leaders of new movements has created an environment of submission to the pope and to Rome and a fierce competition between the various movements and the local churches, and within the same movements as well. The new movements have largely dismantled—at the level of ecclesial praxis, not of theological reflection—what Vatican II had tried to accomplish in order to limit the excesses of Vatican I with regard to the extremes of papalism in the Catholic Church.

During the final period of John Paul II's pontificate, associations such as Catholic Action, which in Italy had maintained a more autonomous profile compared to the new movements' "ultramontanism," reestablished a more regimented line with regard to relations with the pope and the Holy See. The "Reconciliation of Loreto" (September 5, 2004) between Catholic Action and Communion and Liberation symbolically sanctioned an ongoing trend: the submission of the old elites of Catholic laity (Catholic Action) to the new movements (Communion and Liberation). In the course of the "Christian-oriented Cultural Project," a series of conferences promoted by the Italian Episcopal Conference under Cardinal Ruini and set in motion at the assembly of the Church of Palermo in 1996, the soul of a "cultural project" sponsored by Catholic Action was replaced over the years by one closer to Communion and Liberation, which meant a progressive marginalization of Catholic Action together with the laity not engaged in movements. These are indications of a trend that saw the Communion and Liberation model as the most valued and supported by the hierarchy. It was a model that the other organizational-ecclesial movements, which were far more illustrious and rich in tradition, such as Catholic Action, were forced to adapt in matters pertaining to obedience.

If Communion and Liberation's old proposal of the creation of "a bishop for the movements" was not achieved during John Paul II's pontificate, it is undeniable that under Benedict XVI a series of appointments of bishops and cardinals were meant to reward this or that movement. Ecclesial movements have thus appointed for themselves not only "protectors" (which in the history of Catholic religious orders and congregations has a very long tradition), but also leading members of the movements who can bring forward—within the conclave, the Roman Curia, the synod of bishops, and the episcopal conferences of any future council—the voice of one single movement, or of the movements in general.

Similarly, the creation of seminaries for the training of the clergy belonging to specific movements became, during John Paul II's long pontificate, a race for the movements' founders and leaders to gain accreditation in Rome, even at the cost of diminishing the already weakened leadership of the diocesan bishops. The creation, at the end of 2007 and early 2008, of Sophia University (established by pontifical decree of December 7, 2007) in the citadel of the Focolare movement, Loppiano (near Florence), marked a further step in the "formative entrepreneurship" of ecclesial movements: the two areas of study—philosophical-theological and political-economical—are evidence of the role of the new institute in creating the "draft of a new society."

In John Paul II's era, the economic and numeric strength of the movements have often represented a clear pressure on the bishops, the theological faculties, and the pastoral guidelines of the local churches. In John Paul II's Church, the local churches experienced a decrease of opportunities to make their voices heard. The voice of the laity was heard only if coming from the movements, and the objections of the bishops and theologians to some problematic aspects of these associations were dismissed and overcome. The convergence of the general theological trajectory of the ecclesial movements and John Paul II's general line of action, during the twenty-seven years of his pontificate, did little to change the face of the movements, yet consolidated their place in the Church, and certainly transformed the balance of power therein. The bishops and the "loose" laity appear to be the truly defeated in a postconciliar Church coping with the "rise of the movements."

CHAPTER 8

The Ecclesial Movements
from Benedict XVI to Francis

1. Pope Benedict XVI and John Paul II's Legacy for the Movements

During Pope John Paul II's final days and funeral, and followed by Joseph Ratzinger's election to the papacy, it was already evident that ecclesial movements were a part of the cumbersome legacy passed on by John Paul II to his successor. On that occasion, the new associations' eagerness to grab the media attention of the Catholic Church worldwide emerged once again, this time without the support of the reigning pope. Nevertheless, they managed to put themselves on the agenda of the post–John Paul II Church.

The newly elected pope, Benedict XVI, was far from unfriendly toward the movements. In the meditations for Good Friday 2005, a few days before John Paul II's death, Cardinal Ratzinger's emphasis on the "filth" in the Church reflected the vision of a cardinal who was the leading exponent of the Roman Curia but who in recent years had chosen to stand as guardian of the faith within the Roman Curia. He did not, however, intend to be identified or recognized with the Curia. Ratzinger's judgment on the filth in the Church had much in common with a recurring theme in the views on the Church expressed by more recent pro-movement Catholicism: only the genuineness and truth of Christians' testimony of faith under the leadership of the pope of Rome, and certainly not the anxieties of ecclesial "reform," were able to restore the true face of the Church. According to this pessimistic understanding of the relationship between faith, Church, and history, the Church's postconciliar reformism advanced by progressive Catholics (on issues of clerical celibacy; collegiality between the Holy See, the bishops, and the local churches; collegiality between the clergy and the laity; and the role of women and theologians in the Church), with its inevitable political and administrative implications, was seen as part of the illusions of modernity creeping within conciliar Catholicism and thus sullying the Church.

Beyond superficial alliances and sympathies, there was a deep affinity between Ratzinger's ecclesiological lines and the movements' ecclesial praxis, as it had been consolidated in the last two decades of the twentieth century. If it is true that the conclave of April 2005 sanctioned (and the conclave of March 2013 confirmed) the principle that "the pope can also sympathize with some movements, or with movements in general, but cannot be their expression,"[1] then the themes of the movements had already emerged during that conclave. Along with the conclave's decision not to elect one of the cardinals close to Communion and Liberation or Opus Dei, we should make sense of the huge media emphasis on John Paul II's final days, death, and funeral. This media coverage ended with what was an almost complete exaltation of the Roman pontificate and the equation between loyalty to the person of the pope and Catholicism. This equation is typical of "Romanized" contemporary Catholicism, and one which many movements have taken as their identifying trait.

In the days between John Paul II's death and Benedict XVI's election, St. Peter's Square saw a huge influx of pilgrims mobilized by the ecclesial movements. The slogan "Santo subito!" (Sainthood now!) coined by the Focolare movement, and so cleverly spread in the square in front of the TV cameras, demanded immediate and unanimous canonization of the just-deceased pope. This slogan soon became more important than the Focolare movement, which was behind it, as well as the original intention that motivated and, to a certain extent, defined the movements' presence in the square: to place their lives as an element of continuity between the two pontificates, thus embodying, in the movements' logic, a loyalty that at the same time was also a petition to the Church and the papacy.

In a meditation to the cardinals held on April 14, 2005, the preacher of the pontifical household, Capuchin friar Raniero Cantalamessa (who

---

[1] Alberto Melloni, *L'inizio di papa Ratzinger. Lezioni sul conclave del 2005 e sull'incipit del pontificato di Benedetto XVI* (Turin, Einaudi: 2006), 17.

was close to the movement Renewal in the Spirit) had touched closely on the issue of the movements' role in the Church:

> *Lumen Gentium* [no. 12] placed charisms back at the heart of the Church. The Lord seems to have confirmed this decision of the council because soon after we have witnessed a widespread reawakening of charisms in the Church. . . . Only the Church expresses the *pleroma*, the fullness of grace and gifts, not only synchronically but diachronically, through the ages.[2]

2. The Ecclesiologies of Benedict XVI and the Movements

As a German ecclesiastic and theologian, less instinctive than John Paul II in supporting the movements, but no less inclined to see the movements as a shield against the anguish of the postconciliar period, Benedict XVI followed a less conspicuous approach, but one that was not far from that of John Paul II. As prefect of the Congregation for the Doctrine of the Faith, Cardinal Ratzinger's *Report on the Faith* in 1985 represented a kind of theological manifesto for the second phase of John Paul II's pontificate. The report cited the cases of the charismatic movement, the Cursillos de Cristianidad, the Focolare movement, the Neocatechumenal Way, and Communion and Liberation, saying that "certainly all of these movements also give rise to some problems. They also entail greater or lesser dangers." The cardinal prefect went on affirming that the movements' intense life of faith—a phenomenon that appeared "right in the heart of the crisis of the Church in the Western world"—was not to be understood as "an escape into intimacy or a retreat into privacy, but simply a full and integral catholicity," and the Church's duty was to make room for them.[3]

Ratzinger's lines of interpretation of Vatican II also led him, well before his election to the papacy, to get closer to the organization of German Catholics whose distinctive trait was their loyalty to the pope and repudiation of the reformist positions. Thus, these German organizations distance themselves from the majority of lay Catholic

---

[2] Quoted in Melloni, *L'inizio di papa Ratzinger*, 47.

[3] See Joseph Ratzinger in Vittorio Messori, *Rapporto sulla fede* (Rome: Paoline, 1985), 42–43 (published in several languages; English edition: *The Ratzinger Report: An Exclusive Interview on the State of the Catholic Church*, trans. Salvator Attanasio and Graham Harrison [San Francisco: Ignatius Press, 1985]).

organizations, which in Germany have a particularly strong base of participation (and far from the spirit of the movements) in the *Zentralkomitee,* the Central Committee of German Catholics. This pro-movement choice, close to the pope and tied to a restrictive interpretation of Vatican II, dated back to the 1970s, namely, to Ratzinger's days as bishop and cardinal, thus before becoming Pope Benedict XVI.

A more clear and definite alignment in favor of movements came from Cardinal Ratzinger in his lecture at the fourth congress of the movements in May 1998. On that occasion, Ratzinger put ecclesial movements beyond an ambiguous "dialectic of principles" (between charism and institution, between Christology and pneumatology, between hierarchy and prophecy), depicting them instead as an answer of the Spirit for cooperation in the Church's universal apostolicity. Thus, Ratzinger clearly distanced himself from the diocesan bishops' criticism (expressed especially at the synod of 1987) of some movements with their ecclesiological drive, their exclusivist and sectarian, if not fundamentalist and extremist, tendencies. The cardinal prefect of the Congregation for the Doctrine of the Faith gave a warning to the movements, however, to remain loyal to the totality of the Church and submit to the exigencies of this totality:

> Both the dangers and ways of overcoming them [sectarian tendencies] exist in the movements. The dangers, but also the ways of overcoming them, that exist in the movements may at this point be glimpsed. One-sidedness is threatened by the over-accentuation of the specific mission that emerges in one particular period or through one particular charism. . . . It can lead to the movement being absolutised. It comes to be identified with the Church herself. It comes to be understood as the one way for everyone, though this one way can take and communicate itself in a variety of forms. It is almost inevitable, therefore, that the vitality and totality of the original charismatic experience should time and again give rise to conflicts with the local community, a conflict in which both sides may be at fault, and both may be spiritually challenged.[4]

---

[4] See Joseph Ratzinger, "The Ecclesial Movements: A Theological Reflection on Their Place in the Church," in *Movements in the Church,* ed. Pontifical Council for the Laity (Vatican City: Libreria Editrice Vaticana, 1999), 23–51. See also Joseph Ratzinger / Benedict XVI, *New Outpouring of the Spirit: Movements in the Church* (San Francisco: Ignatius Press, 2007).

But the local churches and bishops, who at least since the mid-1980s started to have growing doubts about the movements' isolationist tendencies and their work within dioceses (especially in pastoral care and liturgy), were given not one but four warnings. First, Ratzinger said that the bishops were not allowed to expect uniformity in pastoral organization and planning. Second, according to the cardinal prefect it was not the bishops' prerogative to affirm what the Spirit is allowed to do. Third, the bishops cannot enforce a concept of communion intended to avoid conflict. Finally, the bishops should avoid an attitude that "brands the zeal of those seized by the Holy Spirit and their uninhibited faith with the anathema of fundamentalism."[5]

Beyond these speeches, an objective convergence between Cardinal Ratzinger's ecclesiology and the movements' work became clear.[6] Around and immediately after the Synod of Bishops of 1985 on the reception of Vatican II, it was Ratzinger's thesis that led the International Theological Commission toward a diminished role of bishops' conferences with respect to the Holy See's authority.[7] Those same bishops who had begun to speak out about the movements' unorthodox tendencies in dioceses and who, at the synod of 1987, spoke of the movements as "parallel churches" were subjected to "discipline" during John Paul II's pontificate, despite the fact that the council had given a glimpse, albeit only for a short time, of the possibility of a new and more balanced power between the pope and bishops. The "new primacy" of John Paul II's papacy, and of Cardinal Ratzinger, favored the implicit ecclesiology of the movements, which was fundamentally different from both the "episcopalist" ecclesiology of the collegiality between the pope and bishops and the "theology of the laity" that leaned toward the de-clericalization of the Catholic Church.

---

[5] Ibid.

[6] Brendan Leahy offers a sympathetic reading of the phenomenon of the movements in *Ecclesial Movements and Communities: Origins, Significance, and Issues* (Hyde Park, NY: New City Press, 2011), 64–70.

[7] See Massimo Faggioli, "Prassi e norme relative alle conferenze episcopali tra concilio Vaticano II e post-concilio (1959–1998)," in *Synod and Synodality: Theology, History, Canon Law and Ecumenism in New Contact*, ed. Alberto Melloni and Silvia Scatena (Münster: LIT, 2005), 265–96 (English translation: "The Regulation of Episcopal Conferences since Vatican II," in *The Japan Mission Journal* 68, no. 2 [Summer 2014]: 82–96).

It was the public controversy between 2000 and 2001 with fellow German theologian and later cardinal Walter Kasper on the relationship between the "universal Church" (i.e., Rome and the Holy See) and the "local church" (i.e., the dioceses and bishops) that permeated the new relationship between the pope and the movements, sanctioned once again by the jubilee of 2000.[8] Ratzinger's thesis, according to which the universal Church is a reality "ontologically and temporally prior to every individual particular church," represented the same "political" choice made by the movements starting in the late 1970s and early 1980s. The movements' winning choice to place themselves under the protective wing of Rome not only emphasized a tactical choice dictated by the difficulty of being incorporated into the Catholic Church but also ex-emplified the movements' loyalty to the pope as the representative of the universal Church—a loyalty to the pope that became, as it was for Communion and Liberation, constitutive of the movements' identity.

At the February 24, 2005, funeral of Fr. Luigi Giussani, the founder of Communion and Liberation, which was held in the Cathedral of Milan, Cardinal Ratzinger recognized in Fr. Giussani the "gift of dis-cernment, of deciphering correctly the signs of the times in a diffi-cult time, full of temptations and of errors." Fr. Giussani escaped the "moralist" temptation of the 1960s to respond to the emergencies of poverty, which said, "For the moment we have to set Christ aside, set God aside." In Ratzinger's view, Fr. Giussani transmitted to Com-munion and Liberation the centrality of Christ, according to a new associative mode that was initially met with hostilities and opposition: "In virtue of the faith, Monsignor Giussani passed fearlessly through these dark valleys and naturally, with the novelty he carried with him, found it difficult to find a niche inside the Church."[9]

3. A Step Backward?

Some observers have pointed out that in some of his off-the-cuff remarks Benedict XVI did not hide but rather hinted, with his usual

[8] See Kilian McDonnell, "The Ratzinger/Kasper Debate: The Universal Church and Local Churches," *Theological Studies* 63 (2002): 227–50.

[9] The homily delivered by then-Cardinal Ratzinger at the funeral of Luigi Giussani (Milan, February 24, 2005) can be found at http://www.vatican.va/roman_curia /congregations/cfaith/documents/rc_con_cfaith_doc_20050224_homily-giussani _it.html.

frankness, at the difficulty for the Church as an institution to welcome and incorporate new associative entities like the movements. But this acknowledgment of the tension between the movements' plurality and overall diversity and the institutional mechanisms did not lead the pope and the Holy See to take a step back in its policy of openness toward the new protagonism of the organized laity. Moreover, the movements did not alter the course of their progressive integration, begun during the previous pontificate, within the body of the Catholic Church.

Even the frequent "incidents along the way" that have plagued the relationship of the ecclesial movements with the Roman Curia (and the media) have not stopped the movements' rise. This rise continued during Benedict XVI's pontificate, even though it was according to a "pecking order" that is still being redefined after John Paul II's death. Nevertheless, the sanctions Benedict XVI's Roman Curia placed on the Neocatechumenal Way and the founder of the Legionaries of Christ between late 2005 and 2006 can hardly be interpreted as the end of a certain "favorable regime" granted to the movements.

Between December 2005 and January 2006, an exchange of letters between the pope and Cardinal Arinze, and among the founders and leaders of the Neocatechumenal Way, Kiko Argüello, Carmen Hernández, and Father Mario Pezzi, renewed the duel between the Holy See and the Neocatechumenal Way. Certain concerns regarding liturgical matters, together with the difficulties of bishops to incardinate priests trained and ordained by the Neocatechumenals in their seminaries were at the center of the bishops' and the Holy See's objections to the Neocatechumenal Way. The pope, during an audience granted to the Neocatechumenals on January 12, 2006, reminded them, in all frankness, that "the Congregation for Divine Worship and the Discipline of the Sacraments recently imparted to you in my name certain norms concerning the Eucharistic Celebration, after the trial period that the Servant of God John Paul II conceded. I am sure you will attentively observe these norms that reflect what is provided for in the liturgical books approved by the Church."[10] The periodic difficulties

---

[10] Benedict XVI, "Address of His Holiness Benedict XVI to Members of the Neocatechumenal Way," January 12, 2006. Translation from http://www.vatican .va/holy_father/benedict_xvi/speeches/2006/january/documents/hf_ben-xvi_spe_ 20060112_neocatecumenali_en.html.

experienced by the movement with Church authorities and the bishops were renewed on February 25, 2007, when a letter from the Catholic bishops of the Holy Land addressed to the Neocatechumenal Way, which since 2000 had been running the international center Domus Galileae, accused the movement not only of disregarding and not conforming to Middle Eastern liturgical and cultural traditions but also of fostering a pro-Israel climate hardly reconcilable within the context of the Palestinian Arab Catholics. Likewise, tensions between the Neocatechumenal Way and some Japanese bishops, managed directly by the Vatican in late 2010 and early 2011, did not lead to a solution, a problem becoming typical of the relationship between this and other movements and many episcopal sees.[11]

The scandal that hit the Legionaries of Christ had repercussions for the Legionaries but not for other movements. At the conclusion of an investigation begun in 1998, following allegations of sexual abuse and violation of the sacrament of confession, Fr. Maciel, founder of the Legionaries of Christ, was convicted in the spring of 2006. Maciel's conviction gave new vigor to the accusers of the movements *tout court*, as some hoped the Holy See might reverse its trend of giving a green light to the movements, while others hoped to turn the balance of power among movements created during John Paul II's pontificate in their favor.

Even earlier, incidents similar to those just mentioned had already emerged and had been resolved during John Paul II's pontificate. Ratzinger, however, brought a style to the papacy that was unquestionably different from John Paul II's energetic, charismatic, and "actorial" approach; this was immediately clear from Benedict's public papal appearances, such as his participation in the twenty-first World Youth Day in Germany in the summer of 2006. But from the beginning of his pontificate, Benedict XVI did not fail to make his voice heard by the movements. In September 2005, during his message to the international conference at Lucca, attended by the charismatic renewal, the Focolare movement, and the Community of Sant'Egidio, the pope stressed the link between the movements' development and the Second Vatican Council. Titling his message "The Signs of the Spirit's

---

[11] See Massimo Faggioli, "The Neocatechumenate and Communion in the Church," in *Japan Mission Journal* 65, no. 1 (Spring 2011): 46–53.

Presence in the Twentieth Century," he described their relationship as a new "Pentecost" for a "humanity sometimes troubled and even frightened when facing the great challenges of the modern era."[12]

A certain line of continuity between Benedict XVI and the previous pontificate regarding the movements can also be seen in Benedict's attitude toward the base Christian communities in Latin America, so different from the ecclesial movements active in Europe, not only in terms of theological and political sensibility, but also in their much less friendly relations with the Holy See. Another side of the Catholic Church's preference for movements loyal to the pope is clearly visible in the case of Latin America during Pope Benedict's pontificate. The gap between the discussion on base communities during the First Meeting of Ecclesial Movements and New Communities in Latin America, held in March 2006 in Bogotá, Colombia, and organized by the Pontifical Council for the Laity and the Latin American Episcopal Council (CELAM), and the role played by these communities in the final text of the CELAM conference voted in Aparecida and mostly "rectified" by the pope (in July 2007) was very visible. This gap revived not only the mistrust of the bishops nominated in thirty-five years by John Paul II and Benedict XVI toward this type of laity more tied to local churches than to Rome, but also marginalized the ecclesial base communities from both mainstream movements within the global Catholic Church. A change of attitude of the papacy toward the base communities came only later with Pope Francis.[13]

The case of Latin America says much more than the Roman Curia's reprimands addressed to the Neocatechumenals and Legionaries of Christ might suggest. The affinities between Benedict XVI and John Paul II seem to be more significant than the dissimilarities. In his message of May 22, 2006, to the participants of the Second World Congress of Ecclesial Movements and New Communities,[14] Benedict XVI drew a parallel between the experience of the movements and the historical progress of Christianity over the centuries communicated

---

[12] *Insegnamenti di Benedetto XVI*, vol. 1/2005 (Vatican City: Libreria Editrice Vaticana, 2006), 597.

[13] Representatives of fifty movements and communities in Latin America, together with forty bishops, attended the meeting in Bogotá, in March 2006.

[14] Again, as in 1998, Communion and Liberation, the Community of Sant'Egidio, the Focolare movement, and the Neocatechumenal Way were all present.

through "the newness of life of individuals and communities able to provide an effective witness of love, unity, and joy." The pope called the movements "schools of communion, groups journeying on," all the more necessary today, in the "darkness of a world overwhelmed by the contradictory messages of ideologies." The deeply pessimistic reading of the historical situation in which the Church lives, where the movements become "a force for the construction of a more just social order . . . that can withstand the advance of barbarity," was followed by a fleeting reference to the relationship between movements and bishops. The pope thanked them "for your readiness not only to accept the active directives of the Successor of Peter, but also of the bishops of the various local Churches. . . . I trust in your prompt obedience. Over and above the affirmation of the right to life itself, the edification of the Body of Christ among others must always prevail with indisputable priority."[15]

The link between the pope's negative perception of the present moment and the movements' positive role remerged once again on June 3, 2006, on the vigil of Pentecost, at the Meeting with the Ecclesial Movements and New Communities, when Benedict XVI spoke of the "missionary zeal" of the movements, using John Paul II's words regarding their "providential" role. Defined as "schools of true freedom" in a world "so full of fictitious forms of freedom," the pope encouraged the movements to preserve "diversity and unity," which are "inseparable." The bishops were openly urged by the bishop of Rome not to limit this diversity: "Pastors must be careful not to extinguish the Spirit and you will not cease to bring your gifts to the entire community."[16]

In addition to the pope's words, even the documents of the Roman Curia and episcopal conferences seem to have continued on the path under Benedict XVI set by the previous pontificate. The approval *ad experimentum* for five years of the Neocatechumenal Way's statute, published on June 29, 2002, was followed by the approval of the Renewal in the Spirit by the Italian Episcopal Conference in January 2007, thus concluding a process of recognition started under John Paul II in 1991. By forgoing the creation of "framework laws" for the move-

---

[15] *Insegnamenti di Benedetto XVI*, vol. 2, 1/2006 (Vatican City: Libreria Editrice Vaticana, 2007), 665. See *La bellezza di essere cristiani. I movimenti nella Chiesa. Atti del II congresso mondiale dei movimenti ecclesiali e delle nuove comunità (Rocca di Papa, 31 maggio–2 giugno 2006)* (Vatican City: Libreria Editrice Vaticana, 2007).

[16] *Insegnamenti di Benedetto XVI*, vol. 2, 1/2006, 757–65.

ments (advocated by some canonists and in 2004 by the Jesuit-run *La Civiltà Cattolica*, as well), the Roman Curia seems to be continuing on the path of incorporation of the movements in the ecclesial body through the approval of their statutes. This method does not touch on the issue of their integration in local churches but submits the movements to the obedience of the national episcopal conferences, which, in the meantime, have seen a rise in the number of bishops close to movements, not only in the Italian Episcopal Conference, but, for example, also in the United States Conference of Catholic Bishops.[17]

4. The Two Approaches

Those expecting a change of course on movements from Benedict XVI, based on his blunt replies during occasional speeches, apparently were destined to be disappointed.[18] The movements' problematic integration in local churches was clear to the pope, but, in his perspective, there were too few elements to warrant a reversal of the trend. The pope's insistence on painting gloomy pictures of the modern world and especially of Europe strengthened not only the "worldview" of many contemporary Catholic movements but also the need to rely on these lay forces—more than on local churches or religious orders—in the effort to proclaim the Gospel in a secularized society.

Several factors support the thesis that there is continuity in the relationship between movements and the Holy See. On the one hand, worth noting is the condensed presence of the Church in the political sphere, evident through the aspirations of direct political engagement of some factions within movements, as happened during "Family Day" on May 12, 2007, in Rome (an event politically expedient for Silvio Berlusconi, who was later condemned for paying for sex with an underage prostitute).[19] On the same day, 250 Christian movements

---

[17] See the program of the Catholic Theology Society annual meeting (May 29–June 1, 2014, at Saint Vincent College in Latrobe, PA) on the theme God Has Begun a Great Work in Us: The Embodiment of Love in Contemporary Consecrated Life and Ecclesial Movements.

[18] See Benedict XVI's speech to the clergy and the diocese of Rome, February 22, 2007. Translation from http://www.vatican.va/holy_father/benedict_xvi/speeches/2007/february/documents/hf_ben-xvi_spe_20070222_clergy-rome_en.html.

[19] The advertisement for the "Family Day," titled *More Family*, was endorsed, among others, by Catholic Action, ACLI, Communion and Liberation, charismatic

gathered together in Stuttgart "to give new hope to Europe," including members of the charismatic renewal in the Evangelical Church of Germany, England's Alpha Course, the Focolare movement, the Schönstatt movement, and the Community of Sant'Egidio.[20] The movements' conspicuous and numerous presence at national and international youth meetings with the pope (such as the massive participation of Renewal in the Spirit and the Neocatechumenal Way at the youth meeting at Loreto in September 2007) continues to be very popular and sought after by the papacy and bishops who organize papal events in their dioceses. Moreover, John Paul II's "mandate" for some movements to control certain ecumenical and interreligious events seems to continue. For instance, in September 2007, Fr. Paolo Pezzi of the Priestly Fraternity of the Missionaries of St. Charles Borromeo (a branch of Communion and Liberation) was appointed as archbishop metropolitan of Moscow, while the international meeting for peace in Naples of October 2007, organized by the Community of Sant'Egidio, was attended by the pope himself. The gathering of the movements in St. Peter's Square, in support of Benedict XVI in the throes of the clergy sexual abuse scandal, on May 16, 2010, testifies to the continuous efforts of papal policy to make use of the movements as a shield not only for papal primacy but also for the Church itself.[21]

It seems unlikely that the Holy See will significantly and swiftly deal in the near future with the movements, which are so essential, albeit broad and internally diversified and even confrontational, as evidenced by the recent initiative of the Focolare movement to create an office for dialogue among movements and new communities. Despite tensions created by the movements' new status, movements played a central role as part of Benedict's vision of the relationship between Church and politics, a vision in which Christianity—as fruit of both biblical revelation and Greek *logos*—provides politics with the rational conditions of its

---

renewal, the Neocatechumenal Way, Movement for Life, Association of Catholic Scouts of Europe.

[20] See http://www.miteinander-wie-sonst.de/_it/presse.html.

[21] For more on the continuity between John Paul II and Benedict XVI, see also the speech of the secretary of the Pontifical Council for the Laity at the international conference for bishops (Rocca di Papa, May 15–17, 2008) organized by the Pontifical Council; and Joseph Clemens, "Papa Ratzinger e i movimenti," *Il Regno-documenti* 13 (2008): 441–49.

existence. Conversely, however, if political and social analysis is brought within the Church to reform the Church, such analysis is perceived as a temptation to the purity of truth. The Catholic movements, which during the postconciliar period were characterized by the preferential choice of loyalty to the pope and the Holy See and rejected any proposal of reform (if only institutional) of the Church, fit perfectly in the vision of the Church and policy pursued by the papacy.[22]

Benedict XVI's detached and dispassionate attitude toward the movements, so different from John Paul II's vision of the new ecclesial groups as genuine fruits of Vatican II, did not seem to be incompatible with a continuation of the Church's policy of officially recognizing the movements. In his pontificate's almost exclusive attention to Europe, Benedict XVI saw in the new lay (but obedient to the clergy) elites of the new ecclesial movements a particular asset for the recovery of the Catholic Church, especially in Europe, which more than others had suffered through the tribulations of the postconciliar period. It is in this perspective that we should read Cardinal Godfried Danneels's initiative in Belgium, where he invited all the movements of the Diocese of Brussels to the preparation of the Brussels 2006 meeting, a project intended for the New Evangelization of the great metropolitan areas.

We can discern in the relationship between the pope and the new ecclesial movements a convergence of purposes and visions, which does not circumvent the problem of articulating different strategies and visions between the papacy and the movements and within the same movements. On the other hand, Benedict's view on the movements had been effectively expressed in terms of "cohabitation," or "condominium," in a less passionate but more realistic acknowledgment than his predecessor's enthusiasm:

> Catholicism in fact can never be merely institutionally and academically planned and managed but appears ever again as a gift, as a spiritual vitality. And in the process it also has the gift of diversity. There is no uniformity among Catholics. There can be Focolare or Catechumenate piety, Schönstatt, Cursillo, and Communion and Liberation spirituality, and so on, as well as a Franciscan, Dominican, and Benedictine piety. The treasury of faith provides many dwelling

---

[22] See Hansjürgen Verweyen, *Joseph Ratzinger—Benedikt XVI. Die Entwicklung seines Denkens* (Darmstadt: WBG, 2007), 114–25.

places within the one house. And we should preserve this dynamic openness. . . . The others must then, of course, be likewise ready to adapt themselves to the service of the Church, to allow themselves to lose something of their peculiarities or of the factors that tend to shut them off.[23]

If it is true that Benedict's vision of the Catholic Church was more disciplined and uniform than that of John Paul II, it is equally true that Benedict's reading of the situation of Catholicism in the modern world (and especially in Europe) was even more negative and troubled. Pope Benedict XVI's pontificate was destined to use the movements as a weapon in the attempt to revive the Church's role in society— unless the papal magisterium's reading on the relationship between the postconciliar Church and contemporary European society were radically changed.

5. Between Pope Benedict XVI's Orthodoxy and "Custom-Made" Faith

As a result of a program that can be summarized with the formula "less organization and more Holy Spirit," the ecclesial movements and Benedict XVI found a broad common denominator for the Catholic Church in the twenty-first century. But it is a *modus operandi* that hides some unknown facts. The new religious movements offer believers a home where they can find protection from a world perceived as alien and inhospitable from a religious, social, political, and cultural perspective. With Pope Benedict XVI's pessimistic reading of the modern world, ecclesial movements played a similar role in the contemporary Catholic Church. There appears to be a resolution between the apparent contradiction or ambivalence—typical of John Paul II's attitude toward the movements—between an opening toward the modern world and the intransigent, sectarian tendency of a large part of the contemporary Catholic movements. Yet, there is still a pending need to harmonize the universal, "Catholic," dimension of the Church

---

[23] See *Dio e il mondo. Essere cristiani nel nuovo millennio* (Cinisello B.: San Paolo, 2001), 416–17; original German edition: *Gott und die Welt: Glauben und Leben in unserer Zeit* (Stuttgart München: Deutsche Verlags-Anstalt, 2000); English edition: *God and the World: A Conversation with Peter Seewald* (San Francisco: Ignatius Press, 2002).

of Rome with the deep European cultural and social roots of ecclesial movements, which outside of Europe exist as a radiation of the European "center" and not as native phenomena.

One of the challenges posed by Benedict XVI, the theologian-pope, to the future of the movements was that of the relationship between a "local" European Church, made of dioceses and parishes, and an ecclesial structure, with the movements at its core, functioning autonomously. In fact, the structure of the new ecclesial movements in Europe is one that does not reach distant Christians but, on the contrary, continues to tap into the pool of the faithful formed by conventional pastoral work in the parishes. At present, there seems to be a competitive dynamic between the diocesan clergy and movements, even with regard to the recruitment and use of the clergy; John Paul II also pointed to the movements as an antidote to the hemorrhage of priestly vocations. In some local situations, the bishops and local clergy have waved the white flag in front of the new fresh energy brought by the movements, and in some dioceses the majority of seminarians are now members of movements. In turn, the movements have started to sublet seminaries directly from bishops.

It also became apparent that there was clear distance between some typical sensitivities of Pope Benedict XVI's theological and liturgical orthodoxy and the concrete praxis of some Catholic movements, showing affinity with Protestant movements of "strong religions" and "new religious movements" of the English-speaking world.[24] In Europe, contrary to what happens in the Americas, the Catholic movements fail to engage and convert the distant ones (the former Catholics, the non-Christians, the non-Catholics, the atheists). Yet, just as in America, the movements in Europe are witnessing a *bricolage des croyances* (custom-made religious beliefs), which represent the other extreme of inherited religious identities, in a *deregulation* of Church membership transcending the oaths of allegiance to the Holy See and the episcopal conferences.[25]

Communities run by charismatic leaders, fascination with the pantheon of the movements' witnesses as guardians of the lived faith,

---

[24] See R. Scott Appleby and Emmanuel Sivan, *Strong Religion: The Rise of Fundamentalisms around the World* (Chicago: University of Chicago Press, 2003).

[25] See Danièle Hervieu-Léger, *Le pèlerin et le converti: la religion en mouvement* (Paris: Flammarion, 1999).

a penchant for spectacularizing events, performance culture: all these elements are constitutive of the new religious movements, and are also part of the genetic code of Catholic pro-movement culture. The distinctive trait of the movements as an expression and combination of religious and modern individualism—within groups who share similar beliefs and are united in the mutual confirmation of each other's beliefs based on personal testimony and exchange of individual experiences— raises some questions about the ability to radiate outside a Church that supports them as its last resort to reach out to a secularized world.

6. Pope Francis's "Theology of the People" and the Movements

The key concept for understanding the ecclesiology of Pope Francis is "theology of the people"—a significant variation in the diversified but coherent theological stream called "liberation theology." In this theology—a very important voice in the post–Vatican II theology in Argentina—the people are active subjects of the evangelization work of the Church. Therefore, the new movements play a role in Francis's idea of the Church, which is less "institution" and more "movement" than under his predecessors.

But there is an interesting evolution in Bergoglio-Francis and a difference between his approach to the movements as a bishop and as the bishop of Rome. Before the election at the conclave, Bergoglio was known for being sympathetic to movements such as Communion and Liberation—something that sparked some worries in the world of liberal Catholicism immediately after the conclave.[26] Since the election in March 2013, though, Francis has chosen a more cautious tone that responds to an appreciation of the role of the movements in global Catholicism. In several occasions during the first year of his pontificate, Francis has spoken to the movements but always inviting them to a more collaborative stance with the rest of the Church, especially with the parishes. In the homily for the Pentecost Mass, on May 19, 2013, Francis told the members of new ecclesial movements and lay Catholic associations:

[26] See Jamie Manson, "One of Pope Francis' Allegiances Might Tell Us Something about the Church's Future," *National Catholic Reporter* (March 15, 2013); http://ncronline .org/blogs/grace-margins/one-pope-francis-allegiances-might-tell-us-something -about-churchs-future.

When we are the ones who want to build unity in accordance with our human plans, we end up creating uniformity, standardization. But if instead we let ourselves be guided by the Spirit, richness, variety and diversity never become a source of conflict, because he impels us to experience variety within the communion of the Church. Journeying together in the Church, under the guidance of her pastors who possess a special charism and ministry, is a sign of the working of the Holy Spirit. Having a sense of the Church is something fundamental for every Christian, every community and every movement. It is the Church which brings Christ to me, and me to Christ; parallel journeys are very dangerous![27]

At the same time, Pope Francis has embraced much more than his predecessors the new ecclesial movements that have always had a difficult relationship with the Vatican. Francis is the first pope to send a message to an official meeting of the basic ecclesial communities (thirteenth inter-ecclesial meeting, Brazil, January 7–11, 2014), thus acknowledging these ecclesial Catholic communities, a reality that comes from the legacy of Vatican II in Latin America but also from the Church of liberation theology. We find an interesting message in the audience of March 8, 2014, to the leaders of the ecclesial movements of the Diocese of Rome, when he invited them to avoid the danger of building a contraposition between the movements and the parishes.[28]

But the most interesting exchange in the relationship between Francis and the movements took place a few weeks before, on February 1, 2014, in his audience with a few thousand members of the Neocatechumenal Way. The audiences between the movement founded by Kiko Argüello and the popes have always played a key role in building the legitimacy of the Neocatechumenal Way. In this audience Francis invited them explicitly to "preserve the communion of the local Churches" where they are active:

> In the name of the Church I would like to give you a few simple recommendations. The first is to take the greatest care to build and preserve *the communion within the particular Churches* where you

[27] Francis, homily of May 19, 2013. Translation from http://w2.vatican.va/content /francesco/en/homilies/2013/documents/papa-francesco_20130519_omelia -pentecoste.html.

[28] Francis had received in audience the parish priests of the Diocese of Rome just two days before, March 6, 2014.

will go to work. The Way has its own charism, its own dynamic, a gift that like all gifts of the Holy Spirit has a profoundly ecclesial dimension; this means listening to the life of the Churches where your leaders send you, appreciating their riches, suffering through their weaknesses if necessary, and walking together as a single flock under the guidance of the Pastors of the local Churches. Communion is essential: at times it can be better to give up living out in detail what your itinerary would call for, in order to guarantee unity among the brethren who form one ecclesial community, which you must always feel a part of.[29]

Francis voiced the same concern for the unity of the Church when he met fifty thousand members of the Renewal in the Holy Spirit gathered in Rome at the Olympic Stadium on June 1, 2014, for the thirty-seventh national convocation; in that same speech, the pope linked the movement with the work of two great leaders of Vatican II: Cardinal Leo Jozef Suenens and Bishop Helder Camera.[30]

Francis never gave any sign about a return to a Church without the movements; on the contrary, his ecclesiology "of the peripheries" entails a great role for the movements. Some movements, like the Community of Sant'Egidio, are particularly close to Francis's agenda and his message on social justice and the poor, as it became evident in the visit of the pope to St. Egidio's parish and headquarters in Santa Maria in Trastevere in Rome on June 15, 2014.[31] But there is little doubt that the concern for the unity of the Church vis-à-vis the particularity of the movements' charism is in Francis's pontificate a more visible motif than in the ones of John Paul II and Benedict XVI.

---

[29] Pope Francis to the Neocatechumenal Way, February 1, 2014. Translation from http://w2.vatican.va/content/francesco/en/speeches/2014/february/documents/papa -francesco_20140201_cammino-neocatecumenale.html.

[30] See http://w2.vatican.va/content/francesco/en/speeches/2014/june/documents /papa-francesco_20140601_rinnovamento-spirito-santo.html.

[31] See http://w2.vatican.va/content/francesco/en/speeches/2014/june/documents /papa-francesco_20140615_comunita-sant-egidio.html.

PART 2

ॐ

The New Issues

CHAPTER 9

New Catholic Movements
and Priestly Formation in the Seminaries

1. The New Catholic Movements:
From Lay Groups to "Multi-Vocational Groups"

Before analyzing the issue of the relationship between the role of formation in the seminaries and the rise of the new Catholic movements, it is necessary to consider critically the peculiar development these movements had in the Catholic Church in the last few decades. It is known that the rise of the new ecclesial movements is usually associated with the Second Vatican Council; as a matter of fact, the new Catholic movements are the only case in which the mention of the "spirit of Vatican II" is considered acceptable in the official public discourse of the Catholic Church. Usually the expression "spirit of Vatican II," if used by a theologian, triggers suspicions of a dangerously liberal Catholic theology. But the history of the new Catholic movements (Opus Dei, Focolare, Neocatecumenal Way, Community of Sant'Egidio, etc.) predates Vatican II and at the same time develops only after Vatican II as an expansion of the "letter" of Vatican II about the role of the laity and lay groups in the Church. The lay character of these new movements was evident in that they were the "product" or the consequence of the crisis of the "classical" way for lay Catholics to be involved in the activities of the Church, that is, through the structures of "Catholic action" in every country between the 1920s and the 1950s.

The rise of the new Catholic movement was significantly boosted by the spirit of Vatican II as it was interpreted by Paul VI and especially by John Paul II, in particular between 1975 and the jubilee in

2000. During the 1980s it became visible in the growth of the existing movements and the creation of new communities and movements, thanks to the benevolence not only of the pope but also of then-Cardinal Ratzinger. As prefect of the Congregation for the Doctrine of the Faith, Ratzinger acknowledged, in his best-selling interview with Vittorio Messori, *Ratzinger Report*, that in the new Catholic movements was visible "a full and integral Catholicity," far from an insulated or fundamentalist version of modern Catholicism.[1] The frequent travels of John Paul II and the World Youth Day (starting in 1984) helped the Church accept the shift from a "Tridentine" idea of local Church to an idea of a more vibrant and missionary Catholic Church, a shift that the new Catholic movements found viable for their particular way of structuring themselves, in silent contrast or often in visible friction with their local bishops and the national bishops' conferences.

This tension finally became visible, and from 1985 on, even the messages of John Paul II to the beloved new Catholic movements stressed the need for them to respect the authority of the bishops in their dioceses. But the emphasis of Rome on the need for the Church to have these new movements as an integral part of the effort to fight secularization made the emerging tensions between the movements and the hierarchical structure of the Church become a "necessary evil" and, in the end, something the bishops should accept as part of the landscape of post–Vatican II Catholicism.[2] At the Synod of Bishops on the laity in 1987 several bishops and cardinals (such as Cardinals Carlo Maria Martini, Aloisio Lorscheider, and František Tomasek) expressed their worries about the growing role of the movements, criticized as "parallel Churches."[3] But the final result of the synod of 1987 did not take into account the criticism coming from many bishops. At that time, the potential conflict between bishops and Catholic movements

---

[1] See Joseph Ratzinger with Vittorio Messori, *The Ratzinger Report: An Exclusive Interview on the State of the Church*, trans. Salvator Attanasio and Graham Harrison (San Francisco: Ignatius Press, 1985). German edition: *Zur Lage des Glaubens* (München: Verlag Neue Stadt, 1985).

[2] See John Paul II's speech to the movements of March 2, 1987, in John Paul II, *Insegnamenti*, vol. 10 1/1987 (Città del Vaticano, 1988), 476.

[3] See Giovanni Caprile, *Il Sinodo dei Vescovi. Settima assemblea generale straordinaria (1–30 ottobre 1987)* (Rome, 1989); Jesus Bogarín Diaz, "Los movimientos eclesiales en la VII Asamblea General Ordinaria del Sinodo de Obispos," *Revista española de Derecho Canónico* 47 (1990): 69–135.

was already evident, even though the issue of the seminaries and the self-exclusion of the movements from the diocesan seminaries was still to come as a global problem for the Catholic Church.

At the end of the 1980s the new movements offered a new kind of activity in the Church that was typical of the laity and that did not modify the educational path of the priests and the structure of the seminary. Representative of this attitude was John Paul II's exhortation *Christifideles Laici* (January 30, 1989) and his emphasis on the five criteria for the ecclesial character of the Catholic movements: the primacy of the universal call to holiness, the responsibility to confess the Catholic faith, the participation in a strong communion, the participation in the apostolic goal of the Church, and the committment to be present in the human society.

The presence and the importance of the new Catholic movements in the magisterium during the pontificate of John Paul II did not vanish in the following years, focused as it was on the need for a "new evangelization." But the teaching of John Paul II increasingly showed a new awareness by the ecclesiastical institution of the theological and sociological complexity of these movements. The growth of the movements was showing the difficulty of making these new "actors" coexist within the traditional structures of recruitment and formation of the clergy, as these movements became something different from the post–Vatican II version of the pre–Vatican II lay movements; they had become a more complex and layered network of groups, communities, and associations in which the lay component was now followed by a clerical component (seminarians, deacons, priests).[4]

The declaration of the Synod of Bishops for Europe in 1991 and the following apostolic exhortation *Pastores Dabo Vobis* of John Paul II (1992) stressed the need to address the issue of the presence of priests in the movements and highlighted the function of these movements for the vocational recruitment of the Church. Moreover, *Pastores Dabo Vobis* clearly mentioned the positive connection between seminarians and clergy on one side and their background in the new Catholic movements:

[4] See Olivier Landron, *Les communautés nouvelles. Nouveaux visages du catholicisme français* (Paris: Cerf, 2004).

It is therefore necessary, in the new community of the seminary in which they are gathered by the bishop, that young people coming from associations and ecclesial movements should learn "respect for other spiritual paths and a spirit of dialogue and cooperation," should take in genuinely and sincerely the indications for their training imparted by the bishop and the teachers in the seminary, abandoning themselves with real confidence to their guidance and assessments. Such an attitude will prepare and in some way anticipate a genuine priestly choice to serve the entire People of God in the fraternal communion of the presbyterate and in obedience to the bishop.

The fact that seminarians and diocesan priests take part in particular spiritualities or ecclesial groupings is indeed, in itself, a factor which helps growth and priestly fraternity. Such participation, however, should not be an obstacle, but rather a help to the ministry and spiritual life which are proper to the diocesan priest, who "will always remain the shepherd of all. Not only is he a 'permanent' shepherd, available to all, but he presides over the gathering of all so that all may find the welcome which they have a right to expect in the community and in the Eucharist that unites them, whatever be their religious sensibility or pastoral commitment."[5]

Also the apostolic letter *Tertio Millennio Adveniente* (November 10, 1994) linked the push for the New Evangelization, the protagonism of the new Catholic movements, and the growth of new vocations within these movements.[6] Similarly, the apostolic exhortation *Vita Consecrata* (March 25, 1996) recognized the importance of the new movements. But for the first time John Paul II hinted at the potentially problematic issue of the participation of consecrated faithful to the "movements":

> In recent years, many consecrated persons have become members of one or other of the *ecclesial movements* which have spread in our time. From these experiences, those involved usually draw benefit, especially in the area of spiritual renewal. Nonetheless, it cannot be denied that in certain cases this involvement causes uneasiness and

[5] John Paul II, apostolic post-synodal exhortation, *Pastores Dabo Vobis*, March 25, 1992, no. 68. Translation from http://www.vatican.va/holy_father/john_paul_ii /apost_exhortations/documents/hf_jp-ii_exh_25031992_pastores-dabo-vobis _en.html.

[6] See John Paul II, apostolic letter, *Tertio Millennio Adveniente*, November 10, 1994, esp. nos. 46–47.

disorientation at the personal or community level, especially when these experiences come into conflict with the demands of the common life or of the Institute's spirituality. It is therefore necessary to take care that membership in these ecclesial movements does not endanger the charism or discipline of the Institute of origin, and that all is done with the permission of Superiors and with the full intention of accepting their decisions.[7]

With the death of John Paul II and the election of Benedict XVI the "Roman policy" toward the new Catholic movements stayed the course and remained consistent with the enthusiasm of Rome and these new realities invigorated the demographics of Western Catholicism. The actions of Rome against the scandals that became public with the Legionaries of Christ are not telling of a policy change of Rome against the new movements. On the contrary: Benedict XVI's often-repeated view of the future of the Church as a "small flock" was a direct encouragement for the new Catholic movements. But new problems arise and old problems keep festering, one of them being the relationship between the movements and the local bishops, especially when it comes to the seminaries.

2. Movements and Seminaries:
The Case of the Neocatechumenal Way

The transformation of the new Catholic movements from local lay groups to global, multi-vocational (and powerful) communities has set in motion, in many cases, the creation of new and specific institutions for the formation of its members. This is not new in Church history, if we look at the history of the mendicant orders or of the Jesuits. But the new ecclesial movements live and prosper in a truly global Church. Therefore, mapping these institutions is difficult and complicated, not only because of the very nature of the movements: available data are usually coming from the same movements interested in emphasizing their "market share." There is also the vast world of the new ecclesial movements outside Europe and the Americas that is largely unexplored by scholars.

---

[7] John Paul II, post-synodal apostolic exhortation, *Vita Consecrata*, March 25, 1996, no. 56. Translation from http://www.vatican.va/holy_father/john_paul_ii /apost_exhortations/documents/hf_jp-ii_exh_25031996_vita-consecrata_en.html.

A few cases are known for their relevance and for the fact that Rome provided the scenario for this important change in the relationship between the Catholic Church in its territorial (diocesan) structure and these new supra-local realities. Opus Dei (hardly a "movement" in its ideal-typical sense) established its own university in Rome, Pontificia Università della Santa Croce, already in the academic year 1984–85. In September 1985, Communion and Liberation created its own fraternity for priests, Fraternità dei missionari di San Carlo Borromeo. More recently, December 2007, the Focolare movement established in Loppiano (central Italy) its own university, Istituto Universitario Sophia. The Pontifical Athenaeum Regina Apostolorum in Rome is sponsored by the Legionaries of Christ and its lay ecclesial movement, Regnum Christi.

But the most interesting case of all, regarding the creation of an institution for the priestly formation of members of a movement, is the case of the Neocatechumenal Way.[8] Created in 1964 in Madrid's shantytown by Kiko Argüello, a young Spanish painter, and a laywoman, Carmen Hernández, who had studied in the institute Misioneras de Cristo Jesús,[9] the Neocatechumenal Way expanded significantly during the pontificate of John Paul II. In 2002 the statutes of the Neocatechumenal Way were approved *ad experimentum* for five years by John Paul II, just five years after an informal request submitted by the "Camino" during an audience of the leaders of the movement with John Paul II in 1997. On June 13, 2008, the formal process ended, with the formal decree of approval of the Neocatechumenal Way sent by the president of the Pontifical Council for the Laity to Kiko Argüello, Carmen Hernández, and to Fr. Mario Pezzi, who had been associated with the movement from the start. This Roman approval of the Neocatechumenal Way seemed a clear overruling of the bishops of Japan, who in 2007 (especially in the *visita ad limina* of December 2007) had

---

[8] See Bernhard Sven Anuth, *Der Neokatechumenale Weg: Geschichte Erscheinungsbild Rechtscharakter* (Würzburg: Echter, 2006); and Bernhard Sven Anuth, "L'istituzionalizzazione del Camino neocatecumenale," *Il Regao–Documenti* 9 (2013): 296–320.

[9] For the official "historical note" on the origins of the Neocatechumenal Way, see www.camminoneocatecumenale.it. See also Kiko Argüello, "Le comunità neocatecumenali," *Rivista di vita spirituale* 2 (1975); Ricardo Blazquez, *Le comunità neocatecumenali: Discernimento teologico*, ed. Ezechiele Pasotti (Cinisello B.: San Paolo, 1995); Paolo Sorci, "Ermeneutica della Parola nel cammino neocatecumenale," *Rivista liturgica* 6 (1997): 867–80.

expressed to Rome formal complaints regarding the pastoral practices of the Camino in the Catholic Church in Japan and its refusal to co-operate with the bishops.

The fight between the Japanese bishops and the leader of the Neo-catechumenal Way did not end with the Roman approval of the statutes of the movement in 2008. During that year the Japanese bishops visited Rome twice to ask for the closure of the seminary for the members of the movement in Japan, and they succeeded in gaining the under-standing of the Vatican for their worries about the pastoral problems caused by the divisive ecclesial praxis of the members of the move-ment and its seminary. The Neocatechumenal Way in Japan resisted the decision, and in March 2009 Rome sent an apostolic visitation, which did not convince the Japanese bishops to change their decision regarding the seminary of the Neocatechumenal Way in Japan. That seminary was transferred to Rome as part of the local seminary Re-demptoris Mater. On December 13, 2010, a special meeting took place in Rome between the Japanese bishops and members of the Roman Curia, including Pope Benedict XVI and six cardinals.[10] The final deci-sion was an "encouragement" from the pope to the Japanese bishops to work closely with the Neocatechumenal Way in order to solve the problems regarding the coexistence between the local Churches and the movement in Japan. A few days later, on December 26, 2010, the *Catechesi* (catechetical handbook) of the movement was approved by Rome and presented to the pope in the special audience granted to the seven thousand members of the movement on January 17, 2011. In a press conference held in Rome on the same day, the three leaders of the movement (Argüello, Hernández, and Fr. Pezzi) defended the role of the Neocatechumenal Way in Japan and denied any disregard for the role of the bishops in the local churches where it is active. At the same time, in that same press conference, the founders used strong words against Cardinal Arinze (former prefect of the Congregation for Divine Worship and the Discipline of the Sacraments, retired in 2008) and against the liberation theologians, both of which were registered as "enemies" of the Neocatechumenal Way. The decision of Benedict XVI was accepted by the Japanese bishops with less than great enthusiasm,

---

[10] See Lorenzo Prezzi and Maria Elisabetta Gandolfi, "A una svolta," *Il Regno— Attualità* 2 (2011): 24–25.

to say the least, and as soon as the bishops got back to Japan they did not hesitate in manifesting their disappointment with the decision made by Rome over their heads.[11]

The history of the difficult relations between the movement and the Church as an institution, both at its local and Roman level, is a long one, and it does not concern only the Catholic Church in Japan. There are two main issues: the liturgical life of the movement (in particular, the exclusive dimension of the eucharistic celebrations) and the pastoral dimension of the life of the movement in the local churches (especially regarding inculturation and the respect of the authority of the bishops). Tensions have arisen in the last few years about the coexistence of the Neocatechumenal Way and the local Church, for example, in the Arabic-speaking Catholic Church in Israel and in the Philippines.[12]

Leaving aside the doubts and questions at the doctrinal level that have been part of the relations between the movement and the Church in the last fifteen years,[13] the issue of the seminaries of the Neocatechumenal Way has become a staple in the relationship between local churches and the movement.[14] In different situations with different bishops, the local churches seem to reject or to accept (or even seek) the presence of the Neocatechumenal Way for reasons having much

[11] For the letter of Bishop Osamu Mizobe (bishop of Takamatsu, January 20, 2011), see http://www.ucanews.com/2011/01/20/bishop-speaks-out-on-neo-cats/.

[12] See "Proposition 17" in the *Elenchus Finalis Propositionum* of the Special Assembly of the Bishops' Synod for the Middle East (October 2010), http://www.vatican.va/roman_curia/synod/documents/rc_synod_doc_20101026_elenco-prop-finali-mo_it.html (available online in only Arabic, French, and Italian); for the letter of the bishop of Lingayen-Dagupan in the Philippines (May 3, 2010), see http://www.lingayen-dagupan.org/ArchBishop/neocat.html.

[13] Between 1997 and 2003, the Congregation for the Doctrine of Faith (chaired by Cardinal Ratzinger with Msgr. Bertone as secretary) examined the thirteen volumes of the oral teaching of Kiko Argüello and Carmen Hernández (now under the title of *Direttorio Catechetico*). The congregation amended those texts and added several hundred links to the text of the *Catechism of the Catholic Church*. The thirteen volumes collecting the oral teaching of the founders and explaining the praxis of the movement received formal approval from Benedict XVI only in 2010.

[14] See B. Esposito, "Un nuovo tipo di seminario? I seminari diocesani missionari 'Redemptoris Mater,'" *Quaderni di diritto ecclesiale* 12 (1999): 95–122. The Redemptoris Mater seminaries have been erected all over the world, in more than fifty countries on five continents.

to do with the imposing activity of their seminaries.[15] The issue of the seminaries of the Neocatechumenal Way and of similar institutions as part of the larger system of "operations" run by the new Catholic movements raises an important ecclesiological and cultural question for the future of the Catholic Church.

3. Canonical and Theological Issues

The canonical issue of the creation of seminaries for the new Catholic movements is made more serious by the actual push, coming from some of these movements, toward the possibility of an incardination of priests in the ecclesial movements instead of in the local churches (diocesan).[16] If in the 1980s and 1990s some members of Communion and Liberation floated the idea (promptly rejected) of appointing a "bishop for the movements,"[17] now the Catholic Church is in the next phase: new Catholic movements able to attract and form new vocations are tempted to "appropriate" these new vocations and to defend them from the bigger Church and its alleged "laxity."

This push presents the Catholic Church with the opportunity to acknowledge the mutation of the new Catholic movements from their origins of lay movements to the actual configuration of multi-vocational communities: laypeople, celibate and consecrated members, seminarians, priests, bishops. This new face of the Catholic movements has to be understood in the history of Catholic laity and in particular as the response of the body of the Church to the crisis of the consecrated life, which had its golden age in the decades immediately before and after World War II. The crisis of the consecrated life and of the priesthood has invited many Catholics to join the new Catholic movements: with the difference that while the canonical regulations

---

[15] On the other hand, in February 2011 the bishop of Trieste (Italy), Giampaolo Crepaldi, made known his invitation to the Neocatechumenal Way to found a Redemptoris Mater seminary in his diocese: see the letter published in the diocesan weekly *Vita Nuova* (February 7, 2011), http://www.vitanuovatrieste.it/content/view/5241/1/.

[16] Opus Dei, among others, clearly pushes in this direction. See Luis Navarro, "L'incardinazione nei movimenti ecclesiali? Problemi e prospettive," *Fidelium Iura* 15 (2005): 63–96. See also Michael J. Mullaney, *Incardination and the Universal Dimension of the Priestly Ministry: A Comparison between CIC 17 and CIC 83* (Rome: Pontificia Università Gregoriana, 2002).

[17] See "Un vescovo per i movimenti?," in *Il Regno—Attualità* 22 (1982): 507.

for consecrated life and priesthood were and are quite clear, the canonical regulations for the new Catholic movements are far from clear,
in the field of *de iure condendo* (still to be defined legally), if not *extra
legem* (a phenomenon that develops in absence of a law regulating
it)—especially for the issue of the formation of its clerical members.

On the other hand, it is clear that the emergence from these new
movements of more "independence" from the local Churches goes
together not only with the request to have separate seminaries and
separate "vocational paths" for their members but also with the development of a "clericalization" of the style of leadership and of the
culture within these movements. The clerical elements still constitute
a minority in these new Catholic movements, but their influence is
growing in terms of the kind of culture, spirituality, and lifestyle.[18] It is
in this broader picture that the request of founding separate seminaries
for the members of the new Catholic movements has to be understood.

From a historical point of view, after the apostolic exhortation of
John Paul II, *Pastores Dabo Vobis* (1992), the will to maintain diocesan seminaries as the normal way to form seminarians coming from
Catholic movements now seems no longer a clear option for the
Catholic Church. That might undermine the authority of local bishops
in Churches, being that episcopal authority was undermined already
during the recent pontificates of John Paul II and Benedict XVI. The
ultra-papalist loyalty of the average new Catholic movement makes the
choice between the local episcopate and these new kinds of laity a very
easy one for Rome. If the future of the Catholic movements will bring
a separation of the formation paths for new priests between "local
priests" and "movements' priests," that will happen at the expense
of the "Catholicity" of the Church, that is, the universal dimension
of contemporary Catholicism: all in the name of a re-creation of a
communional-sectarian mind-set that rejects the call of the faithful
(and the ministers) to serve in the local Church and not in an elective
and self-selected milieu, as hospitable as it may be in comparison to
the "big chill" of the outer world.[19]

---

[18] See Gianni Ambrosio, "Cammino ecclesiale e percorsi aggregativi," *La Scuola
Cattolica* 116 (1988): 441–60.

[19] For the "ticket mentality" in some of the new Catholic movements, see Shmuel N.
Eisenstadt, *Fundamentalism, Sectarianism, and Revolution: The Jacobin Dimension
of Modernity* (Cambridge, UK, and New York: Cambridge University Press, 1999).

The election of Pope Francis has brought a new awareness about the potential divisiveness of the new ecclesial movements in local churches. The audience of the pope with the members of the Neocate-chumenal Way on February 1, 2014, sent a clear message about the view of the movements typical of the pontificate:

> I would like to propose to you some simple recommendations. The first is to have the utmost care to build and to preserve the communion within the particular Churches in which you will work. The Way has its own charism and dynamic, a gift, which like all of the gifts of the Spirit, has a profound ecclesial dimension; this means paying attention to the life of the Churches to which your leaders send you, to enhance the riches, to suffer for the weaknesses if necessary, and to walk together, like one flock, under the guidance of the pastors of the local Churches. Communion is essential sometimes it can be better to renounce living in all the details that your itinerary demands, in order to ensure the unity among those who form one ecclesial community, of which you must always feel that you are part.[20]

---

[20] Pope Francis, audience with about eight thousand members of the Neo-catechumenal Way on February 1, 2014, in the Aula Paul VI. Text from http://en .radiovaticana.va/news/2014/02/01/pope_to_neocatechumenal_way:_build _ecclesial_communion,_evangelize/en1-769304.

Catholic Movements
and the "Apologetics of Enmity"
in the Postconciliar Church

1. Ecclesiology of the Tridentine Period, of Vatican II, and of the *Reconquista*

For those patient enough to read and understand the significance of the Second Vatican Council in the contemporary Catholic Church, it becomes clear that "something happened *at* Vatican II."[1] Less simple is the answer to the question "what happened *to* Vatican II?" in the decades after the council.[2]

In 1990, toward the end of the twenty-first century, at a point that we can now situate chronologically in the middle of John Paul II's pontificate, Italian theologian Giuseppe Ruggieri addressed the issue of the relationship between Church and world in the theology of the twentieth century and the postconciliar period from an ecclesiological perspective. He detected in the reaction of the Christian Churches to its "exclusion" from modern Western consciousness an "apologetics of enmity":

> Facing exclusion, the Christian Churches, especially the Catholic Church, react by developing an apologetics of enmity, which is different from the "monastic withdrawal" that characterized past cen-

---

[1] See John W. O'Malley, *What Happened at Vatican II* (Cambridge MA: Belknap Press of Harvard University Press, 2008).

[2] See Massimo Faggioli, *Vatican II: The Battle for Meaning* (Mahwah, NJ: Paulist Press, 2012).

turies. In fact, "monastic withdrawal" was never intended to advance claims on the world, while the Church's enmity toward the modern world is entirely aimed at regaining a place for itself in the world, the same position of privilege that had been essentially suppressed by the wars of religion, and that the French Revolution would bury forever under the rubble of the *Ancien Régime*.[3]

In light of such observation, Ruggieri advanced a reasonably cautious prognosis on the evolution of this relationship between Church and world in the postconciliar Church:

> Current theology has therefore sought to develop alternative models for the Church's presence in the world, from the new "political theology" to the various forms of liberation theology. . . . The ecclesial and theological conscience seems at present to be experiencing a phase of "fluidity" and uncertainty in determining the relationship that ought to connect the experience of the Christian faith with "this" world. Conversely, this "fluidity" is perhaps the result of Vatican II's shattering effects on the relationship between Church and world.[4]

The period between the Jubilee of 2000, the end of John Paul II's pontificate, and the unfolding of Benedict XVI's political doctrine offers an opportunity to reexamine Ruggieri's notion, formulated in 1990, of "fluidity" in postconciliar Catholicism. After almost thirty years since it had been first expressed in the middle of John Paul II's pontificate and five years after the 1985 Synod of Bishops on the reception of the council, it certainly is important to rethink Ruggieri's notion to try to understand how the relationship between Church and world has changed in the Church's "theology in the public square." The ecclesial movements are a natural point of reference, because they undoubtedly are one of the most "advanced," complex, and ambivalent instruments emerging out of postconciliar Roman Catholicism for the articulation of the relationship between the Church and the modern world.

To understand the ecclesial movements' role in the Catholic attitude toward Church and world, this new reality of the Catholic experience should be seen in the context of a more extensive discourse on the ecclesiological models of the Church of Rome, before placing it

---

[3] Giuseppe Ruggieri, "Chiesa e mondo," in *Cristianesimo, chiese e Vangelo* (Bologna: Il Mulino, 2002), 307–38, esp. 319.

[4] Ibid., 321–22.

within the debate on the reception of Vatican II.[5] In fact, the experience of the variable and diverse ecclesial movements that emerged during the twentieth century, especially starting from the end of the council, substantiates a fact in the history of ecclesiology: on the one hand, the historicity and discontinuity between ecclesiological models during the history of the pre-Tridentine and post-Tridentine modern Church; on the other, the influence of cultural and political (broadly speaking) models on the Church's theological self-understanding.[6]

One of the ways in which an ecclesiology differs from another can be detected in the selection and formation of its leadership and the quality of the prosopography of the Church's leader elites. This element takes on a particular importance in our case, because the history of the postconciliar Catholic movements lies at the turning point from a Catholic Church guided by an episcopal leadership to a Church where the episcopate is paired with the alternative model: that of the movements. This new model has been sometimes endorsed by the papacy (especially under John Paul II and Benedict XVI) as the quintessential example of the postconciliar Church and is seen as an alternative to the "lay notables" of the late nineteenth century and early twentieth century, as well as the "mature laity" of the late twentieth century and the episcopal "old Catholic elite."

In effect, one of the decisive moments in the transition from a pre-modern to a modern functioning model of the Church coincided with the creation at the Council of Trent in the second half of the sixteenth century of a new episcopate with a residence requirement; bishops selected no longer on the basis of lineage or census but rather on the basis of characteristics corresponding to that of a modern official (legal, rather than theological, education); residence in the assigned episcopal see (but also willingness to travel if requested); moral reliability; ability to supervise subordinates; and obedience to Rome.[7] As the system of selection of bishops and training of the clergy changed between the pre-Tridentine and the Tridentine era, a new model of

[5] See Yves Congar, *L'Église de Saint Augustin à l'époque moderne* (Paris: Cerf, 1970).

[6] See the classic essay by Hubert Jedin, "Zur Entwicklung des Kirchenbegriffs im 16. Jahrhundert," in *Relazioni del X Congresso internazionale di Scienze storiche (congresso di Roma, 4–11 settembre 1955)*, vol. 4 (Florence, 1955), 59–73.

[7] See Massimo Faggioli, "La disciplina di nomina dei vescovi prima e dopo il concilio di Trento," *Società e Storia* 92 (2001): 221–56.

the Church as an institution emerged.[8] This is also true for the post–Vatican II Church, in which ecclesial movements have come to fill the role of a particular "ruling class" with different visions of the relationship between Church and modern world. Within the vast and diverse galaxy of associations, groups, and communities, however, there are some shared values and ecclesiological visions. This is particularly evident in the movements of the *reconquista* such as Opus Dei, the Legionaries of Christ, and Communion and Liberation, whose tormented reading of modernity seems to have taken firm root in the Catholic Church's body.

2. The First Three Stages of the Contemporary Catholic Movements (1870–1970)

As we have seen in chapter 1, the lowest common denominator of an ecclesial movement is a charismatic founder, a particular charism, some form of ecclesial expression, a predominantly lay membership, a form of theological training closely linked to its charism, and a commitment to bringing its own emphasis or understanding into the life of the Catholic Church.[9] But this definition must be complemented by an understanding of the historical origin of these new forms of association within Western Catholicism.

The history of the new ecclesial movements begins well before Vatican II, at a time when the ecclesiastical institution understood that the changes underway in the modern world required a new Catholic

---

[8] See Giuseppe Alberigo, "L'istituzione e i poteri nella chiesa. L'episcopato nel cattolicesimo riformato (XVI–XVII sec.)," in *L'institution et le pouvoirs dans l'église, de l'antiquité à nos jours*, Miscellanea historiae ecclesiasticae, 8 (Brussels and Leuven, 1987), 268–86; Hubert Jedin, "La riforma del processo informativo per la nomina dei vescovi al concilio di Trento," in *Chiesa della fede chiesa della storia* (Brescia: Morcelliana, 1972), 316–39 (previously published in *Archiv für katholisches Kirchenrecht* 116 [1936]: 389–413); Joseph Bergin, "L'Europe des évêques au temps de la réforme catholique," in *Bibliothèque de l'École des Chartes* 154 (1996): 509–31; Wolfgang Reinhard, "Introduction: Power Elites, State Servants, Ruling Classes, and the Growth of State Power," in *Power Elites and State Building*, ed. Wolfgang Reinhard (Oxford: Oxford University Press, 1996), 17–18.

[9] See Charles Whitehead, "The Role of Ecclesial Movements and New Communities in the Life of the Church," in *New Religious Movements in the Catholic Church*, ed. Michael A. Hayes (London and New York: Continuum, 2005), 18.

laity to work alongside (without replacing) the episcopate and clergy. In dealing with the French Revolution, the end of the *Ancien Régime*, and the shock of its aftermath, the papacy leading the Church from the Restoration to the First Vatican Council (1869–70), namely, from Pope Gregory XVI to Pope Pius IX, realized that directing bishops and clergy was not going to be enough: to regain society the Church needed to mobilize the laity, but more important, the laity needed to be closely supervised. In this perspective, the birth of the "Catholic movement" has more to do with an antiliberal political culture than with an anticommunist one, which is a relevant aspect for a theological reading of the relationship between Church and world. The training and supervision of the newly organized laity was achieved in three stages between the end of the nineteenth century and the era of Vatican II.

During the *first stage*, from the birth of the "social question" after Vatican I to the First World War, the Catholic movement in Europe was sustained and controlled by the hierarchy on a local basis and geared toward socio-economic and political objectives of predominantly local relevance, with the creation of a solidarity network still relatively flexible and indirectly dependent on the bishops and the papacy. During this first moment, the laity's leadership in Europe was still entrusted to Catholic notables: members of the upper class whose social views were expressed through works of philanthropy and charity but also through a democratic ethos that was visible in their way to organize the Catholic movement, that is, in structures and procedures with some kind of visibility and accountability. Toward them the bishops acted more as an organ of control than of mobilization and formation, as evidenced by the episode of the dissolution of the Opera dei Congressi (congresses of Catholic laity) in Italy in 1904.[10] It was essentially a social movement focused on activities *ad extra* the European church but within the liberal states and was not intended for, nor to bring about, changes in the way members lived the Church.[11] Above all, this Catholic social movement did not find common ground with the

---

[10] See Francesco Traniello and Giorgio Campanini, introduction to *Dizionario storico del movimento cattolico in Italia, 1860–1980*, vol. 1/1 (Genova: Marietti, 1981).

[11] See Severino Dianich, "L'ecclesiologia in Italia dal Vaticano I al Vaticano II," in Traniello and Campanini, *Dizionario storico del movimento cattolico*, vol. 1/1, 162–80; Giuseppe Alberigo, "Le concezioni della Chiesa e i mutamenti istituzionali,"

emerging movements for liturgical, ecumenical, and biblical reform between the two councils of Vatican I and Vatican II.[12]

During the *second stage*, from the 1920s to the Second World War, we witness the creation by the Vatican of Catholic Action, which had to forcibly give up a political involvement, managed independently by the laity, to focus instead on the formation of a mass movement with broader educational aims, in view of a future change of the political regime.[13] In his encyclical of 1922, *Ubi Arcano Dei* on Catholic Action, Pius XI stated that "Christ reigns where the position in society which He Himself has assigned to His Church is recognized, for He bestowed on the Church the status and the constitution of a society which, by reason of the perfect ends which it is called upon to attain, must be held to be supreme in its own sphere; He also made her the depository and interpreter of His divine teachings, and, by consequence, the teacher and guide of every other society whatsoever."[14] Thus, Catholic Action became an active part in the Church's design of "restoration of the Kingdom of Christ," in a modern society considered corrupt by modern politics as a secular activity and lacerated by struggles between classes, political parties, and families. The reestablishment of peace must pass through the reestablishment of the *societas Christiana* under the guidance of the ecclesiastical authority. Catholic Action was thus characterized by a strong loyalty to the pope and bishops, and a capillary system of formation and supervision extended to virtually every member of the Church by virtue of an ancillary vision of Catholic Action within the larger context of the Church's action. Catholic Action was also a "big tent for the movements in the Church"

---

in *Chiesa e papato nel mondo contemporaneo*, ed. Giuseppe Alberigo and Andrea Riccardi (Roma-Bari: Laterza, 1990), 65–121.

[12] See André Haquin, *Dom Lambert Beauduin et le renouveau liturgique* (Gembloux, 1970); Maria Paiano, *Liturgia e società nel Novecento: percorsi del movimento liturgico di fronte ai processi di secolarizzazione* (Rome: Edizioni di Storia e Letteratura, 2000); Bernard Montagnes, *Marie-Joseph Lagrange. Une biographie critique* (Paris: Cerf, 2005).

[13] See Liliana Ferrari, *L'Azione Cattolica in Italia dalle origini al pontificato di Paolo VI* (Brescia: Queriniana, 1982); and Liliana Ferrari, *Una storia dell'Azione cattolica. Gli ordinamenti statutari da Pio XI a Pio XII* (Genova: Marietti, 1989).

[14] Pius XI, encyclical, *Ubi Arcano Dei*, December 23, 1922, no. 48. Translation from http://www.vatican.va/holy_father/pius_xi/encyclicals/documents/hf_p-xi _enc_19221223_ubi-arcano-dei-consilio_en.html.

compared to other organizations mobilized in the clash/encounter between Church and authoritarian-totalitarian political ideologies.

During this time, the leadership cadres were no longer recruited only among the members of the Catholic aristocracy (both social and intellectual upper class). More effort was invested in their formation, which was more centralized, standardized, and aimed to unify the Church during the transition from the end of the totalitarian regimes (in Italy, Germany, and Spain, which had all signed concordats with the Holy See) to the socio-political reordering of the postwar era in the West.[15] From the point of view of the new movements' development, the period between 1945 and the beginning of Vatican II is a moment of transition, which saw the birth of experiences such as Gioventù Studentesca led by Fr. Giussani in Milan in 1954, the Opera di Maria (Focolare) shortly after, and the Neocatechumenal Way, which emerged even before the council ended, that is, in 1964. Nevertheless, their relationship with Catholic Action, from which these new movements would distance themselves in a more or less polemical way, represented the prelude to a dynamic that characterized the next stage.

The *third stage*, from Vatican II and the first postconciliar period to the late 1960s and 1970s, saw the end of Catholic Action's preeminence and, starting with the 1960s, the proliferation of Catholic movements that originated from within Catholic Action. Despite the fact that this period represented the moment of maximum tension between the Western–northern Atlantic identity of Roman Catholicism, on the one hand, and the Communist ideology on the other, the new Catholic movements, for which the political sphere had very different meanings and boundaries, thrived. In the United States in 1967, between the East Coast and the Midwest, the Catholic charismatic renewal movement was born (at the University of Notre Dame in Indiana and beyond) and reached Italy in 1972; in 1968, the leaders of the Neocatechumenal Way arrived in Rome and also spread throughout Italy; during Lent 1975, Communion and Liberation received in Rome a first provisional, but no less public, recognition by Paul VI, who until then had been hesitant regarding the ecclesiology of this new association.[16]

---

[15] See Ernesto Preziosi, *Obbedienti in piedi. La vicenda dell'Azione Cattolica in Italia* (Turin: SEI, 1996).

[16] See Massimo Faggioli, "Tra referendum sul divorzio e revisione del Concordato. Enrico Bartoletti segretario della CEI (1972–1976)," *Contemporanea* 2 (2001): 255–80.

During the third stage, among the diversity of experiences and visions of the world, those associations whose culture of reference was based on a negative view of the Church-world relationship became stronger. Once the experience of the Catholic left faded away, on the one hand, the movements of the Christian *reconquista* of the world (Opus Dei, Communion and Liberation, the Legionaries of Christ) came to life.[17] On the other hand, there emerged less visible forms, but no less relevant, of Pentecostalism/Catholic evangelicalism (Renewal in the Spirit, the Neocatechumenal Way, the Focolare movement).[18] Regardless of the enthusiasm or criticism it aroused, during this time the Second Vatican Council intersects only tangentially with the history of the new Catholic movements, except for the case of those movements that more openly embraced the conciliar ecclesiology (the Community of Sant'Egidio, the Franco-Belgian Catholic Scout Associations, and the movements in Italy and France with roots in the experience of Jeunesse Ouvrière Chrétienne). Both the conciliar debates and the final documents of Vatican II, however, neglect this new phenomenon, still on the rise, to focus instead on a structure for the lay apostolate with Catholic Action at its center.[19] Despite this

[17] See *Ai quattro angoli del fondamentalismo. Movimenti politico-religiosi nella loro tradizione, epifania, protesta, regressione*, ed. R. Giammanco (Scandicci: La Nuova Italia, 1993); R. Scott Appleby and Emmanuel Sivan, *Strong Religion: The Rise of Fundamentalisms around the World* (Chicago: University of Chicago Press, 2003).

[18] See Edward O'Connor, *Le renouveau charismatique: origines et perspectives* (Paris: Beauchesne, 1975), esp. 221–96; Randy R. McGuire, *Catholic Charismatic Renewal: The Struggle for Affirmation (1967–1975)* (PhD diss., Saint Louis University, 1998), esp. 100–104; Kevin and Dorothy Ranaghan, *Catholic Pentecostals* (Paramus, NJ: Paulist Press, 1969); Kevin and Dorothy Ranaghan, *Catholic Pentecostals Today* (Notre Dame, IN: University of Notre Dame Press, 1983); Kilian McDonnell, *The Charismatic Renewal and Ecumenism* (New York: Paulist Press, 1978); Francis A. Sullivan, *Charisms and Charismatic Renewal: A Biblical and Theological Study* (Ann Arbor, MI: Servant Books, 1982); Paolo Maino, *Il post-moderno nella Chiesa? Il Rinnovamento carismatico* (Cinisello B.: San Paolo, 2004); Mario Panciera, *Il Rinnovamento nello spirito in Italia: una realtà ecclesiale* (Rome: RnS, 1992); Peter Zimmerling, *Die charismatischen Bewegungen. Theologie–Spiritualität–Anstöße zum Gespräch* (Göttingen: Vandenhoeck & Ruprecht, 2001).

[19] See Massimo Faggioli, "Tra chiesa territoriale e chiese personali. I movimenti ecclesiali nel post-concilio Vaticano II," in *I movimenti nella storia del cristianesimo. Caratteristiche—variazioni—continuità*, ed. Giuseppe Alberigo and Massimo Faggioli, *Cristianesimo nella Storia* 24, no. 3 (2003): 677–704.

incipient and mutual estrangement between Vatican II and the new Catholic movements of the *reconquista*, the organization and role of these new associations changed along the way between the council and the postconciliar period.

At the height of the postconciliar period, we witness the beginning of a *fourth stage* in the history of the new Catholic movements, characterized by self-reproduction processes (in the sociological sense) within the Catholic Church as well as by distinct ecclesiologies and reference cultures.

3. The Fourth Stage of Catholic Movements (1980–)

Starting in the 1980s, with the full unfolding of John Paul II's pontificate in relation to the question of the reception *ad intra* of Vatican II, this fourth stage in the movements' history was "institutionalized" by the postconciliar papacy. Through a series of public acts, initially relevant only for the local Italian Church (for example, in favor of Communion and Liberation), and defining moments for the universal Church (for example, with the creation of Opus Dei's personal prelature in 1982 and its recognition in the new Code of Canon Law of 1983), Pope John Paul II embraced the phenomenon of the movements, interpreting their ecclesiology of the relationship between Church and world according to a complex, but not ambiguous, equation.[20]

In 1980 there was the first congress of the movements organized by the Pontifical Council for the Laity, and in 1982 the first world congress of the movements at Rocca di Papa. Further, in 1980 the Rimini Meeting of Communion and Liberation was launched, and in 1982 its Fraternity was recognized. The bestowal of a particular canonical status, in the form of a personal prelature to Opus Dei in 1982 and the new Code of 1983 represent two signs of the new direction taken by

---

[20] Different opinions on John Paul II can be found in Alberto Melloni, *Chiesa madre, chiesa matrigna. Un discorso storico sul cristianesimo che cambia* (Turin: Einaudi, 2005); Daniele Menozzi, *Giovanni Paolo II. Una transizione incompiuta?* (Brescia: Morcelliana, 2006); Giovanni Miccoli, *In difesa della fede. La chiesa di Giovanni Paolo II e di Benedetto XVI* (Milan: Rizzoli, 2007); Andrea Riccardi, *Giovanni Paolo II. La biografia* (Cinisello B.: San Paolo, 2011). These authors share a clearly dissimilar view from George Weigel's works on John Paul II.

John Paul II, who abandoned Paul VI's previous calculated prudence toward the new movements.[21] In 1983, John Paul II approved the constitutions of the Legionaries of Christ; in 1985 Communion and Liberation (and not Catholic Action) was invited to participate in the Extraordinary Synod of Bishops, twenty years after the conclusion of the council. The Extraordinary Synod of 1985 dealt with the reception of Vatican II and ultimately gave more authority to the papacy (and not to the episcopal conferences) in promoting the knowledge and application of Vatican II. Thus, it advanced a more flexible and special interpretation of the papal role *ad extra* (especially with regard to interreligious dialogue), and one more of the "law and order" type *ad intra*.[22]

Between the 1980s and 1990s, the movements became an active part of John Paul II's new direction through the New Evangelization project.[23] The recruitment was such that at the Synod of Bishops on the laity in 1987 eminent cardinals talked about the risk of "parallel churches" created by the movements.[24] This fear had little effect on the Vatican recognition policy: in 1990, the pope recognized the Neocatechumenal Way's itinerary of Christian formation; in 1991, the third international congress on ecclesial movements was held in Bratislava, and that same year the Legionaries of Christ opened their international center in Rome; in 1992, the founder of Opus Dei, Josemaría Escrivá de Balaguer was beatified in record time (and later canonized in 2002).[25] Finally, the international conferences of ecclesial

---

[21] See Bruno Forte, "Associazioni, movimenti e missione nella chiesa locale," *Il Regno—Documenti* 1 (1983): 29–34.

[22] On the synod of 1985, see *Synod 1985: An Evaluation*, ed. Giuseppe Alberigo and James Provost (Edinburgh: T. & T. Clark, 1986).

[23] See Forte, "Associazioni, movimenti e missione nella chiesa locale," 29–34; Juan José Etxeberría, "Los movimentos eclesiales en los albores del siglo XXI," *Revista Española de Derecho Canonico* 58 (2001): 577–616.

[24] See *Il Sinodo dei vescovi: settima Assemblea generale ordinaria (1–30 ottobre 1987)*, ed. G. Caprile (Rome: La Civiltà Cattolica, 1989). On the papal magisterium on the movements up to the synod, see Franco Giulio Brambilla, "Le aggregazioni ecclesiali nei documenti del magistero dal concilio fino ad oggi," *La Scuola Cattolica* 116 (1988): 461–511.

[25] See *I movimenti della Chiesa negli anni Ottanta. Atti del I Convegno internazionale (Roma, 23–27 settembre 1981)*, ed. Massimo Camisasca and Mario Vitali (Milan: Jaca Book, 1982); *I movimenti nella chiesa. Atti del II Colloquio internazionale su Vocazione e missione dei laici nella Chiesa oggi (Rocca di Papa, 28 febbraio–4 marzo 1987)* (Milan: Nuovo Mondo, 1987); *I movimenti nella Chiesa. Atti del Congresso mondiale*

movements represented the first step in a series of events culminating with a day dedicated to John Paul II's meeting with ecclesial movements in 1998, and the Jubilee of 2000.[26]

The Vatican policy of recognition of the movements' statutes represents (as in the case of the Neocatechumenal Way and the Renewal in the Spirit) only one step in the movements' résumé; a step that turns out to be incapable of influencing the theological culture and praxis (both ecclesial and liturgical) of the single movements and of their founders yet confirms their newly acquired canonical "legal" status.[27] This moment of official recognition often coincides with a rereading of the Catholic associative experiences prior to those of the new movements, and is substantiated by the conversion of the lay movements, rooted in Vatican II, to the postconciliar ethos of the *reconquista*, which actually has very little in common with those first associative experiences. The peace agreement signed in Italy in 2004, at the meeting in Loreto, between Catholic Action and Communion and Liberation, in reality represented Communion and Liberation's taking over the supremacy from Catholic Action. Further, the transition in 2005 from John Paul II's to Benedict XVI's pontificate did not mark a discontinuity in the Vatican policy toward the movements, despite the conviction in 2006 of Fr. Marcial Maciel, founder of the Legionaries of Christ, when his double life was brought to light.[28]

---

dei movimenti ecclesiali (Roma, 27–29 maggio 1998) sponsored by the Pontificium Consilium pro Laicis (Vatican City: Libreria Editrice Vaticana, 1999).

[26] See John Paul II's message in Pontificium Consilium pro Laicis, *Movements in the Church: Proceedings of the World Congress of the Ecclesial Movements* (Vatican City: Libreria Editrice Vaticana, 1999), 16.

[27] See Barbara Zadra, *I movimenti ecclesiali e i loro statuti* (Rome: Pontificia Università Gregoriana, 1997); Velasio De Paolis, "Diritto dei fedeli di associarsi e la normativa che lo regola," in *Fedeli Associazioni Movimenti* (Milan: Glossa, 2002), 127–62.

[28] See Joseph Ratzinger / Benedict XVI, *Nuove irruzioni dello spirito. I movimenti nella Chiesa* (Cinisello B.: San Paolo, 2006); *La bellezza di essere cristiani. I movimenti nella Chiesa. Atti del II congresso mondiale dei movimenti ecclesiali e delle nuove comunità (Rocca di Papa, 31 maggio–2 giugno 2006)* (Vatican City: Libreria Editrice Vaticana, 2007); Benedict XVI's speech to the clergy and diocese of Rome, February 22, 2007, at http://www.vatican.va/holy_father/benedict_xvi/speeches/2007/february/documents/hf_ben-xvi_spe_20070222_clergy-rome_en.html; and the message of the Secretary of the Pontifical Council for the Laity at the international conference for bishops organized by the Pontifical Council (Rocca di Papa, May 15–17, 2008), Joseph Clemens, *Papa Ratzinger e i movimenti*, in *Il Regno—Documenti* 13 (2008): 441–49.

4. *Weltanschauung* and the Ecclesiology of the *Reconquista*

If it is too extreme to define the movements as an "opportunistic" phenomenon in relation to the Church's crisis of authority as an institution during the postconciliar period, it is equally gratuitous and incorrect to identify them with the "spring" of the postconciliar Church. Not only because the explosion of this phenomenon is more linked to the history of the postconciliar pontificates than to the postconciliar period as such, but also because the "rise of the movements" is also founded on an opposition—at times oblique, at times more direct—to post–Vatican II theology at the height of the debate on the reception of the council in the early 1980s. It is a moment that can be viewed, however, as the fourth stage of the development of the phenomenon of the movements with its own specific traits.[29]

First, it should be noted that from a sociological point of view the most characteristic and identifying trait of the new movements of the *reconquista* is the reception—at times creative, but more often than not inaccurate—of Vatican II's message, a reception undoubtedly more ruminated and withdrawn than open and outgoing. This aspect is particularly important because it is more explicative of the "apologetics of enmity": various movements are founded on a reception of Vatican II that is closer to the neo-Augustinian school than to the neo-Thomistic.[30] The "communitarian" development (in an experiential more than theoretical sense) of the latest generation of Catholic movements has a clearly negative take on modernity and modern freedoms. The very idea, formulated by Pope Benedict XVI, of the movements as "creative minorities" within a "minority" Church in the modern world posits a situation of *enmity* between Christianity and the modern world, an enmity created by modernity, to which Christianity responds defensively with the creation of a communitarian world aimed at establishing an identity-based, social, and affective support community in the face of adversity.

Second, from a historical perspective this distinctive group was awarded the dividend of the end of the short-lived Catholic dissent

---

[29] A recent survey of the movements is available in Agostino Favale, *Segni di vitalità nella chiesa. Movimenti e nuove comunità* (Rome: LAS, 2009).

[30] See Joseph A. Komonchak, "Augustine, Aquinas, or the Gospel *Sine Glossa*?," in *Unfinished Journey: The Church 40 Years after Vatican II; Essays for John Wilkins*, ed. Austin Ivereigh (New York and London: Continuum, 2005), 102–18.

saga without being affected (neither from an ideological nor a socio-logical point of view) by that debacle.[31] This development represented not only a rejection of European Catholic leftism but also a radical reversal of preconciliar and conciliar theology. If some Catholic movements approach politics by participating in the seasonal battles launched by bishops, a typical reaction of all movements is to run away from the intra-ecclesial debate. In this sense, it is easy to see how the term "movements" is at times used inaccurately. Weighing either the new Catholic movements' ecclesial praxis against the meaning of the term, or the new movements against the movements for litur-gical, biblical, ecumenical, and patristic reform of the first half of the twentieth century, the contribution of the "new movements of the *reconquista*" to the life of the Church is removed from the concept of movement as an element within the dialectic between "movement" and "institution."[32] Reversing the progress of twentieth-century theology that freed contemporary Catholicism from the stereotypes of *liberal* anti-Catholicism thanks also to an intra-ecclesial theological battle,[33] the theological culture of the movements of the *reconquista* refrains from any intra-ecclesial debate to engage instead in the apologetics of enmity between Church and world. On the one hand, there is a need on their part to distance themselves from the Catholic dissent style of the 1970s, as well as to protect the precarious existence of these newly formed ecclesial entities that are still essentially and by definition *extra legem* (outside canon law)—if not *contra legem* (against canon law). But on the other, which is far more important, there is the reception of the idea of the Church as a citadel besieged and attacked by external and internal enemies, an idea that breeds group solidarity and unity

[31] See Mario Cuminetti, *Il dissenso cattolico in Italia 1965–1980* (Milan: Rizzoli, 1983); Denis Pelletier, *Le crise catholique: religion, société, politique en France 1965–1978* (Paris: Payot, 2002); Daniela Saresella, *Cattolici a sinistra. Dal modernismo ai giorni nostri* (Rome-Bari: Laterza, 2011); Denis Pelletier, *A la gauche du Christ: Les chrétiens de gauche en France de 1945 à nos jours* (Paris: Seuil, 2012).

[32] See Étienne Fouilloux, "I movimenti di riforma nel pensiero cattolico del XIX e XX secolo," in Alberigo and Faggioli, *I movimenti nella storia del cristianesimo*, 659–76; for the United States, see James M. O'Toole, *The Faithful: A History of Catholics in America* (Cambridge, MA: Harvard University Press, 2008), esp. 144–265.

[33] See John McGreevy, *Catholicism and American Freedom: A History* (New York: W. W. Norton & Company, 2004), 189–215.

with the ecclesiastical hierarchy more than with other members of the Church or in the contemporary world.

In this sense, these movements, autonomously organized but very close to some of John Paul II's positions, between the mid-1970s and the 1980s, promoted themselves as the Catholic vanguard fighting (in the political and social spheres) against secularization and the legalization of divorce and abortion; but their fight was more symbolic and had little political impact. The rise of these movements coincided chronologically with the almost total disappearance from official Church teaching of Vatican II's message in favor of a "Church of the poor," and they spread in the wake of the repression of liberation and feminist Catholic theology starting from the mid-1980s.

Moreover, with the fourth postconciliar stage of the movements and starting from the early 1980s, the great diversity of the movements was brought into line with different (yet not conflicting) spiritual models, theological cultures, a particular ideological and political *Weltanschauung*, liturgical styles, forms of governance, and types of membership. Despite the obvious differences, mainly attributable to the initiators' personalities, the movements' fourth stage reveals some common features. Throughout John Paul II's and Benedict XVI's pontificates, we witnessed the substantial failure of the bishops' attempts to oversee certain aspects of the movements at the local level, such as the practice of eucharistic celebrations behind closed doors. Yet, supported by Rome, the movements could bypass the local bishops' authority. This phase is also marked by the failed attempt to bring about the unity, by means of the movements' statutes, of an extremely varied galaxy of movements. In any case, the ultimate tools for fostering the "apologetics of enmity" are precisely the movements of the *reconquista*, which feed on two sources.[34]

On the one hand, there are movements whose political ideology is antiliberal, antimodern and "apolitical." In these movements (such as Communion and Liberation) the culture has remained largely unreceptive to the link between conciliar Catholic culture and the antiauthoritarian, democratic, and progressive trends that in Western culture is typically associated with the 1960s. More than just a polemical critique

---

[34] See Piersandro Vanzan, "Elementi comuni e identificativi dell'attuale fenomeno movimentista intraecclesiale con cenni a rischi e speranze," in *Fedeli Associazioni Movimenti* (Milan: Glossa, 2002), 187–206.

of modernity tout court, the critique is directed toward "liberal" modernity and its influence on Catholicism.

On the other hand, there are movements with leader-centered and communitarian tendencies and a strong subcultural drive. These movements (the model being Opus Dei) call for the creation of new social spaces of confessionalization, whereas associations animated more by the "spirituality of the *reconquista*" and the "culture of presence" started to build new *ecclesial* spaces of confessionalization, aiming to increase their presence at the top of the Catholic Church (in the episcopal hierarchy, the Roman Curia, the leadership controlling the Holy See's political and media agenda). In these movements, the apologetics of enmity toward the modern world does not amount to a *contemptus mundi* (contempt of the world) but to the demonization of modernity aimed at the creation of a subculture.

5. Winners and Losers of the Apologetics of Enmity: The Bishops

These two models are different and opposite but also convergent, and both have a say in shaping a new type of Catholic elite. Today, the stakes are in favor of the movements' autonomy, which signals the defeat (not only symbolic) of a number of other players within the ecclesial body.

First, among the defeated are the bishops. Squeezed between the papacy on the one side and the ecclesial movements on the other, the episcopate is less able to act as agent of conciliar reception at a national or international level. In this context, the intra-ecclesial handling of the various sex abuse scandals (from the American cases to those in Europe, from 2001 onward) reveals a heterogenesis of purposes that has objectively strengthened the protagonists of the apologetics of enmity between the Church and the modern world. It also represented the final blow to a postconciliar episcopate ideologically redefined by John Paul II and his successor Benedict XVI and, for at least three decades, openly relegated to passive addressees of the pontifical magisterium.

Moreover, the episcopate and the episcopal conferences are continually overridden by a media-friendly papacy, and these same weakened bishops tend to chase after ecclesial movements as privileged interlocutors of the new militant Church. Thus, the transition from "the Catholic movement" to "the ecclesial movements" seems to foreshadow a structural transition in an ecclesiological sense as well. We are moving, with the new vanguards, from a Church led by the bishops and clergy toward a Church that is replacing the primeval model of pastoral ministry of bishops and priests (as pastors of local territorial churches) with the remote government of the pope (who represents the unique, indisputable, global point of confessional identity) and the direct guidance of the community leaders (whether they be of the laity or clergy, as long as it is someone whose authority comes from the base, or the community, and not directly from the Church's institutional apparatus). The immediate consequence is that within the new Catholic elites there is certainly a lower degree of cultural and political pluralism when compared to what is present in Churches with deep local roots. In the late nineteenth and early twentieth centuries, the Catholic hierarchy managed to stir and control the mobilization of the laity within a framework that did not put at risk the Church's traditional power structure. At present, we are witnessing instead a profound transformation of the legitimacy of foundations of the lay Catholic elites of the nineteenth and twentieth centuries thanks to Catholic movements, secularization, and the Church's mobilization efforts.

Given the unchanging mechanisms for the selection of bishops, which have officially remained almost the same since the Council of Trent (despite Vatican II and the first fifty years after Vatican II), the short-lived moment of self-representation and self-selection of the Catholic laity is already over. That Catholic laity as such has given way to the new selected members of the laity representative only of the associations or communities to which they belong. Their action is only apparently in support of the role of the laity at large; in reality, they represent a return to the past when weighed against the progress of the laity during the late twentieth century.[35] In this view, the proliferation of more centralized and leader-oriented movements represents a case of non-reception of the message of Vatican II, which had explicitly among its objectives a more decentralized Church.[36]

[35] See Sabine Demel, *Zur Verantwortung berufen. Nagelproben des Laienapostolats* (Freiburg-Basel-Wien: Herder, 2009).

[36] See Massimo Faggioli, *Il vescovo e il concilio. Modello episcopale e aggiornamento al Vaticano II* (Bologna: Il Mulino, 2005); Nicholas Lash, *Theology for Pilgrims* (Notre Dame, IN: University of Notre Dame Press, 2008), 234.

It is a fact that the new movements of the *reconquista* tend to promote themselves as the twentieth-century equivalent of the mendicant orders in the Middle Ages or the Jesuits in the Tridentine Church. Even if their self-promotion corresponded to the truth, it only proves the ecclesiological orientations of these new associations, which not only disregard the teachings of Vatican II but also tend to ignore its essential theological recentering of the Church-world relationship, on the one hand, and that of the local and universal Church, on the other. Despite the differences between single movements, their success is built at the expense of the ecclesiology of the local church and undermines the balance between the center and periphery in the contemporary Church. The new balance is instead based on a globalized ecclesiology, founded on the Roman papacy, combined with an apologetics of enmity between the Church and the modern world and a low awareness of the relationship between the collegial Church and the bishops' role in the universal and local Church.

6. Winners and Losers of the Apologetics of Enmity: The Clergy

The diocesan clergy and religious have been overshadowed by ecclesial movements both in terms of the mission *ad gentes* (to the nations) and in terms of contemporary Catholicism's emphasis on family and marriage. The spheres of action that until a few decades ago were in the hands of the episcopate, the clergy, the religious and monastic orders, and the Catholic nobility and notables are now managed by a new elite that largely stands out for its anonymous or unrecognizable theological position, or for its opposition-resistance to the teachings of the council and the postconciliar experiences of reception of new associative models within the Church. The action of this new elite, however, is likely to develop into a less collegial and more centralized Church. In the words of Montesquieu's *The Spirit of the Laws*: "The most natural intermediate and subordinate power is that of the nobility. The nobility, in a way, is of the same essence of monarchy, whose fundamental maxim is: *no monarch, no nobility; no nobility, no monarch*; or else, one has a despot."[37] To paraphrase, we could say

---

[37] "Le pouvoir intermédiaire subordonné le plus naturel, est celui de la noblesse. Elle entre, en quelque façon, dans l'essence de la monarchie, dont la maxime fondamentale est, *Point de monarque, point de noblesse; point de noblesse, point de*

that the Catholic Church was a monarchy (the papacy) supported by a nobility (the episcopate and the old elite of the associated laity). Today, thanks to the new ecclesial movements, the Catholic Church is trying to bypass the "nobility" and is supported by a new elite that rejects the work of renewal of the conciliar bishops and of the twentieth-century laity. The end of a Church governed by the bishops and clergy did not mark the beginning of a more participatory and synodal model of Church but has led instead to the adoption of a "communitarian" model in local churches, which has had deep repercussions in terms of theology of mission and Church-world relations.[38]

7. Winners and Losers of the Apologetics of Enmity: The "Lay Laity"

Among the losers of this phenomenon in the postconciliar Church is the unorganized, unaffiliated Catholic laity, whose loyalty to a local Church (usually translated into the percentage of Mass-goers) has no longer any relevance. The situation changes, however, when members of the unorganized laity join an association or ecclesial movement. This often becomes a form of marginalization for the "simple" faithful without the support of a Catholic association, especially when it prevents them from taking active part in the life of the local church.[39]

Finally, among the losers we also find the "liberal" Catholic culture (in the broadest sense), which sees the movements' victory as a postmodern revival of nineteenth-century Ultramontanism, turning Catholic culture into a new "Catholic ghetto," as the American-educated, Italian political scientist Nicola Matteucci clearly put it in 1970, when he identified Catholic movements, and their now disavowed offshoots, with the ultra-left: "One almost gets the impression that the ancient aversion of reactionary Catholicism to the state and

---

monarque; mais on a un despote." Montesquieu, *De l'esprit des lois:* book 2: Des lois qui dérivent directement de la nature du gouvernement. Chapter 4: Des lois dans leur rapport avec la nature du gouvernement monarchique.

[38] See Jacques Palard, "L'istitution catholique en recherches. L'acteur, le théologien et le sociologue," in *Le gouvernement de l'église catholique. Synodes et exercice du pouvoir* (Paris: Cerf, 1997), 7–57; Ghislain Lafont, *Imaginer l'église catholique* (Paris: Cerf, 1995).

[39] See Ciro García Fernández, "De la 'teología de los laicos' de Lumen gentium a los 'movimientos eclesiales' posconciliares," *Burgense* 48, no. 1 (2007): 45–82.

modern civilization, against liberalism and the middle class, long kept alive in Catholic organizations, is today re-exploding on the left, on the strength of revolutionary political ideas, while keeping intact the old traditionalist and clerical imprint."[40]

On the political-associative side, with the transition from the "Catholic movement" to "ecclesial movements" we witness the end of the formative experience of a Catholic political and social leadership that managed to free itself from the old notability and clerical supremacy and embrace systems of selection and succession of an assembly, or participatory, nature. With the new ecclesial movements this era is not only superseded but also denied and relegated to the archive of the conciliar era. The new Catholic movements have leaders but no decision-making meetings, appointments but no elections. Thus, in a Catholic Church still based on a pyramid structure, we witness the arrival on the scene of a new generation of *homines novi* (new men and women) largely disconnected from the decades of struggle of the organized Catholic laity to be recognized with a dignity that is proper to the layperson.

In addition, some of these new Catholics movements reproduce— in clear contrast with the Catholic culture that during the twentieth century developed its own thought about the state and its legitimacy— a vision of the state and government as usurper of the true supremacy, namely, that of Church over society. In the context of the nonprofit sector and solidarity economics, this perception breeds a type of activism that actually created, in recent decades, a culture of social service within contemporary Catholicism. This activism has a corresponding theological stance, however, which often shapes the formulation of the Catholic Church's social and economical doctrine. This aspect not only has an impact on the Church's vision on issues of social justice but is also accompanied by a preliberal, or antiliberal, vision of the state's and government's role in the management of welfare and the economy.[41] From a sociological perspective, both those in power in

---

[40] Nicola Matteucci, "La cultura politica italiana: fra l'insorgenza populista e l'età delle riforme," *Il Mulino* 19 (1970): 5–23 (republished in Nicola Matteucci, *Sul Sessantotto. Crisi del riformismo e "insorgenza populistica" nell'Italia degli anni Sessanta*, ed. Roberto Pertici [Soveria Mannelli: Rubbettino, 2008], 72).

[41] See *Religions and Philanthropy: Global Issues in Historical Perspective*, ed. Giuliana Gemelli (Bologna: Baskerville, 2007).

the Catholic Church, that is, the clergy and episcopate (whose authority is considered by the movements to be inferior to that of their own
leaders), and the "lay laity" (which after the brief parenthesis of Vatican
II has once again assumed a subdued and passive attitude) seem to have
been replaced in the local churches by an "ecclesial professionalism of
the laity" (to use more conventional terminology) and a "dictatorship
of volunteerism" (to paraphrase Karl Marx) in the social, political,
and economic spheres. It is a *dictatorship* because the old elite and
the previous mechanisms of accreditation and succession have been
swept away; and *vanguard* because the theology aiming to overcome
the secular, lay, and capitalist world is turned into mobilization. Further, it is a type of *professionalism* because it replaces and excludes that
section of the Catholic faithful whose lower social awareness and less
resolute concern to comply with the Church hierarchy prevents them
from sustaining the level of commitment and efficiency guaranteed
by the new ecclesial movements as the new "divisions of the Church."

8. The Movements of the *Reconquista* and Current *Loci Theologici*

It is difficult to escape, in the current ecclesial and theological
debate on the new ecclesial movements, both the triumphalism that
sees these new entities as the answer to the crisis of European Catholicism (especially in terms of attendance and participation) and
the conspiracy theories that consider this important phenomenon as
the new "fundamentalist" face of Catholicism, if not the "elite troops"
taking control of the Church's government in Rome. Both readings,
the apologetic and the conspirationist, are exaggerated with regard
to the ability of these movements to intervene in the course of the
postconciliar Church. But one aspect worth considering, in relation to
Ruggieri's remark made twenty years ago and mentioned earlier, is the
role played by some of these movements in promoting the "apologetics of enmity" in the postconciliar Church, as an attitude essentially
at odds with the message of Vatican II.

On the one hand, there is the question of the movements' development within the Church and in a direction that sees the crisis of
conciliar theology in standalone groups impervious, both ideologically
and existentially, to the rest of the ecclesial communion. This phenomenon is visible in the movements regardless of their theological
orientation, but it is all the more evident in those movements that

have programmatically rejected some fundamental elements of the theology of Vatican II.

If it is true that movements live the contradictions of the contemporary Church like the rest of the faithful, there is also no doubt that, in matters pertaining to some fundamental aspects of the conciliar redefinition of the relationship between Church and world, the movements of the *reconquista* remain in defensive, restorationist positions, especially with regard to the relations *ad extra*, of the Church with the larger world: globalization, ecumenism, interreligious dialogue, and religious freedom.[42] This resistance to conciliar innovation is grounded in the rejection of Vatican II, seen as a sort of "counter-syllabus"; it also tends to breathe new life into some of the fundamental theses of Pius IX's *Syllabus* of 1864 against the political and doctrinal errors of modernity.

But the most radical difference with the conciliar theology on the relationship between Church and world is the rejection of some of contemporary Christianity's current *loci theologici*: missionary expansion, pluralism of human civilization, ecumenical movement, and apostolate of the laity. Marie-Dominique Chenu's emphasis on the "signs of the times" (which ultimately had an impact on the pastoral constitution of Vatican II, *Gaudium et Spes*) is now sometimes completely reversed with a sentence of condemnation on the modern world based on a negative reading of those same signs. There are two cultural roots behind this pessimistic reading. On the one hand, there is the political culture of the founders of the new ecclesial movements, which generally is more intransigent and ecclesiologically traditionalist than conservative. On the other, there is a "radical" theology, which can be traced back to the seminal *Christ and Culture* by Helmut Richard Niebuhr, who defined five different types of Christian attitudes toward human culture: "Christ against culture, the Christ of culture, Christ above culture, Christ and culture in a relationship of paradox, and Christ as transformer of culture." In our case, the movements of the *reconquista* fall into the category of "Christ against culture." According to Niebuhr, what distinguishes this category is that "the radicals fail to

---

[42] See Massimo Faggioli, "Il Vaticano II come 'costituzione' e la 'recezione politica' del concilio," *Rassegna di Teologia* 50 (2009): 107–22.

recognize what they are doing, and continue to speak as though they were separated from the world."[43]

The most conservative wing of the ecclesial movements is defined precisely by a vision of the world marked by the apologetics of enmity, along lines not far from a certain neo-Augustinian tendency typical of the theological debate of the postconciliar period, a tendency that sets "church and world in a situation of rivals; it sees the world in a negative light; evil and sin abound in the world that the church should be always suspicious and distrustful of it. Any openness to the world would be 'naïve optimism.'"[44] In Avery Dulles' words, the neo-Augustinian tendency depicts "the Church as an island of grace in a world given over to sin."[45]

The difference between this neo-Augustinian reading of the post-conciliar situation and the ecclesiology experienced by many ecclesial movements lies in the interpretation of the Church as an "island of grace" as opposed to a world regarded as a victim of sin. The island of grace ceases to be—in the real experience of some ecclesial groups—the Church as such, becoming instead one's own community. In this perspective, the postconciliar ecclesial movements' revival of the apologetics of enmity is directed not only at the relationship between the Church and the modern world but also at the relationship between different Church identities, while undermining the conciliar Church's trust in being "a symbol of unity of history itself, and of the world," capable of creating "in the world and history metaphors of reconciliation."[46]

---

[43] Helmut Richard Niebuhr, *Christ and Culture* (New York: Harper & Row, 1951 [new edition HarperCollins, 2001]), 76.

[44] Ormond Rush, *Still Interpreting Vatican II: Some Hermeneutical Principles* (Mahwah, NJ: Paulist Press, 2004), 15.

[45] Avery Dulles, "The Reception of Vatican II at the Extraordinary Synod of 1985," in *The Reception of Vatican II*, ed. Giuseppe Alberigo, Jean-Pierre Jossua, and Joseph A. Komonchak (Washington, DC: Catholic University of America Press, 1987), 353.

[46] Giuseppe Ruggieri, *Chiesa e mondo*, republished as *Cristianesimo, chiese e Vangelo* (Bologna: Il Mulino, 2002), 332.

CHAPTER 11

Inclusion and Exclusion in the Ecclesiology of the New Catholic Movements

1. The New Catholic Movements' Ecclesiology

The central place of the new Catholic movements in the contemporary Catholic Church is beyond dispute, especially during and after the pontificate of John Paul II. By "new Catholic movements" I mean, of course, such institutions as Communion and Liberation, the Community of Sant' Egidio, Focolare, Neocatechumenal Way, Cursillos de Cristiandad, the Regnum Christi movement of the Legionaries of Christ, and others. But the history of the movements in twentieth-century Catholicism begins with the reform movements (biblical movements, liturgical movement, patristic renewal, ecumenical movement) that renewed Catholic theology and made possible the crucial changes of Vatican II.[1] These movements built much of the theology of Vatican II, but they were eventually absorbed by Vatican II: most of their protagonism and vitality in pre–Vatican II Catholicism was transformed (or, according to some, lost) during the implementation of the reforms of the council.[2]

It is difficult therefore to map out the genes of the pre–Vatican II theological movements and find those genes in the new Catholic

---

[1] On the history of the debate on Vatican II see Massimo Faggioli, *Vatican II: The Battle for Meaning* (Mahwah, NJ: Paulist Press, 2012).

[2] A fundamental difference exists between the "new Catholic movements" and the "basic ecclesial communities": see Richard R. Gaillardetz, *Ecclesiology for a Global Church: A People Called and Sent* (Maryknoll, NY: Orbis, 2008), 122–26.

movements. In the new Catholic movements whose date of birth predates Vatican II (such as Opus Dei and the Legionaries of Christ, both a product of the 1920s and 1930s), their rejection of the new impulses coming from the council is clear: for example, collegiality in the Church and Church reform, ecumenism, and interreligious dialogue.

For other movements, the issue of their conciliar identity is more complex and spread along a very wide spectrum of attitudes. (Enough here to say that Communion and Liberation and the Community of Sant' Egidio are on the two opposite extremes of this spectrum.) For still other movements (such as Focolare) the acceptance of the issues *ad extra* of Vatican II (ecumenism and interreligious dialogue) is not accompanied by the same enthusiasm in calling for more collegiality and structural reform in the Church. What is clear is the difference between the pre–Vatican II theological movements and the contemporary new Catholic movements: worldview, internal structure, ways to become a member and to leave the movement, and relationship between the movement and the ecclesiastical hierarchy.[3]

Sociologically the main difference is in the organizational principles of the two different movements: at the beginning of the twentieth century, the old reform movements were made of the theological elites of Catholicism, working mostly underground and trying to open the field to new ideas and involve the whole Church and the laity in embracing these new theological developments, in spite of or against the lack of official ecclesiastical approval for these ideas. With the new Catholic movements we have now *a new kind of movement* whose primary goal is not to "move" new ideas in the Church but to rally particular sections of the Church (ordained and laypeople together) around a charismatic founder and his or her message and/or around a particular issue (social, cultural, or otherwise) that defines the activity of the members, the number of members in the movement being crucial for their survival in the market of the contemporary Catholicism.

This need for strong visibility (particularly evident in events like the 1997 World Youth Day in Paris for the movement L'Emmanuel) is a result of the fact that the new Catholic movements were somehow given the task to replace, in the structure of the Church, the role

---

[3] See Massimo Faggioli, "Il movimentismo cattolico e l'«apologetica dell'inimicizia» nella chiesa post-conciliare," in *Tutto è grazia. In omaggio a Giuseppe Ruggieri*, ed. Alberto Melloni (Milano: Jaca Book, 2010), 441–56.

played by Catholic Action in the first half of the twentieth century. It is important to remember that until at least the 1980s the very survival of the Catholic movements within Catholicism was an important issue, nobody being sure about the "juridical grounds" on which the Catholic movements could survive at the end of the benevolence of one pope after his death (especially in the passage between Paul VI and John Paul II and between John Paul II and Benedict XVI).

Once the monopoly of Catholic Action on the laity in the Church was over, the market was divided between different brands competing for their share of Catholic laity—but now a very different kind of Catholic laity. If the pre–Vatican II laity belonging to Catholic Action had an immediate commitment to the parish priest and the bishop and only an indirect one with the pope in Rome, with the new Catholic movements the relationship between these different references changed direction: the pope has become the first and most important direct channel of identification with the Church.

In this sense, it is accurate to define the new Catholic movements as "postconciliar movements" and not as "conciliar movements," given the gap between the ecclesiology of the laity of Vatican II and the later developments—more faithful to a certain "spirit of Vatican II" than to its "letter."[4]

But it is certainly true that the new Catholic movements did not go, differently from the local churches and the unaffiliated Catholics in the Western hemisphere, through the uncertain and trying times of the post–Vatican II period—at least publicly.[5] The vertically structured and charismatic leader-driven structure preserved the new Catholic movements from the culture of "collegiality" in the Church—but with a price. The price the movements had to pay theologically was, in some cases, the refusal of the impulse of Vatican II for a new synthesis between tradition and modernity, being now the theological culture of some of the movements built *per oppositionem*, against modernity, theological and otherwise. For each and every one of the new Catholic movements it is clear, on the other hand, that the defining dimension

---

[4] See Massimo Faggioli, "Between Documents and Spirit: The Case of the 'New Catholic Movements,'" in *After Vatican II: Trajectories and Hermeneutics*, ed. James Heft and John W. O'Malley (Grand Rapids, MI: Eerdmans, 2012), 1–22.

[5] There is a serious lack of objective and independent studies on the new Catholic movements such as Opus Dei, Communion and Liberation, and the Legionaires.

is the refusal to update the institutional culture of the governance of Vatican II according to the ecclesiology of collegiality of Vatican II.

2. Antimodern *Weltanschauung* and Catholic *Weltanschauung*

In terms of worldviews, it can be said that the new Catholic movements are a product of 1968 more than of Vatican II.[6] That is to say that their worldviews reflect a variety of cultural and political elements that are not only theological.

A first element, quite new if compared with the culture of the origins of the Catholic movement in the early twentieth century, is the *centrality of the founder and/or leader of the movement*. The worldview of the founder is the worldview of the members of the movement, and the attitude of the movement toward inclusion or exclusion is driven by the word of the founder or his or her successor, usually elected in order to perpetuate the fidelity of the movement to the charism of the founder.

A second element, relevant for the issue of inclusion and exclusion, is the drive to rebuild Catholicism *around the sociological idea of "community"* more than on the theological concept of "communion."[7] This element is sustained, in many cases, by a negative worldview, in which the rejection of the Rahnerian term "world Church"[8] matches an idea of the world as inherently negative and threatening the Christian identity. It is clear that the inclusiveness of the "political theologies" of the early postconciliar period are no longer part of the theological identities of the new Catholic movements, their self-definition no longer being attached to any political reading of the historical-political reality of the world.[9]

[6] See Massimo Faggioli, "The New Elites of Italian Catholicism: 1968 and the New Catholic Movements," *The Catholic Historical Review* 98, no. 1 (January 2012): 18–40.

[7] The cultural relationship between new Catholic movements and "communitarism" are still to be explored.

[8] See Karl Rahner, "Basic Theological Interpretation of the Second Vatican Council," in *Concern for the Church* (New York: Crossroads, 1981), 77–90.

[9] The new Catholic movements fit the current trend of a Catholicism that has undermined "l'engagement politique au profit d'une revalorisation concurrentielle des pratiques chrétiennes de charité"; see Catherine Fino, "L'autorité des pratiques chrétiennes de la charité en contexte de pluralisme. L'impulsion de Vatican II et le

A third element relevant to the issue of inclusion and exclusion, and part of the *Weltanschauung* of the most important new Catholic movements imported from Spain, is a "spirituality of the *reconquista*" that drives these movements' indifference or hostility toward ecumenism, their marked clericalist identity, and their aggressive relationship with the local churches in which they operate.[10]

A fourth element of their theological culture, which can be seen as a perversion of *ressourcement*, is the conspicuous nostalgia for a premodern world or for a modernity tamed by ecclesiastical ideology, a sort of *regressus ad uterum*[11] that longs for a pure origin in the pre–Vatican II period, in the pre–French Revolution period, or in the Council of Trent—more rarely in the patristic era or in early Christianity, for theologically obvious reasons.[12] The material (if not formal) rejection of the liturgical reform by some of the new Catholic movements is nothing but a visible way to reject the ecclesiology of Vatican II, especially its *ressourcement* and *rapprochement*.[13]

These cultural-theological options reveal a basic "apologetics of enmity" that receives its theological justification from a fundamentally negative worldview.[14] It is interesting that the negative prejudice against the modern world also affects the new Catholic movements' perception of the universal dimension of contemporary Catholicism, which they see as theologically sustainable only if closely identified

---

travail à poursuivre," in *L'autorité et les autorités. L'herméneutique théologique de Vatican II*, ed. Gilles Routhier and Guy Jobin (Paris: Cerf, 2010), 211.

[10] For the history of the conversation about the Neocatechumenal Way between Rome and Japan, see Massimo Faggioli, "The Neocatechumenate and Communion in the Church," *Japan Mission Journal* 65, no. 1 (Spring 2011): 31–38. The Focolare movement and Sant'Egidio are two exceptions here.

[11] See Mircea Eliade, *Myth and Reality*, trans. Willard R. Trask (New York: Harper & Row, 1975); Shmuel Noah Eisenstadt, *Fundamentalism, Sectarianism, and Revolution: The Jacobin Dimension of Modernity* (Cambridge, UK, and New York: Cambridge University Press, 1999).

[12] For the "primitivist" mind-set in the theology of and after Vatican II, see Ormond Rush, *Still Interpreting Vatican II: Some Hermeneutical Principles* (Mahwah, NJ: Paulist Press, 2004), 69–85.

[13] See Massimo Faggioli, "*Sacrosanctum Concilium* and the Meaning of Vatican II," *Theological Studies* 71 (June 2010), 437–52.

[14] See Giuseppe Ruggieri, "Chiesa e mondo," in *Cristianesimo, chiese e vangelo* (Bologna: Il Mulino, 2002), 307–38.

with Roman identity, and therefore they judge it at grave risk when associated with "inculturation."

3. Membership and Relationship with the Ecclesiastical Institution

The presence of the new Catholic movements in the Church also has to be understood in light of their institutional behavior and the response of the institution (to which the movements should be "dialectical," at least from a semantic point of view). Their activism has provided contemporary Catholicism with an element of further centralization and "fragmentation" of the Church at a global level, creating a kind of new version of the old motto *duo genera christianorum* ("in the Church there are two different kinds of Christians"). Once the parting criterion was the belonging (or not) to the clerical order; now it is about belonging (or not) to a Catholic movement.

This new consequence coming from the existence of the new Catholic movements has been encouraged by a kind of "spoils system" adopted by the institutional Church when it comes to ecclesiastical appointments (especially bishops' appointments) and to the prominence given on the occasion of particular global Church events. The existence of the new Catholic movements provided the Catholic Church with a new kind of disciplined and organized laity, not at all willing to enter the stage with a distinct voice as laity, but available to present themselves as the "elite troops" of the papacy. The new Catholic movements's visibility, fidelity, and readiness to mobilize for the defense of the institution has proved difficult to beat in the last decades, especially since John Paul II's pontificate.

It is true that we deal here with visible and invisible movements, but the trend in the vast world of the new Catholic movements in the last two decades has been to give more emphasis to the visibility of and to receiving an official endorsement by Rome and less emphasis to the development of a real dynamic as a "movement in the Church-institution." The institutional dynamics of the life of the movements in the Church forced the movements to accept or to embrace the official doctrinal policies of the Church or of the pontificate, giving up the chance to develop a genuine theological identity. On the other side, weakened local churches often feel compelled to accept the offer (new members, seminarians, resources) coming from these thriving new Catholic movements.

In a way, the present danger of the development of the competition between movements in the Church, or between certain movements and bishops in a given area (like for Neocatechumenal Way in Asia), is that the movement become a recruiting tool for the new ruling elite in the Church—in some cases as an opposition of local church to the authority of the bishops. In this respect, John Paul II's definition of the new Catholic movements as "schools of communion" must be read as an encouragement more than as an actual description of their perception in the Church.[15]

All that has to be seen together with the recent tendency of the new Catholic movements to "clericalize" their structures and to build their own seminaries, separately from diocesan seminaries.[16] After John Paul II's attempt to appeal to the movements to use diocesan seminaries for the formation of their candidates to the priestly ministry (apostolic exhortation *Pastores Dabo Vobis*, 1992),[17] the trend of the last few years is to grant the movements the chance to build and run their own formation institutions.

4. The Impact of the Movements on the Issue of Inclusion and Exclusion

One of the reasons for the success of the new Catholic movements is the immediacy of the experience of Christian faith within that kind of Catholicism. But it is also a problematic connection between the praxis of this new kind of Catholic experience and its relationship with the Catholic Church at large—at the levels of the local and of the universal Church.

4.1. Inclusiveness in the Local Church

The new Catholic movements have made the Church more *plural* and less *pluralistic* at the same time. This can be seen in the local

---

[15] See Piero Coda, "Movimenti ecclesiali e chiesa in Italia. Spunti ecclesiologici," *Communio* 149 (September–October 1996): 64–73.

[16] See Jean Beyer, "Movimento ecclesiale (Motus ecclesialis)," in *Nuovo Dizionario di Diritto Canonico*, ed. Carlos Corral Salvador, Velasio De Paolis, Gianfranco Ghirlanda (Cinisello B.: Paoline, 1993), 707–12. See the example of the Redemptoris Mater seminaries of the Neocatechumenal Way. (The first one was founded in Rome in 1990.)

[17] See John Paul II, apostolic exhortation, *Pastores Dabo Vobis* (March 25, 1992), no. 68.

churches where the movements are more rooted and active. (The example of the United States is not as telling as some examples in secularized areas, like Western Europe, or in "mission countries" or former mission countries, like Japan and Southeast Asia.)

The epoch-making shift made possible by Vatican II from a hierarchical, institutional ecclesiology to one centered on *communio* implied a new pattern of relationship between pope, bishops, clergy, and laity, and between Rome and the local churches. At the local level, the new ecclesiology meant not only the resurgence of synods, provincial councils, and plenary councils, the need for which had been ignored for four centuries, but also the creation of a series of new councils and boards at the diocesan and parish levels. The goal of the creation of these new institutions for the governance of the Church was to *include* more of the Christian people and give way to some representation of the laity in modern Catholicism (even if this did not include features typical of liberal democracy like elections).[18]

According to Vatican II, these institutions were supposed to redress the balance of power within the local church, stressing the ordinary powers of bishops alongside the pope's extraordinary powers in the government of dioceses and enabling the participation of laity in the life of local churches, not just through liturgy and social action, but also through taking part in the theological reception of Vatican II. Vatican II invites the faithful to take part in the life of the local church as individuals and families building a community, that is, the local church at the parish level and at the diocesan level. Participation at this local level was encouraged for individual Catholics through liturgy, parish life, and evangelization.

This ongoing process has been influenced by some important and still little considered factors. On one side, the secularization and the new self-consciousness of the laity gave a considerable push to the weakening of the power of clergy and bishops. On the other side, the rise of the movements was not only a reaction against secularization along the lines of John Paul II's slogan of New Evangelization but also

---

[18] About this, see Massimo Faggioli, *Il vescovo e il concilio. Modello episcopale e aggiornamento al Vaticano II* (Bologna: Il Mulino, 2005); *Synod and Synodality: Theology, History, Canon Law and Ecumenism in New Contact*, ed. Alberto Melloni and Silvia Scatena (Münster: LIT, 2005); *Repraesentatio: Mapping a Keyword for Churches and Governance*, ed. Alberto Melloni and Massimo Faggioli (Berlin: LIT, 2006).

a reaction of the new laity as *parvenus* against the old elite within the Catholic Church—the old elite being formed on one side by the bishops (heirs of a European tradition in which being a bishop was a class symbol just like having land and real estate) and on the other side by the "old school" laity formed along the *théologie du laïcat* from the 1930s to the 1950s.[19] It is time to notice that this pivotal shift in the life of Catholicism had a fairly negative impact on "inclusion" at the local level. In the last three decades the practical ecclesiology of the movements has initiated the end of the "bishop- and clergy-led local church."

Even if one considers that the relative decline of bishops in the overall balance of Church power has a positive side, this situation is not immune from deep consequences, and not only for the sake of the ecclesiological tradition that sees in the episcopacy a necessary link to the *paradosis* of Christian faith.

The end—or crisis—of a "bishop- and clergy-led local church" has not been in the direction of a more participatory local church. Rather, the movements have replaced the inclusive model opened by Vatican II with a more leader-driven model of Christian community, where inner diversity is paradoxically far less present and less welcome than in the past. For example, in Italy, after the post–Vatican II wave of diocesan synods, the celebration of such events within the local churches has become very uncommon in the last twenty years. The need for debate between laity and clergy—so strongly felt in the 1960s and 1970s— has been replaced by the creation of strong, personal ties between ever weaker bishops and ever stronger leaders of the movements at the diocesan level. This partition of the local church is graphically represented in liturgies celebrated separately behind closed doors by different communities (especially the Neocatechumenate).

Within the movements, the need for free speech inside the public sphere of the Church—strongly represented by twenty centuries of local councils and synods, by the very example of Vatican II, and also

---

[19] For the historical ties between the episcopate, the clergy and the social elites in Europe, see Joseph Bergin, "L'Europe des Évêques au temps de la réforme catholique," *Bibliothèque de l'École des chartes* 154 (1996): 509–31; *Power Elites and State Building*, ed. Wolfgang Reinhard (Oxford: Clarendon Press, 1996); Christoph Weber, *Senatus divinus: Verborgene Strukturen im Kardinalskollegium der frühen Neuzeit (1500–1800)* (Frankfurt a.M.: Peter Lang, 1996).

by the late institutional and theological development of Catholic Action—is often dismissed as a concession to current social and political taste and is seen as jeopardizing their new Catholic way of living within the social community.[20]

This negative and pugnacious *Weltanschauung* has peculiar effects on the shape of the new movements. Given the emphasis on the coherence of the group and on its success in perpetuating itself in face of a world perceived as secularist and hostile, the spiritual needs of the less "employable" members of the community easily become marginal within both the movement and the local church, with obvious consequences on the inclusiveness of contemporary Catholicism.

Offered this new model of obedient and active Catholicism, local bishops rarely grasp the movements' long-term challenge to the "catholic" (in the sense of plural and inclusive) set-up of the local church. Driven by the need to fight back secularization at all costs, bishops and clergy tend to perceive the movements as "the real Church," as the ultimate asset for the counterattack against the crisis of authority of Catholicism, a crisis that they see related to its inclusive character. In this sense, the new Catholic movements provide the example of a new kind of Catholicism that is clustered in separate and noncommunicating cells—a Catholicism whose diversity is now much more limited than the diversity that could show up from a more representative look at the intellectual and spiritual identities of Catholicism.

The creation of networks of Catholic welfare and the protection of the vested interests attached to this volunteerism give the movements active in this area a political, economic, and moral power that few people dare to question with regard to its relations with the role of individual Christians in the Church and in society at large. The rest of the local church and the Catholics not active in the movements are left in a sort of a "dead zone" between this new, front-page Catholicism and the outer world. In a sense, the rise of the movements has re-created within the Catholic Church the medieval *duo genera christianorum* ("two types of Christian faithful"): a Church where the distinction between the power holders on one side and the subjects on the other side is crystal clear. The movements' founders and their successors

---

[20] See Massimo Faggioli, "Chiese locali ed ecclesiologia prima e dopo il concilio di Trento," in *Storia della Chiesa in Europa tra ordinamento politico-amministrativo e strutture ecclesiastiche*, ed. Luciano Vaccaro (Brescia: Morcelliana, 2005), 197–213.

are held up as examples of the new *ecclesia docens* over against a once again patronized lay Church supposed to be the *ecclesia discens*.

At the local and diocesan level, the important distinction is no longer between clerics and laypeople, but between movement-belonging Catholics (where the individualism of contemporary Western culture is accommodated through the creation of a variety of different movements for different tastes) and ordinary, "loose" Catholics (whose cultural, social, and moral subjectivity is considered the definitive victory of secularization over the old, comforting, yet gone "shepherd-leading-sheep Catholicism").[21]

The coexistence between the ecclesiological role of the local church and the "globalized character" of the new Catholic movements is still a building site, in part overlapping the theological debate of the early 2000s on the relationship between local church and universal Church. But it is clear that, if at the beginning the rise of the new Catholic movements was a direct accusation against the effectiveness of the pastoral life in the local churches, now their role in some local churches puts at risk the very life of a local church existing independently from the activity of a new Catholic movement. In some areas of the world there is an evident competition between the territorial Catholic Church and the Church of the movements: in this fight, the first casualty is inclusiveness and diversity in the Church.

Strange as it may seem, inclusiveness and diversity are much better protected in a Church that works under the leadership of a bishop willing to enact the procedures and governing bodies created by Vatican II—much better than in a Church led by movements whose procedures and governing bodies are part of the *arcana imperii*.[22]

---

[21] See Danielle Hervieu-Léger, *Le pèlerin et le converti. La religion en mouvement* (Paris: Flammarion, 1999).

[22] See Alberto Melloni, "Movimenti. De significatione verborum," *Concilium: "Movimenti" in the Church*, ed. Alberto Melloni (2003/3): 13–34; Jean Beyer, "De motu ecclesiali quaesita et dubia," *Periodica* 78 (1989): 437–52; Gianni Ambrosio, "Cammino ecclesiale e percorsi aggregativi," *La Scuola Cattolica* 116 (1988): 441–60; Agostino Favale, *Movimenti ecclesiali contemporanei. Dimensioni storiche, teologico-spirituali ed apostoliche*, 2nd ed. (Rome: LAS, 1982 [4th ed., 1991]); Piersandro Vanzan, "Elementi comuni e identificativi dell'attuale fenomeno movimentista intraecclesiale con cenni a rischi e speranze," in *Fedeli Associazioni Movimenti* (Milano: Glossa, 2002), 187–206.

4.2. The Impact at the Level of the Universal Church

At the universal level the effects of the new movements on inclusion within the Catholic Church are no less critical. One of the roots of the success of the movements is their embrace of the "ecclesiology of the universal Church" (pushed by Cardinal Ratzinger from the mid-1980s) and their rejection of the "ecclesiology of the local church." Besides all the elements that distinguish one movement from another, one key point constitutes the basic ecclesiology of most of them: the ideological acknowledgment of the pope as their only and real pastor, the *episcopus episcoporum* or *episcopus universalis*.

This "globalized ecclesiology," which acts as an undeclared disowning of Vatican II collegiality and goes far beyond Vatican I–style infallibility, is at the core of the new movements' identity. It has heavy implications for the issue of inclusion in the Church. The twentieth-century struggle to rediscover the ancient, patristic conciliar and synodal tradition in the Church has had a short life. The post–Vatican II, antimodern anguish embodied by the movements has contributed to the failure of the conciliar and synodal institutions in the Church and to the suppression of subsidiarity in the relations between Rome and the local churches in favor of a modernistic presidential style of leadership that is not traditional and not Catholic.

This latter element does not derive from the development of ecclesiology in the twentieth century, nor from the great ecclesiological tradition from the late second century on. Rather, it represents the appropriation of some features of antiliberal political culture by the Catholic Church in Europe. This "Jacobin attitude"[23] of the new elites within the Catholic Church explains the movements' refusal to address the most debated issues in the Church today (sexual ethics, inculturation, ecumenism, interreligious dialogue) and reflects their and their leaders' refusal to enter a theological debate not only about the Vatican's policies and their enforcement but also about the theological agenda of global Catholicism now.

Their increasingly important presence in the institutions of the Roman Curia and their effort to establish institutions for higher educa-

---

[23] See Shmuel N. Eisenstadt, *Fundamentalism, Sectarianism, and Revolution: The Jacobin Dimension of Modernity* (Cambridge, UK, and New York: Cambridge University Press, 1999).

tion in Rome tells much about their success in creating a "Roman nest," which is necessary in order to have a voice and a face inside the very heart of universal Catholic Church government. Some movements' apparently unlimited financial resources and the esteem in which they are held in the Catholic mainstream are creating inside the Vatican a fierce market of vocations. The most prestigious universities, such as the Gregorian, are now fighting with the new movements' academically anemic but politically stronger universities and seminaries, which educate priests for the movements' needs around the world.

Surprisingly, the ecclesiology of the movements embodies identity-driven papalism but at the same time embodies a more "horizontal" conception of the Church, as a community rich in charisms but with no intermediate level (episcopate, clergy, theologians) between the founder-leader (the pope) and the base (the individual faithful). In this respect, it is unlikely that the new European-based Catholic movements will contribute to the vitality of theological debate within a Church facing the intellectual challenges of bringing the Gospel to the contemporary world.

The institutionalization of the movements in the body of the Roman Church has come a long way. The juridical status of each of them differs. They represent the richness and the variety of the spiritual traditions within contemporary Catholicism, and in this sense they are a true manifestation of freedom. But it is a freedom that is given only to the members of the movements and comes at the expense not only of the old Church elites but also of the unorganized laity.

It is fair to say that the role the movements have acquired in the Catholic Church is not helping to foster debate within the Church but on the contrary is strengthening anti-intellectual sentiment and rebuffing calls for the freedom of individual, "unlabeled" Catholics within Catholicism.

5. A Setback for Inclusiveness in the Church?

There is no doubt that the phenomenon of the new Catholic movements represents a new face of the relations between the faithful and the ecclesiastical hierarchy. The blessing currently given by the papacy and the bishops to the new movements should not cause us to forget how at their beginning in the 1960s and 1970s, the founders and members of these movements struggled with the hierarchy in order to get permission to act as Catholics outside of the institutional and recognized Catholic lay associations. The new style of leadership, the lay identity of the leaders, their mission to reach out to a new society, and their early independence from clerical authority made for an uneasy relationship between the movements, the bishops, and the Vatican—at least until the mid-1970s. Carried on the wave of 1968 in Europe and America, the movements represented the long-waited chance (in Italy especially) for a revolutionary *prise de parole* inside the Catholic Church.

But this fight for freedom inside the Catholic Church, waged by the new movements *against* the institutional establishment and *for* a new model of organized Catholicism, soon turned into the slow but steady development of a new kind of "movement Catholicism," which has given this network of communities and movements the same kind of power in the Church that they questioned and fought against immediately after Vatican II. For the movements and for some of the members of the movements, freedom in the Church has expanded significantly. Since they are not under ecclesiastical surveillance anymore, their members enjoy considerable liberty in terms of self-government and independence from the institution, liturgical creativity, autonomy of pastoral projects, and social and economical entrepreneurship. On the other hand, the movements tend to form inner communities in order to maintain "spiritual warmth" and to meet their spiritual and material needs, causing a selection of the members on the basis of their capability to protect the group identity and to perform the group's mission.

The need for these movements to compete aggressively in the dynamic market of Catholic identities manifests itself with the call for an intense and high-cost activism in order to carry out the mission of the community inside the Church. This process comes frequently at the expense of the spiritual and intellectual freedom of the members, the diversity and the inclusiveness of their community. The selection of the members of these movements and communities involves not only the ideological and theological personality of the faithful but also their willingness to devote their entire life—family life, social relations, job opportunities, *Weltanschauung*—to the movement's mission. The very minor role of theological reflection in these communities and in the members' education reflects this attitude, as do the refusal to share the language of the old Catholic elites and the adoption instead of an idiom of social action, allegiance to the community, proud obedience to the pope and to the official teaching of the Church.

The rise of many of the new Catholic movements is a sign of the path "from the open Church to neo-exclusivism," as it has been accurately put by Gerard Mannion.[24] This lay mobilization of the Catholic Church for the *reconquista* of the contemporary world leaves little room for the exercise of freedom inside the movements. While the movements have enhanced the new media-friendly face of world Catholicism, their "community Catholicism" is quite different from "Catholicism as a communion." It is enacted in a Church made up of small communities highly committed to sharing their members' faith and to making their faith visible and effective, but also to silencing the voices that put in jeopardy the "ticket mentality."[25] Harmony becomes far more important than pluralism; obedience to the leader overrides spiritual freedom; a sound-bite theology replaces daily contact with the Bible and with theology as an intellectual effort to read the Gospel in the world as it is.

Vatican II is the council that introduced religious freedom as correlated both to human dignity and to the freedom of the Church. The council's ecclesiology opened the gates toward the future, toward a Church capable of addressing the issue of balance of power within itself and of solving the contradictions between its liturgical-communional identity and an overwhelmingly inherited institutional framework of the *Ancien Régime*.

After Vatican II the institutional framework has somehow changed, and the supremacy of bishops and clergy has been reduced, but this change did not create new balances and new room for freedom in the Church. After the shock of 1968, Catholicism seems to be more and more afraid of freedom in the Church. A major part of the new Catholic movements embodies reaction to this shock and a spirit of fear.

The rise of the new movements is leading to a Church that is effectively no longer run by bishops and clergy (as in Tridentine Catholicism) but that is not renewed by a participatory and theologically educated laity either (as the mid-twentieth century theology of the laity dreamed).

---

[24] See Gerard Mannion, *Ecclesiology and Postmodernity: Questions for the Church in Our Time* (Collegeville, MN: Liturgical Press, 2007), 43–74.

[25] See Theodore W. Adorno et al., *The Authoritarian Personality* (New York: Harper, 1950); Elias Canetti, *Masse und Macht* (Hamburg, 1960).

Rather we see a new alliance between a hyperactive papacy and a highly motivated and mobilized spectrum of movements strongly tied to the pope as the symbolic badge of theological orthodoxy. This could mean the precipitous end of Vatican II's attempt to reconcile Catholicism with the ancient tradition of councils and synods governing the Catholic Church on one side and with democratic, human rights–based and participative culture on the other side.

The movements' "political" option for an ecclesiology based almost exclusively on obedience to the pope and to the culture of their community, applied through an intense communitarianism that almost completely bypasses communion with the local churches (their bishops and parishes), has heavy implications for the issue of freedom and dialogue in the Church.[26] Accessibility and inclusion in the Church are witnesses to the accessibility of God, "the gate" (John 10:9). It is time to ask whether the accessibility of the Church has been increased by the new Catholic movements or if these new movements have introduced new filters for the accessibility of God.[27]

The new Catholic movements have gained a special legitimacy within Catholicism, one that seems above criticism—until the secrecy of their inner life becomes a problem for the public relations of world Catholicism. The mobilization brought about by the new Catholic movements in the Church offered, in the first decades of their rise, hospitality to a more diverse population of Catholics. Now, after the biblical forty years of their life in the Church have elapsed, it is time to ask ourselves some questions about the overall outcome of this new phenomenon from an ecclesiological point of view.

---

[26] See Bradford Hinze, *Practices of Dialogue in the Roman Catholic Church: Aims and Obstacles, Lessons and Laments* (New York and London: Continuum, 2006), esp. 238–67.

[27] See Jürgen Werbick, *Grundfragen der Ekklesiologie* (Freiburg i.B.: Herder, 2009), 243–46.

The Ecclesial Movements and Post–Vatican II Catholicism: An Assessment

1. Beyond the Apologetics on the New Catholic Movements

This book is not an indictment of the new Catholic movements. Rather, it is written by a historian and theologian trying to reconstruct a unified historical narrative of the Catholic movements that during the late twentieth century have spread throughout the world, with quite unique theological and sociological characteristics and with ecclesiological consequences that still need to be assessed. This is one of the reasons why the new Catholic movements are not only a European phenomenon and why this book is not only intended for Church historians and Catholic theologians.

There are two basic premises of this book. First, the new Catholic movements originated in Europe alongside and from within Catholic Action. Although the fortune of Catholic Action was different in the United States, it was crucial in other parts of the Catholic world, such as continental Western Europe, where it became the matrix of twentieth-century Catholic laity.[1] Pius XI's and Pius XII's strategic option for the presence of the Catholic Church in European states at the crossroads between nationalistic ideologies (Fascist Party in Italy, Nazism in Germany, National Catholicism in Spain) and the Communist threat

---

[1] See John W. O'Malley, *What Happened at Vatican II* (Cambridge, MA: Belknap Press of Harvard University Press, 2008), 229–30; and James O'Toole, *The Faithful: A History of Catholics in America* (Cambridge, MA: Belknap Press of Harvard University Press, 2008), 145–98.

(in Eastern Europe) was the creation of a "Catholic Action" founded on the roots of the late nineteenth-century "social Catholicism," but more closely controlled by the pope, the bishops, and the clergy in every single group and community. The "diaspora of Catholic Action" has affected Europe more directly than other continent, but the consequences will be no less visible in America and in other continents.

Second, the central position of the new Catholic movements in the contemporary Catholic Church needs to be addressed from the point of view of their historical origins and relationship with the Second Vatican Council. From an ecclesiological perspective and in order to understand the challenge to the "structure" of Catholicism today, we must remember that, according to Nicholas Lash, "there are, at present, few more urgent tasks facing the Church than that of realizing the as-yet-unrealized program of Vatican II by throwing into reverse the centralization of power which accrued during the twentieth century, and restoring episcopal authority to the episcopate."[2]

In this sense, Catholic movements play an important role in both the decentralization and centralization of Catholicism, which is still in its early stages. I am not nostalgic about the enthusiasm of the years of Vatican II (and not only for biographical reasons), but I am also convinced that the Catholic Church cannot afford to turn its back to the theology, and especially the ecclesiology, of Vatican II.

It is clear that the phenomenon of the movements is one from which the global Catholic Church cannot turn away: it is one of the prices to pay at the end of the Constantinian era and of the marriage between Church and state in the Western world. It is also clear that Catholic movements are not only very different from each other but even more so in different cultural and ecclesial contexts within the same groups. For instance, Communion and Liberation and the Community of Sant'Egidio in Italy are, to a certain extent, different from their North American counterparts, especially from the point of view of the relations between the leaders of these movements and the political world. And the same is true for other movements, which is a topic that would require another book. One of the key elements for understanding the importance of the movements today, however, is

[2] Nicholas Lash, *Theology for Pilgrims* (Notre Dame, IN: University of Notre Dame Press, 2008), 234.

precisely the complexity of an only apparently homogeneous globalized contemporary Catholicism.

The effort to understand the history and the true meaning of new
ecclesial movements is made more arduous by the fact that around this
theme there is a kind of taboo. It is a complex that drives those who
belong to the movements to talk about them mostly in enthusiastic
terms, with resulting repression of open issues, while inducing many
of those who do not engage in movements to talk about them in terms
of conspiracy and ultimately as the cause of many of the ills that afflict
the contemporary Church.

The history of the new Catholic movements is intimately intertwined with the history of modern papacy and the contemporary
Catholic Church. Inevitably, the more our reconstructions zoom in on
the present, the more difficult it is to unravel the knot and make sense
of the different statements, acts, positions, and theological-ideological
approaches that distinguish each single movement, group, or ecclesial
association. As a whole, however, the history of the movements has
followed a specific path, which we should try to summarize by focusing on its outcomes.

2. Continuity and Ruptures between Movement and Movements

If there is a certain continuity between the ideological-political
reading of the modern world by the first Catholic movement and the
political attitudes of the postconciliar Catholic movements, no less
important are the discontinuities and ruptures between the two.

After the Catholic "social movement" of the late nineteenth century, organized in several associations and groups engaged in social
issues, with Pius XI emerged the one-size-fits-all Catholic movement,
equally faithful to the pope and the bishops but without the mandate to
get involved in the socio-economic arena. In the 1920s, the supremacy
of Catholic Action arose in connection with an effort on the part of
the Holy See to protect the laity from the threat of the authoritarian
regimes, while protecting itself from the autonomy of a laity that risked
destabilizing alliances with political powers.

The supremacy of Catholic Action came to an end between the end
of the Second World War and the Second Vatican Council, when the
socio-political conditions for the existence of the Church in Western

democracies changed and when the theology of the laity began to address the issue of the dignity—not only socio-political, but also theological—of the "people of God." From Catholic Action in the 1960s and 1970s there was an outpouring and blossoming of Catholic movements, characterized by a variety of associative models, types of membership, reference cultures, and fields of action. The Catholic Church of John Paul II did not attempt to suppress this variety but rather attempted to regulate and support, recognize and encourage. By doing so, John Paul II played a fundamental role in the shift from a Church founded on the authority of the bishops to a Church in which the episcopate must begin to come to terms with the power of a "new laity" allied to a new "hypertrophic" and media-friendly papacy.

While the ecclesial associations born before the Second World War kept their approach aimed at the *reconquista* of the modern world and the creation of new confessional spaces, the majority of the community-movements emerging during and after Vatican II stemmed from religious experiences that did not have urgent theological, philosophical, or political demands to be put on the agenda of the global Church. But all of these new ecclesial entities have reshaped the face of Catholicism and its impact on European society. Being in contact with different social and political scenarios has further diversified the movements' development in different geographical areas. Latin America has seen the success of the base Christian communities, which in Europe have always remained marginal. The phenomenology of "parallel churches" instead, taken by the ecclesial movements in secularized Europe, did not have the same impact in other parts of the world where Catholicism is still firmly grounded in dioceses and parishes and is only indirectly affected by these new associations. On the other hand, Catholicism in North America, where there has never been a history of the "throne-altar" alliance, but rather a close connection with the Protestant and evangelical culture, has always been much more movement-oriented than European Catholicism.[3]

---

[3] For more on the situation in the United States, see Vincent Gragnani, "A Symphony of Church Life," *America Magazine* (August 14, 2006); Renée M. LaReau, "Super Catholics? Sizing Up the New Lay Movements," *U.S. Catholic* (February 2006): 12–17.

3. Catholic Movements and the European Political Arena

The recent "religion and politics" type of studies on the new leading role of religion in world politics tends to consider the phenomenon of the movements as a novelty of the last thirty to forty years. But the Catholic movement of the late nineteenth century had already come to light for socio-political purposes, and not to pursue an agenda of reform of the Church or in response to the maturation of a particular theological, liturgical, or spiritual sensitivity. Only in the twentieth century did Catholic movements take on a more "ecclesial" character, yet without completely losing their original genetic code.

Therefore, the history of Catholic movements should be understood as part of the narrative of the attempt of the European Catholic Church to react to the shock of the loss of its temporal power in Italy and on the entire continent at the end of the *Ancien Régime*. Defeated on the international political scene with the loss of the Papal States between 1861 and 1870, the Catholic Church at the First Vatican Council proclaimed the dogma of papal infallibility and then chose the "social" path through which the Catholic laity, under the leadership of the pope and bishops, was asked to restore the supremacy of the Catholic Church. Later on, the Catholic movement born in the late nineteenth century as a programmatically antiliberal and antidemocratic entity gained in the period following the First World War a certain political autonomy and became open to an anti-Bolshevik, anticommunist, moderate democracy. At that point, the Catholic socio-political movements found themselves caught between the emergence of totalitarian and authoritarian regimes in Europe and the primacy of the Holy See, which chose to deal directly with dictators, thus silencing the voice of Catholics involved in politics.

Although the more intellectual currents of the Catholic movements for ecumenical, liturgical, biblical, and patristic reform were still alive but under the radar, between the 1930s and the 1950s the Catholic movements organized under the banner of Catholic Action were still interconnected and unified in their obedience to the bishops and the pope. They were also engaged in animating the activity of the laity in the Church and following the political and doctrinal directions of the ecclesiastical hierarchy.

At that same time, however, the countries where the "clash of civilizations" had been stronger between Catholicism and the socialist and national-liberal political cultures (as in Spain and Mexico) and where the bishops were left almost without Rome's protection, thus more vulnerable to the anticlerical political forces, saw the rise of new ecclesial movements and associations (such as Opus Dei and the Legionaires of Christ). These new movements were all inspired by the culture of the *reconquista* and were undoubtedly the strongest, most lucid, and most reliable political cultures in the history of the Catholic movements of the first half of the twentieth century.

From a political point of view, the "progressive" label attributed in the 1970s to a part of the Catholic postconciliar movements has proven to be for many a disappointed hope and, in any case, a misunderstanding. From a theological and institutional perspective, the event of Vatican II made life easier for the movements that already existed and for those emerging shortly thereafter. From a theological and political perspective, however, Catholic movements have remained largely unreceptive to the connection between the conciliar Catholic culture and the anti-authoritarian, democratic, and progressive currents that Western culture associates with the "1960s." Hence, in order to grasp the movements' public dimension, the recurring analyses of the political tendencies of Catholic movements should begin with the pontificates of the late nineteenth and early twentieth centuries, and from the papal *non expedit* addressed to Catholics engaged in politics ("it is not expedient" for Catholics to participate in politics), rather than from the period of Vatican II and the political categories of right and left.

The dichotomy between "culture of presence" and "culture of mediation"[4] well captures the ecclesial movements' political tendencies in that it reflects a more general vision of the relationship between Christianity and history, without dwelling on fleeting alliances and similarities between Catholic movements and political alignments. Consequently, the rejection of socio-political (environmentalist, pacifist, Christian socialist) readings of the Gospel—readings so much in vogue in the 1960s and 1970s—was, between the pontificates of John Paul II and Benedict XVI, not an involutional turn but a return to Catholic movement's true theological-political origins.

---

[4] See Italo Mancini, *Tornino i volti* (Genova: Marietti, 1988).

There is no doubt that in recent history the preferences of the majority of Catholic movements have gone to different groups and political parties of the conservative right. But we should first and foremost emphasize the conscious instrumentality and transient nature of these convergences and then point to the fact that in non-European scenarios (like the United States) Catholic movements are not inclined to be absorbed by the "religious right"—as it has at times been feared in Europe—not only because of certain "issues," but also because there is a fundamental gap between the theological cultures of the two phenomena.

Despite the accusations of sectarianism and inflexibility, even from a political standpoint the movements have shown a certain "modern" trait, and even though they refuse the progressive utopias of emancipation and social or individual change, they do not reject the technological and organizational aspects of modernity. Far from being naive, ecclesial movements know how to make use of politics. For instance, Communion and Liberation in Italy, on the basis of its pre-liberal and antiliberal political culture, in the early years decided to support the socialist Bettino Craxi, then the media mogul Silvio Berlusconi, and now it is left without clear political reference points at the end of Berlusconi's twenty-year era.

4. Between Secularization and the End of Confessionalization

The visible rise of the new ecclesial movements is often interpreted as a sign of the Catholic Church's regaining power against modernity and politics. In light of the history of contemporary movements, which emerged thanks to the protection of the Roman papacy at the very moment of its greatest crisis at the end of the nineteenth century, we should resist this triumphalist reading. Then, as now, the zenith of the power of the papacy *over* the Church (ratified at Vatican I) coincided with a substantial loss of power of the papacy and the Church *over* European society; the solution was to send on the ground an organized Catholic laity closely controlled by the pope and bishops.

This moment marked the progress of secularization (in sociological terms) and de-confessionalization (in theological-political terms) that caused a revival of Catholic movements in Europe. The prolongation of this historical moment and the corresponding social and political weakness of the Church in Europe helped to strengthen the "weapon" of the movements in the hands of the leadership of world Catholicism. The power of the contemporary ecclesial movements is therefore equivalent to denouncing not only the prolongation of an uncomfortable situation for the Church but also the immutability of the socio-historical reading of the situation by the papacy. In other words, the new ecclesial movements can be identified as a Catholic alternative version of the "social" conversion experienced by the Protestant and Reformed churches of northern Europe and Scandinavia, which in those countries have become at the social level an organic resource of the welfare state.[5]

But within the Catholic Church this acceleration of the social protagonism of the papacy in defense against secularism has also led to a transformation of the forces of this lay protagonism. The need to "count" the number of members in the Catholic Church of the lay movements, in order to reassure the institutional Church (and the political factions leaning on it), has led to the identity crisis of the clergy and bishops, on the one hand, and the unorganized laity, on the other.[6] In particular, the transition from "Catholic movement" to "ecclesial movements" seems to foreshadow the transition from a Church led by the bishops and clergy to a Church that replaces the traditional model of the pastoral ministry of bishops and priests (the pastors of the local churches) with the government of a *remote* pope (who represents the unique, indisputable, global point of confessional identity) and with the *direct* guidance of the community leaders (whether they be of the laity or clergy, but one who enjoys legitimacy from the base, from their communities, and not directly from the institutional mechanisms of the Church).

The revitalization of the laity in the Catholic Church seems in many cases only the fictitious ransom of a laity that actually has became more clerical in its attitude and worldviews. The "theology of the laity" of the 1940s and 1950s, intended to form baptized Christians with their own autonomy within the Catholic Church and society, has penetrated only in small doses in contemporary Catholic movements,

---

[5] See *Welfare and Religion in 21st Century Europe*, ed. Anders Bäckstrom, Grace Davie, Ninna Edgardh, and Per Pettersson, 2 vols. (Farnham, UK: Ashgate, 2010 and 2011).

[6] See Massimo Faggioli, *Il vescovo e il concilio. Modello episcopale e aggiornamento al Vaticano II* (Bologna: Il Mulino, 2005).

if only because the "theology of the laity" was linked to a "theology of earthly realities" (Gustave Thils, Marie-Dominique Chenu, Yves Congar) adjacent to socio-political readings that are not part of the cultural heritage of the ecclesial movements that prospered in John Paul II and Benedict XVI's Church.

The new international Catholic movements are today closer to the "ecclesiology of the papacy," coeval with their birth at the end of the nineteenth century, than to the "theology of the laity" of the mid-twentieth century. In the life of many movements, the importance of the papacy (the "papalist identity" typical of the Catholic reaction to modernity) is so significant that it can "Catholicize" a "low" ecclesiology—an ecclesiology that does not look to the priesthood and the episcopate as defining elements of the conception of the Church, but the ecclesiology of the new Catholic movements is also a "communitarian" one, equally removed from the ecclesiology of the undivided Church as well as from the great tradition of Catholic ecclesiology, and close instead to other Christian movements of the Anglo-Saxon world. The contemporary Catholic movements, however, are among the few that in the European Catholic Church live and convey a visible message of hope, linked to the creation of a subset of communities and groups within the broader, and less enthusiastic, Catholic body.

But if the Catholic movement's goal was the "*reconquista* of the territory," at this stage and from a social perspective the movements, which recruit members only from within the Church and not from outside, seem implicitly to have failed their mission. The communitarian model that animates many of the Catholic movements makes them look not like bearers of the New Evangelization but rather like the expression of a Catholicism of migration and diaspora in a place—Europe—that they consider foreign and hostile. It remains to be seen what kind of reading of American cultural and religious identity the new Catholic movements active in this part of the world Church will have.

The experience of the ecclesial movements has helped change the public image of Catholicism, which, rather than "communion," seems to be moving on a different path (and, in the long run, one full of legal and political implications) of "community." This might even entail a higher intensity of the experience of faith, of its sharing and "effectiveness," but at the risk of conformism (what Theodore Adorno called "ticket mentality," which also explains the unreceptive side of some of these movements with regard to ecumenical and interreligious dialogue) typical of social realities where the pursuit of harmony prevails over pluralism.[7] In some cases, the phenomenon of the movements in the Church may endorse a tendency toward silent (coerced?) consensus rather than openness toward both people and issues considered problematic by the Church magisterium, or the social context with which the community-movements mostly interact; in the words of Bradford Hinze, "excluded people, taboo topics."[8]

The tendency to exclusivism results in the difficulty for the movements to recognize not only the unaffiliated Catholic laity but also other ecclesial movements. It is not yet clear how the recurring world congresses of Catholic movements and the World Youth Days have changed this situation. If it is true that there is a certain *plurality* in the Church thanks to the movements and the diversity among them, and if it is true that every movement is home to different trends, experiences, and attitudes, nonetheless, we should ask to what extent space for *pluralism* is actually possible within single movements, especially in light of the dynamics, which in the movements are idiosyncratic, of the relationship between generational issues, the role of the leader-founder, and loyalty to the Church authority. On the other hand, the experience of the new Catholic movements outside Europe, where the reality of the parish is different, often shows that there is greater diversity (social, ethnic, cultural) in them than in local parishes. In many cities of the United States, parishes can be far more ethnically and economically uniform because of the increasing cultural polarization, which is also reflected in the geographical boundaries of the parish, and in these cases the new Catholic movements offer a more inclusive model of Church.[9]

5. Conciliar and Anticonciliar Legacies

Among the critics of the ecclesial movements, the defenders of the culture of Vatican II are very vocal, as if between the movements

---

[7] See Theodore W. Adorno et al., *The Authoritarian Personality* (New York: Harper, 1950).

[8] Bradford Hinze, *Practices of Dialogue in the Roman Catholic Church: Aims and Obstacles, Lessons and Laments* (New York and London: Continuum, 2006), 238–67, quotation at 246.

[9] See Bill Bishop with Robert G. Cushing, *The Big Sort: Why the Clustering of Like-Minded America Is Tearing Us Apart* (Boston: Houghton Mifflin, 2008).

and the council there is a contradiction in terms. But both the link between Vatican II and the "spring of the movements" and the antagonism between the two events trivialize the complexity of the relationship between the Catholic Church and the experience of Vatican II. This trivialization is similar to the observation made by some that the movements are "the fruit of Vatican II," thus inferring that the council is the cradle of a new and discontinuous element in the history of the Church while indirectly supporting a "hermeneutic of separation" that is generally imputed to the theological and historiographical culture of the conciliar type.

The reference to Vatican II as the source behind the explosion of charisms within the movements is especially present in the "multi-vocational communities" that gather together single, married, widowed, and divorced laypeople as well as priests, religious, seminarians, and deacons. During the second half of the twentieth century, which for the Catholic Church coincided with the crisis of consecrated life, the movements appear sometimes to have taken the traits of a "pseudo-consecrated life," where the communities are the result of strong vocations, but at the same time are more institutionally flexible than the vocational paths of ordained ministries, and where the acceptable (and sometimes obligatory) vows are more temporary and revocable.[10]

But above all, the movements consider themselves to be the heirs of Vatican II because, as movements, they have lived through a post-conciliar period different from that experienced by the unorganized laity. This postconciliar experience has certainly been more uncertain in terms of the institutional and juridical rights of the movements in the Catholic Church (at least until John Paul II) but theologically less fickle and troubled because it is more tied to the figure of a leader, or to the practice of obedience to the institution, which during the postconciliar period was certainly not among the most evident and practiced virtues by the movements.

Contrary to the local churches (parishes and dioceses), the movements have not experienced the crisis of theology that originated

---

[10] See Ian Ker, "The Priesthood and the New Ecclesial Movements," *Louvain Studies* 30 (2005): 124–36; Gianfranco Ghirlanda, "Movimenti ecclesiali e istituti di vita consecrata nella chiesa e nella società di oggi," *Periodica* 101 (2012): 7–65; Ciro Mezzogori, *Vocazione sacerdotale e incardinazione nei movimenti ecclesiali. Una questione aperta* (Roma: Pontificia Università Gregoriana, 2012).

with Vatican II, the decline of the teaching authority of the bishops and clergy, and the redefinition of the parish pastoral praxis, which are all destabilizing phenomena typical of the postconciliar period. In the movements of the "self-taught theologians," it is no coincidence that bishops and theologians play the role of patrons, sponsors, and representatives to the ecclesiastical institution but do not have an influence on the general guidelines set by the founders and preserved by their successors (in the very few cases where there has been a real succession and not a simulated one). Many of the initiators were teachers and professors at the time of the "foundation"; almost all of them became teachers after founding their communities and movements, thus shaping a "Church of the new teachers," which was not in the intentions of those who wished to overcome the ancient dualism between "teaching Church" and "learning Church."

Within the long history of the new Catholic movements, the Second Vatican Council represents only a brief moment in history; within their foundational narratives, it is a particularly significant moment (positive or negative, depending on the cases). But for many it was a circumscribed and isolated event and overshadowed by their pre-existing genetic code. Some actually have taken from Vatican II the basis for openness and *rapprochement*—either explicitly, as in the case of the Community of Sant'Egidio with its focus on the emergencies of poverty, AIDS, and ecumenical and interreligious dialogue,[11] or in a more mediated manner, as in the case of the Focolare movement with its "path of dialogue" in the Church, between movements, including other churches, Judaism, and other religions.[12] The majority of the other groups place themselves "on the other side," that is, before Vatican II, either because they emerged before the council, thus remaining "preconciliar" (Opus Dei, the Legionaries of Christ), or because they grew and developed during the conciliar and postconciliar period on existential, associative, and ideological premises (such as Communion and Liberation in Italy) that have gone from an intransigent culture to the radicalism of the student culture of the 1960s, and finally to a rejection of the conciliar culture as a rejection of the force of historicity in the Church.

[11] See Robert Calderisi, *Earthly Mission: The Catholic Church and World Development* (New Haven, CT, and London: Yale University Press, 2013), 227–30.

[12] See Roberto Catalano, *Spiritualità di comunione e dialogo interreligioso. L'esperienza di Chiara Lubich e del Movimento dei Focolari* (Rome: Città Nuova, 2010).

If Vatican II was for most of the movements more a parenthesis in their history than a foundational event, John Paul II's pontificate represented instead a watershed moment, but more in terms of the ecclesial movements' legal recognition and existence in the institutional Church than of content proposed by the movements. The unreceptive character of many of the Catholic movements to ecumenical and interreligious dialogue as well as solidarity with the Jews should therefore be interpreted not only as a rejection of the teachings of Vatican II, but also as a failed (or still incomplete) reception of some of the specific directives of John Paul II's pontificate, during which the movements passed their "entrance examinations." Hence, the persistence of an "intransigent" core in most of the movements puts into question the impact of Pope John Paul II's teachings, in both words and deeds. Observing the movements, we are left with the impression that the "personalization" of the papacy meant focusing all the attention exclusively on the person of the pope, to the point that a part of these new associations feel connected to the grateful memory of the "pope of the movements" but are disconnected from the most prophetic and *ad extra* part of his legacy. On the other hand, one of the effects of the "Romanization" of the movements in the last twenty years has meant that the Church has lost much of the ecumenical potential in its relationship with the Protestant world.

While the intent of Vatican II was to pursue a program of *aggiornamento*, if not a "synthesis," with modernity in order to be able to communicate again to the world, the movements seem to be at ease in a Church that has started again to create divisions, between Church and world, the Catholic Church and other churches, Christianity and other religions, seeing the Church as the "little flock." In this perspective, there are no "conciliar movements," only "preconciliar" or "anticonciliar" movements and "postconciliar" movements (which become "single-issue groups" when they focus on one essential theme of Vatican II, such as ecumenism, interreligious dialogue, peace, and so forth). To a certain extent, it is one aspect of the complex relationship between movements and Vatican II, which goes beyond the simple reference in the theology of Vatican II to the *theological* movements as the "missing in action" of twentieth-century Christianity.[13]

---

[13] See *La théologie catholique entre intransigeance et renouveau. La réception des mouvements préconciliaires à Vatican II*, ed. Philippe J. Roy, Gilles Routhier, and Karim Schelkens (Leuven: Bibliothèque de la Revue d'Histoire Ecclésiastique, 2011).

The *nouvelle théologie* of the mid-twentieth century, which was an important source for the movements for patristic, liturgical, ecumenical, and biblical reform, was entirely dedicated to providing Vatican II with themes but without being able to give life to its own recognized and legitimate movements in the years after Vatican II. The interest in biblical scholarship, the theology of the fathers of the Church, and the traditions of the Christian East has remained very strong in the new French ecclesial communities, but it is only marginal in Italy and mostly absent in the Spanish-speaking movements. Conversely, the lack of rootedness of the charismatics in Italy and France and the development in America of the Catholic evangelical movements is one of the facts confirming the distance between the European culture of Latin Catholicism and the religious culture in North America. In the English-speaking world outside the orbit of Catholicism, the fragmentation of the historic churches in America (the Evangelical Lutheran Church in America and the Anglican Communion) around issues of gender and homosexuality is pushing groups and factions to organize themselves into movements. In this sense, it will be interesting to follow its development in order to trace parallels and differences with the Catholic experience of the movements.

6. Between Revanchism in the World and Redemption in the Church

One of the most important aspects in the history of the movements is their shift from the margins of the ecclesial structure to the center of attention and consideration of the pope and bishops during the pontificates of the postconciliar period. Some groups and movements, who claim to be (among others) the true inheritors of the progressive conciliar culture, were never able to follow in the same path and still live at the extreme periphery (barely visible, but very crowded) of Catholicism. These movements are marginal to the mainstream of contemporary Catholicism, orphans of a strong theological culture reference (given the crisis of conciliar theology), faithful to a reform agenda more and more dialectic with regard to the doctrinal and ecclesiastical policies pursued by the papacy.[14]

---

[14] Among these are the following: Comunità cristiane di base italiane, Noi siamo Chiesa–Wir sind Kirche, Catholics for Free Choice (CFFC), Catholics for a Changing

Along with a certain political-theological vision of the world and dreams of a *revanche du Catholicisme* (comeback of Catholicism), in the praxis and self-representation of ecclesial movements more loyal to the Holy See there is now a certain awareness of redemption in a Catholic Church that for a long time, in the first decade of the postconciliar period, feared, marginalized, and scrutinized them— before promoting them *en bloc.* More than the conviction to reaffirm the division of God's people in the *duo genera christianorum* (clergy and movements on one side and unorganized laity on the other), it is the memory of their suffering that is at the root of the current self-awareness and conviction on the part of these movements that only they represent the "real" Catholic laity.

The success of this trajectory of the movements within Catholicism is at the heart of the accusations made by numerous critics and observers against this new type of laity, accused of attempting to climb the ecclesial ladder and take the place of, or alongside, the traditional holders of power in the Church. Compared with the laity of the movements, the "anonymous" laity represented by individuals, families, and parishes has been unable to face the competition and comparison, not only with regard to orthodoxy and orthopraxy (on which there is a certain leniency toward the movements on the part of the Vatican), but in terms of proclaimed loyalty to the pope, ostentatious obedience, mobilization capacity, effectiveness on the social front, and management of visibility.

If it is true that the momentum given by the movements to the ecclesial praxis goes against the aspirations of a greater collegiality and dialogue in the Church, it is equally true that these are accusations launched in large part by those who over the last thirty years have been "defeated" by the new "winning" laity in terms of mobilization. At the core of the movements' success there is a dramatic transformation of the foundation of legitimacy of the lay Catholic elites of the nineteenth and twentieth centuries—against the immutability of the mechanisms for the selection of bishops, which have remained almost the same in the last five centuries, since the Council of Trent.

Church (UK), Partenia 2000, Demain l'Église, Femme et hommes en Église, Fraternité Agapé, Equipe National et d'Animation des Communautés de Base, Initiativgruppe "Fur eine lebendigere kirche." See also *Katholische Reformbewegungen Weltweit,* ed. Susanne Preglau-Hämmerle (Innsbruck-Wien: Tyrolia, 2012).

7. A Difficult Symbiosis

The theories of "conspiracy" or "ascent to the top" of the Catholic Church ladder regarding the movements tend to underestimate the great variety and complexity of this ecclesial galaxy, both internally and in terms of different geographical areas. Diverse in their place and date of birth; membership type, size, and rootedness; mission within the Church; and theological orientation, the new ecclesial movements within Catholicism occupy all possible positions of the broad political spectrum. The ecumenism of the international summits and the "neo-Orientalism" of the Community of Sant'Egidio are opposed to the "Romanism" of the Spanish-speaking movements like Opus Dei and the Legionaries of Christ; the interreligious inclusivism of the Focolare movement is at the opposite end of the exclusivist stance of other groups; and the participatory and democratic culture of the Catholic Scout Associations is far from the elitist and para-masonic mentality of Opus Dei.

Further, the movements live in a difficult symbiosis among themselves; to return to the effective image chosen by then-Cardinal Ratzinger, they live in somewhat chaotic "dwelling places within the one house."[15] If it is an exaggeration to paint a grim picture of a flock of natural enemies in a precarious state of symbiosis, it is not too radical to define the overall picture as one marked by a difficult coexistence, a mind-set of competition, and an ongoing search for balance:

> The movement-associations characterized by a high degree of institutionalization and autonomy from the Church hierarchy (Catholic Action, Catholic Scout Associations)

> The *revanche* movements linked to a political/religious antiliberal and anticommunist culture (Opus Dei, Communion and Liberation, the Legionaries of Christ, Cursillos de Cristianidad)

> The movements of a spiritual-charismatic type (Renewal in the Spirit, the Neocatechumenal Way, the Focolare movement)

> The "lay" and monastic spiritual elites, heirs of Vatican II's *ressourcement* and *rapprochement*, that is, the "return to the sources" of the great tradition of Christianity, and the undivided

[15] See chapter 8, p. 139.

rapprochement with other churches and with the men and women of our time (Community of Bose, Community of Sant'Egidio, Taizé)

A second, more difficult symbiosis is the one between the movements in general, on the one hand, and the local churches (clergy and laity), on the other. In biology, the symbiotic live together, both taking advantage of their co-existence yet suffering a disadvantage by the crisis and the weakness of the other subject of the interaction. It is still not clear whether this is the case regarding the relationship between movements and local churches. It is evident, however, that during the postconciliar decades the movements emerged and developed as an opportunistic phenomenon when faced with the debilitation of the body of the "local churches."

In the face of a "warm" faith lived experientially in communities and movements of one's choice, local churches (parishes and dioceses) are at risk of becoming more and more a sort of "cold" sacramental vending machine: the distribution of the sacrament could no longer correspond to the idea of belonging to a parish community, a parish catechesis, a human and social reality inevitably more varied and more real than that of the small community-movement of one's choice. From the perspective of vocations and ministry, the "lay laity" (which after the brief parenthesis of Vatican II has assumed once again a subdued and passive attitude) and the clergy (whose authority is considered by the movements to be inferior to that of their own leaders) seem to have been replaced in the local churches with a "dictatorship of volunteerism" (to paraphrase Karl Marx), or an "ecclesial professionalism of the laity" (to use a more conventional terminology). In other words, membership in Catholic movements sometimes requires a professionalism that replaces and excludes that section of the Catholic faithful, whose lower social awareness values and less resolute concern to comply with the Church hierarchy, prevents them from sustaining the level of commitment and efficiency guaranteed by the new "divisions of the Church." For this reason, the movements' impact on the body of the Catholic Church is much higher than the relative numerical strength of this new type of laity.

In the late nineteenth and early twentieth centuries the Catholic hierarchy managed to stir and control the mobilization of the laity within a framework that did not put at risk the traditional power structure of the Church. The historical role of the ecclesial movements during the second half of the twentieth century consisted in interpreting (even at an ideological level), translating (into reality, well before the ecclesiastical recognition), and representing (more at an existential than theological level) a solution to the problem of living and bearing witness to the Catholic faith in a society like that of Europe, in the critical transition from a rooted confessional heritage to a radical secularization. The strong self-importance of this new elite is the source of the allegations leveled against the movements of trying to take over the top positions inside the Church that until a few decades ago were in the hands of the episcopate, the clergy, the religious orders, and the Catholic aristocracy. From the "we are the Church" of the conciliar theology of the laity, it seems that with the Church of John Paul II and Benedict XVI we have come to the movements that sometimes seems to say: "The Church is us."

The rise of the new ecclesial movements means undoubtedly a new wave of energy in the Catholic Church and new possibilities for lay Catholics to express spiritual gifts and ministerial roles in ways that were simply not thinkable only two generations ago. But the movements have also produced in these last few decades, after Vatican II, a kind of "big sort" of Catholicism, the fragmentation of Catholics in homogeneous communities. This implies also fewer occasions for the "people of God" to experience their faith with other Catholics coming from different social backgrounds, leading different lifestyles, and with different theological and spiritual inclinations. In this sense, the new movements are also the symptom of the dissolution of the "Constantinian Church" but also a reaction against some optimistic predictions about the compatibility of Catholicism and modernity: the new visibility of Catholic traditionalism (gathered around the pre–Vatican II Latin Mass and around an apparatus of symbols representing an antimodern Catholicism) is part of the rise of the new ecclesial movements.

These movements are a complex phenomenon that shapes the Church now more than before: not only members of the movements and Church leaders but also scholars of Catholicism need to understand it, because the new ecclesial movements play a key role for the future of Catholicism as a global community on all continents. The ongoing reset of the relationship between the bishop of Rome, the universal Church, and the local churches will also have an impact on all the ecclesial movements. If the passage of the pontificate between John Paul II and Benedict XVI in 2005 was not in any way a moment of change in the history of Catholic ecclesiology, the conclave of March 2013 and the election of Francis clearly marked a new beginning. The pontificate of Francis represents the possibility of an updating of the ecclesiology of the Catholic Church, for the Church of Vatican II that Karl Rahner called, right at the end of the council, *Weltkirche*, a world Church.[16] From this perspective, the role of the movements takes on even greater importance for global Catholicism, and it would be a mistake to think that the phenomenon of the new ecclesial movements concerns only the members of the movements or only the members of the Catholic Church.

[16] About Pope Francis and Catholic ecclesiology, see Massimo Faggioli, *Papa Francesco e la Chiesa-mondo* (Rome: Armando, 2014); English translation: *Pope Francis: Tradition in Translation* (New York: Paulist Press, forthcoming).

Bibliography

Sociology of Christianity and New Movements

Appleby, Scott R., and Emmanuel Sivan. *Strong Religion: The Rise of Fundamentalisms around the World*. Chicago: University of Chicago Press, 2003.

Casanova, José. *Public Religions in the Modern World*. Chicago: University of Chicago Press, 1994.

Davie, Grace. *Religion in Britain since 1945: Believing without Belonging*. Oxford, Cambridge MA: Blackwell, 1994.

Dawson, Lorne L. *Comprehending Cults: The Sociology of New Religious Movements*. Toronto and New York: Oxford University Press Canada, 1998 (2nd ed., 2006).

Giammanco, Roberto, ed. *Ai quattro angoli del fondamentalismo. Movimenti politico-religiosi nella loro tradizione, epifania, protesta, regressione*. Scandicci, Florence: La Nuova Italia, 1993.

Hervieu-Léger, Danièle. *Vers un nouveau christianisme? Introduction à la sociologie du christianisme occidental*. Paris: Cerf, 1986.

————. *Le pèlerin et le converti. La religion en mouvement*. Paris: Flammarion, 1999.

Kepel, Gilles. *La Revanche de Dieu. Chrétiens, juifs et musulmans à la reconquête du monde*. Paris: Seuil, 1991 (*The Revenge of God: The Resurgence of Islam, Christianity, and Judaism in the Modern World*, translated by Alan Braley [University Park: Pennsylvania State University Press, 1994]).

Rusconi, Gian Enrico, and Chiara Saraceno. *Ideologia religiosa e conflitto sociale*. Bari: De Donato, 1970.

Origins of the Catholic Movement

Alberigo, Giuseppe, ed. *History of Vatican II*, 5 vols. English edition edited by Joseph A. Komonchak. Maryknoll, NY: Orbis, 1995–2006.

Congar, Yves. *Jalons pour une théologie du laïcat.* Paris: Cerf, 1954. English translation by Donald Attwater. Westminster, MD: Newman Press, 1957.

De Rosa, Gabriele. *Storia del movimento cattolico in Italia.* Bari: Laterza, 1966.

Dianich, Severino. "L'ecclesiologia in Italia dal Vaticano I al Vaticano II." In *Dizionario storico del movimento cattolico in Italia, 1860–1980,* 3 vols., edited by Francesco Traniello and Giorgio Campanini, vol. 1/1, 162–80. Genova: Marietti, 1981.

Minvielle, Bernard. *L'apostolat des laïcs à la veille du Concile (1949–1959). Histoire des congrès mondiaux de 1951 et 1957.* Fribourg (Suisse): Editions Universitaires Fribourg, 2001.

Moro, Renato. *La formazione della classe dirigente cattolica (1929–1937).* Bologna: Il Mulino, 1979.

O'Malley, John W. *What Happened at Vatican II.* Cambridge, MA: Belknap Press of Harvard University Press, 2008.

Rosart, Françoise, and Guy Zelis, eds. *Le monde catholique et la question sociale (1891–1950).* Bruxelles: Vie ouvrière, 1992.

Steinmaus-Pollak, Angelika. *Das als katholische Aktion organisierte Laienapostolat: Geschichte seiner Theorie und seiner kirchenrechtlichen Praxis in Deutschland.* Würzburg: Echter, 1988.

Traniello, Francesco, and Giorgio Campanini, eds. *Dizionario storico del movimento cattolico in Italia, 1860–1980,* 3 vols. Casale Monferrato and Genova: Marietti, 1980–1995. (in *Aggiornamento 1980–1995.* Genova: Marietti, 1997).

Tranvouez, Yvon. *Catholiques d'abord: approches du mouvement catholique en France (XIXe–XXe siècle).* Paris: Editions Ouvrières, 1988.

Overview of the New Catholic Movements

La bellezza di essere cristiani. I movimenti nella Chiesa. Vatican City: Libreria Editrice Vaticana, 2007.

Camisasca, Massimo, and Maurizio Vitali, eds. *I movimenti della Chiesa negli anni Ottanta.* Milan: Jaca Book, 1982.

Castellano Cervera, Jesús. *Carismi per il terzo millennio. I movimenti ecclesiali e le nuove comunità.* Rome: OCD, 2001.

Favale, Agostino, ed. *Movimenti ecclesiali contemporanei. Dimensioni storiche, teologico-spirituali ed apostoliche.* Rome: LAS, 1980 (4th ed., 1991).

Giolo, Antonio, and Brunetto Salvarani. *I cattolici sono tutti uguali? Una mappa dei movimenti della Chiesa.* Genova: Marietti, 1992.

González Fernández, Fidel. *I movimenti. Dalla Chiesa degli apostoli a oggi.* Milan: Rizzoli, 2000.

Hayes, Michael A., ed. *New Religious Movements in the Catholic Church.* London and New York: Continuum, 2005.

Landron, Olivier. *Les Communautés nouvelles. Nouveaux visages du catholicisme français.* Paris: Cerf, 2004.

Leahy, Brendan. *Ecclesial Movements and Communities: Origins, Significance, and Issues.* Hyde Park, NY: New City Press, 2011.

I movimenti nella chiesa. Atti del II colloquio internazionale. Vocazione e missione dei laici nella chiesa oggi. Milan: Nuovo Mondo, 1987.

Movements in the Church, edited by the Pontifical Council for the Laity. Vatican City: Libreria Editrice Vaticana, 1999.

I Movimenti ecclesiali nella sollecitudine pastorale dei Vescovi, edited by the Pontifical Council for the Laity. Vatican City: Libreria Editrice Vaticana, 2000.

Porteous, Julian. *New Wine and Fresh Skins: Ecclesial Movements in the Church.* Leominster: Gracewing, 2010.

Preglau-Hämmerle, Susanne, ed. *Katholische Reformbewegungen Weltweit.* Innsbruck-Wien: Tyrolia, 2012.

Sauer, Joseph, ed. *Lebenswege des Glaubens: Berichte über Mönchtum heute, Gemeinschaften Charles de Foucaulds, Fokolar-Bewegung, Gemeinschaften christlichen Lebens, Schönstatt-Bewegung, Équipes Notre-Dame.* Freiburg i.B.: Herder, 1978.

Secondin, Bruno. *I nuovi protagonisti, movimenti, associazioni, gruppi nella Chiesa.* Cinisello B.: San Paolo, 1991.

———. *Segni di profezia nella Chiesa. Comunità, gruppi, movimenti.* Milan: O.R., 1987.

Theology and Canon Law of the New Catholic Movements

Beyer, Jean. "I movimenti ecclesiali." *Vita consacrata* 23 (1987): 143–56.

———. "Movimento ecclesiale (Motus ecclesialis)." In *Nuovo Dizionario di Diritto Canonico*, edited by Carlos Corral Salvador, Velasio De Paolis, and Gianfranco Ghirlanda, 707–12. Cinisello B.: San Paolo, 1993.

Corecco, Eugenio. "Profili istituzionali dei movimenti nella Chiesa." In *Ius et Communio. Scritti di diritto canonico*, edited by Eugenio Corecco, vol. 2, 143–74. Casale M.: Facoltà di Teologia di Lugano, 1997.

Etxeberría, Juan José. "Los movimentos eclesiales en los albores del siglo XXI." *Revista Española de Derecho Canonico* 58 (2001): 577–616.

Fedeli Associazioni Movimenti. XVIII Incontro di Studio (2–6 luglio 2001), edited by Gruppo Italiano di Docenti di Diritto Canonico. Milan: Glossa, 2002.

Gerosa, Luciano. "Carismi e movimenti ecclesiali. Una sfida per la canonistica postconciliare." *Periodica* 82, no. 3 (1993): 411–30.

Zadra, Barbara. *I movimenti ecclesiali e i loro statuti*. Rome: Pontificia Università Gregoriana, 1997.

Studies of the New Movements

Ambrosio, Gianni. "Cammino ecclesiale e percorsi aggregative." *La Scuola Cattolica* 116 (1988): 441–60.

Angelini, Giuseppe. "I 'movimenti' e l'immagine storica della chiesa. Istruzione di un problema pastorale." *La Scuola Cattolica* 116 (1988): 530–57.

Brambilla, Franco Giulio. "Le aggregazioni ecclesiali nei documenti del magistero dal concilio fino ad oggi." *La Scuola Cattolica* 116 (1988): 461–511.

Coda, Piero. "Movimenti ecclesiali e chiesa in Italia. Spunti ecclesiologici." *Communio* 149 (September–October 1996): 64–73.

Dianich, Severino. "Le nuove comunità e la 'grande chiesa': un problema ecclesiologico." *La Scuola Cattolica* 116 (1988): 512–29.

Faggioli, Massimo. *Nello spirito del concilio. Movimenti ecclesiali e recezione del Vaticano II*. Milano: San Paolo, 2013.

———. "Between Documents and the Spirit: The Case of the New Catholic Movements." In *After Vatican II: Trajectories and Hermeneutics*, edited by James L. Heft with John O'Malley, 1–22. Grand Rapids, MI, and Cambridge, UK: Eerdmans, 2012.

———. "Tra chiesa territoriale e chiese personali. I movimenti ecclesiali nel post-concilio Vaticano II." In *I movimenti nella storia del cristianesimo. Caratteristiche—variazioni—continuità*, ed. Giuseppe Alberigo and Massimo Faggioli, *Cristianesimo nella Storia* 24, no. 3 (2003): 677–704.

———. "I movimenti cattolici internazionali nel post-concilio. Il caso della recezione del Vaticano II in Italia." In *Da Montini a Martini. Il Vaticano II a Milano. I. Le figure*, edited by Gilles Routhier, Luca Bressan, and Luciano Vaccaro, 455–71. Brescia: Morcelliana 2012.

———. "The New Elites of Italian Catholicism: 1968 and the New Catholic Movements." *The Catholic Historical Review* 98, no. 1 (January 2012): 18–40.

Forte, Bruno. "Associazioni, movimenti e missione nella chiesa locale." *Il Regno-documenti* 29, no. 1 (1983): 29–34.

Fouilloux, Étienne. "I movimenti di riforma nel pensiero cattolica del XIX e XX secolo." In *I movimenti nella storia del cristianesimo. Caratteristiche—variazioni—continuità*, ed. Giuseppe Alberigo and Massimo Faggioli, *Cristianesimo nella Storia* 24, no. 3 (2003): 659–76.

Hanna, Tony. *New Ecclesial Movements*. New York: Alba House; Staten Island, NY: Society of St. Paul, 2006.

Hinze, Bradford. *Practices of Dialogue in the Roman Catholic Church: Aims and Obstacles, Lessons and Laments*. New York and London: Continuum, 2006.

Lehmann, Karl. "I nuovi movimenti ecclesiali." *Il Regno—Documenti* 1 (1987): 27–31.

Melloni, Alberto. "Movimenti. De significatione verborum." In *Concilium: "Movimenti" in the Church*, ed. Alberto Melloni (2003/3): 13–35.

Ratzinger, Joseph / Benedict XVI. *New Outpouring of the Spirit: Movements in the Church*. San Francisco: Ignatius Press, 2007.

Sartore, Domenico. "Nuove forme di aggregazione nella chiesa. Tra il particolare e l'universale." *Rivista liturgica* 84, no. 6 (1997): 841–51.

Toniolo, Alessandro. "Nostalgia delle origini: profezia o anarchia celebrativa?" *Rivista liturgica* 84, no. 6 (1997): 787–812.

Catholic Action

Casella, Mario. *L'Azione Cattolica nell'Italia contemporanea: 1919–1969*. Rome, AVE, 1992.

———. *L'Azione cattolica del Novecento. Aspetti, momenti, interpretazioni, personaggi*. Rome: AVE, 2003.

De Marco, Vittorio. *Storia dell'Azione Cattolica negli anni Settanta*. Rome: Città Nuova, 2007.

Ferrari, Liliana. *L'Azione Cattolica in Italia dalle origini al pontificato di Paolo VI*. Brescia: Queriniana, 1982.

———. *Una storia dell'Azione cattolica. Gli ordinamenti statutari da Pio XI a Pio XII*. Genova: Marietti, 1989.

Formigoni, Guido. *L'Azione Cattolica Italiana*. Milan: Ancora, 1988.

Preziosi, Ernesto. *Obbedienti in piedi. La vicenda dell'Azione Cattolica in Italia*. Turin: SEI, 1996.

The Catholic Worker Movement

Ellsberg, Robert, ed. *The Duty of Delight: The Diaries of Dorothy Day*. Milwaukee, WI: Marquette University Press, 2008.

———, ed. *All the Way to Heaven: The Selected Letters of Dorothy Day*. Milwaukee, WI: Marquette University Press, 2010.

Hehir, Bryan J., ed. *Catholic Charities USA: 100 Years at the Intersection of Charity and Justice*. Collegeville, MN: Liturgical Press, 2010.

McKanan, Dan. *The Catholic Worker after Dorothy: Practicing the Works of Mercy in a New Generation*. Collegeville, MN: Liturgical Press, 2008.

Post–Vatican II Catholic Dissent

Cuminetti, Mario. *Il dissenso cattolico in Italia, 1965–1980*. Milan: Rizzoli, 1983.

Horn, Gerd-Rainer. *The Spirit of '68: Rebellion in Western Europe and North America, 1956–1976*. Oxford and New York: Oxford University Press, 2007.

Pelletier, Denis. *À la gauche du Christ. Les chrétiens de gauche en France de 1945 à nos jours*. Paris: Seuil, 2012.

Saresella, Daniela. *Dal Concilio alla contestazione. Riviste cattoliche negli anni del cambiamento, 1958–1968*. Brescia: Morcelliana, 2005.

———. *Cattolici a sinistra. Dal modernismo ai giorni nostri*. Rome-Bari: Laterza, 2011.

Communion and Liberation

Abbruzzese, Salvatore. *Comunione e Liberazione. Identité catholique et disqualification du monde*. Paris: Cerf, 1989.

Bianchi, Sandro, and Angelo Turchini, eds. *Gli estremisti di centro: il neo-integralismo cattolico degli anni '70. Comunione e liberazione*. Rimini-Florence, 1975.

Camisasca, Massimo. *Comunione e Liberazione. Le origini (1954–1968)*. Cinisello B.: San Paolo, 2001.

———. *Comunione e Liberazione. La ripresa (1969–1976)*. Cinisello B.: San Paolo, 2003.

———. *Comunione e Liberazione. Il riconoscimento (1976–1984). Appendice 1985–2005*. Cinisello B.: San Paolo, 2006.

Dadder, Anke M. *Comunione e Liberazione. Phänomenologie einer neuen geistlichen Bewegung*. Konstanz: UVK, 2002.

The Charismatic Movement

Maino, Paolo. *Il post-moderno nella Chiesa? Il Rinnovamento carismatico*. Cinisello B.: San Paolo, 2004.

Panciera, Mario. *Il Rinnovamento nello spirito in Italia: una realtà ecclesiale*. Rome: RnS, 1992.

Sullivan, Francis A. *Charisms and Charismatic Renewal: A Biblical and Theological Study*. Ann Arbor, MI: Servant Books, 1982; Eugene, OR: Wipf and Stock, 2004.

Zimmerling, Peter. *Die charismatischen Bewegungen. Theologie—Spiritualität —Anstöße zum Gespräch*. Göttingen: Vandenhoeck & Ruprecht, 2001.

The Focolare Movement

Fondi, Enzo M., and Michele Zanzucchi. *Un popolo nato dal Vangelo. Chiara Lubich e i Focolari*. Cinisello B.: San Paolo, 2003.

Hegge, Christoph. *Rezeption und Charisma. Der theologische und rechtliche Beitrag Kirchlicher Bewegungen zur Rezeption des Zweiten Vatikanische Konzils*. Würzburg: Echter, 1999.

———. *Il Vaticano II e i movimenti ecclesiali. Una recezione carismatica*. Rome: Città Nuova, 2001.

Lubich, Chiara, and Igino Giordani. *"Erano i tempi di guerra . . ." Agli albori dell'ideale dell'unità*. Rome: Città Nuova, 2007.

Masters, Thomas, and Amy Uelmen. *Focolare: Living a Spirituality of Unity in the United States*. Hyde Park, NY: New City Press, 2011.

Robertson, Edwin. *The Fire of Love: A Life of Igino Giordani, 'Foco,' 1894–1980*. London: New City, 1989.

The Cursillos de Cristianidad

Bonnín, Eduardo. *Historia de un carisma*. Madrid: Libroslibres, 2003.

Matas Pastor, Joan Josep. "Origen y desarrollo de los Cursillos de Cristianidad (1949–1975)." *Hispania sacra* 52, no. 106 (2000): 719–42.

Nabhan-Warren, Kristy. *The Cursillo Movement in America: Catholics, Protestants, and Fourth-Day Spirituality*. Chapel Hill: University of North Carolina Press, 2013.

The Neocatechumenal Way

Argüello, Kiko. "Le comunità neocatecumenali." *Rivista di vita spirituale* 2 (1975).

Anuth, Bernhard Sven. *Der Neokatechumenale Weg: Geschichte, Erscheinungsbild, Rechtscharakter*. Würzburg: Echter, 2006.

———. "L'istituzionalizzazione del Cammino neocatecumenale." *Il Regno— Documenti* 9 (2013): 296–320.

Blazquez, Ricardo. *Le comunità neocatecumenali. Discernimento teologico*. Edited by E. Pasotti. Cinisello B.: San Paolo, 1995.

Sorci, Pietro. "Ermeneutica della Parola nel cammino neocatecumenale." *Rivista liturgica* 84, no. 6 (1997): 867–80.

The Schönstatt Movement

Brantzen, Hubertus, ed. *Schönstatt-Lexikon: Fakten—Ideen—Leben*. Vallendar: Patris Verl., 1996.

Klein, Josef Maria. *Albert Eise: aus der Gründungszeit der Schönstatt-Bewegung*. Vallendar: Patris Verl., 1995.

Monnerjahn, Engelbert. *Pater Joseph Kentenich. Ein Leben für die Kirche*. Vallendar: Patris Verl., 1975 (English translation: *Joseph Kentenich: A Life for the Church*. Cape Town: Schoenstatt Publications, 1985).

The Catholic Scout Associations

Ardigò, Achille, Costantino Cipolla, and Stefano Martelli. *Scouts oggi*. Rome: Borla, 1989.

Cheroutre, Marie-Thérèse. *Le Scoutisme au féminin. Les Guides de France, 1923–1998*. Paris: Cerf, 2002.

Dal Toso, Paola. *Nascita e diffusione dell'ASCI 1916–1928*. Milan: Angeli, 2007.

Guérin, Christian. *L'utopie Scouts de France. Histoire d'une identité collective, catholique et sociale 1920–1995*. Paris: Fayard, 1997.

Laneyrie, Philippe. *Les Scouts de France. L'évolution du Mouvement des origines aux annés 80*. Paris: Cerf, 1985.

Schirripa, Vincenzo. *Giovani sulla frontiera. Guide e Scout cattolici nell'Italia repubblicana (1943–1974)*. Rome: Studium, 2006.

Sica, Mario. *Storia dello scautismo in Italia*. Florence: La Nuova Italia, 1973 (4th ed., Rome: Fiordaliso, 2006).

The Community of Sant'Egidio

Oschwald, Hanspeter. *Bibel, Mystik und Politik. Die Gemeinschaft Sant'Egidio*. Freiburg i.B.: Herder, 1998.

Riccardi, Andrea. *Sant'Egidio, Rome et le monde*. Entretiens avec Jean-Dominic Durand et Régis Ladous. Paris: Beauchesne, 1996 (Italian edition: *Sant'Egidio, Roma e il mondo*. Colloquio con Jean-Dominique Durand e Régis Ladous. Cinisello B.: San Paolo, 1997).

The Neo-Monastic Communities

Brico, Rex. *Frère Roger et Taizé. Una primavera nella chiesa*. Brescia: Morcelliana, 1982.

Favale, Agostino. *Comunità nuove nella Chiesa*. Padova: Messaggero, 2003.

Gutiérrez, Anastasio. *Cristiani senza sconto. Anatomia di un gruppo ecclesiale*. Rome: Pontificia Università Lateranense, 1980 (2nd ed., Rome: Gruppo Laico Seguimi, 2001).

Majocchi, Paola, and Vittoria Prisciandaro. *In cordata. La storia del gruppo Seguimi*. Padova: Messaggero, 2005.

Spink, Kathryn. *Una vita di comunione. Jean Vanier e l'Arca*. Cinisello B.: San Paolo, 2007.

Torcivia, Mario. *Guida alle nuove comunità monastiche italiane*. Casale M.: Piemme, 2001.

———. *Il segno di Bose*. Casale M.: Piemme, 2003.

Vanier, Jean. *Nuovi movimenti. Sette cristiane o segni dello Spirito*. Casale M.: Piemme, 1999.

The "We Are the Church" Movement

Katholische Reformbewegungen weltweit. Ein Überblick. Edited by Susanne Preglau-Hämmerle. Innsbruck/Wien: Tyrolia, 2012.
Noi siamo Chiesa. Un appello dal popolo di Dio: più democrazia nella chiesa. Turin: Claudiana, 1996.
Reihe der Plattform "Wir sind Kirche." 6 vols. Thaur: Kulturverl., 1995–99.

Opus Dei

Allen, John, Jr. *Opus Dei: An Objective Look behind the Myths and Reality of the Most Controversial Force in the Catholic Church*. New York: Doubleday, 2005.
Fuenmayor, Amadeo de, Valentin Gomez Iglesias, and José L. Illanes. *L'itinerario giuridico dell'Opus Dei. Storia e difesa di un carisma*. Milan: Giuffré, 1991.
Rocca, Giancarlo. *L'Opus Dei. Appunti e documenti per una storia*. Milan: Paoline, 1985.
Romano, Giuseppe. *Opus Dei. Il messaggio, le opere, le persone*. Cinisello B.: San Paolo, 2002.

Legionaries of Christ

Berry, Jason, and Gerald Renner. *Vows of Silence: The Abuse of Power in the Papacy of John Paul II*. New York: Free Press, 2004.
Conde, Angeles, and David J. P. Murray. *The Legion of Christ: A History*. North Haven, CT: Circe Press, 2004.

Index of Names

Index of Subjects